HEAD, HEART, AND HAND

HEAD, HEART, AND HAND

John Brown University and Modern Evangelical Higher Education

RICK OSTRANDER

With a Foreword by George Marsden

The University of Arkansas Press
Fayetteville
2003

Manufactured in the United States of America

07 06 05 04 03 5 4 3 2 1

Designer: John Coghlan

♾ The paper used in this publication meets the minimum requirements of the American National Standard for Permanence of Paper for Printed Library Materials Z39.48-1984.

Library of Congress Cataloging-in-Publication Data

Ostrander, Richard, 1965–
Head, heart, and hand : John Brown University and modern evangelical higher education / Rick Ostrander ; with a foreword by George Marsden.
p. cm.
Includes bibliographical references and index.
ISBN 1-55728-761-9 (cloth : alk. paper)
1. John Brown University—History. 2. Church colleges—United States—History. 3. Brown, John Elward, 1879–1957. 4. College presidents—United States—Biography. I. Title: John Brown University and modern evangelical higher education. II. Title.
LD2601.J8O78 2003
378.767'13—dc21

2003009193

CONTENTS

ILLUSTRATIONS

FOREWORD

The history of John Brown University, which Rick Ostrander here engagingly portrays, is part of a larger history of a recovery of a Christian heritage. Higher education in the Western world has deep roots in Christianity, dating back to the founding of the first universities in the medieval era. Christianity's affinity with scholarship can, in turn, be traced back to the Apostle Paul. Although the Gospel message had its greatest appeal among common people, the leadership of Paul indicates that there was always a significant place for the highly educated. As Paul himself famously put it, the church is "one body," but of "many members," each having various gifts that complement each other (1 Cor. 12, Rom. 12). According to that image, neither the ordinary Christian nor the learned scholar is more essential to the church. Each needs the other.

During the early centuries of American history, piety and learning were usually seen as allies. New England Puritans founded Harvard and Yale. By the era after the American Revolution, the great vitality of American Protestantism was being sustained by the popular revivalism. Not dependent on state churches, American Protestantism was being most effectively cultivated by evangelists. As a result, evangelical piety took deeper root among the common people than it had in the Old World. At first revivalism retained a strong educational wing. Many colleges were founded under evangelical auspices and until the mid-1800s college revivals were common occurrences, even at some of the most prestigious institutions.

From about the Civil War until the 1960s, however, popular Christianity and the culture of higher education in American life split apart from each other. Higher education became associated with secularizing forces and scientific outlooks that explicitly excluded traditional theological concerns. Although leading colleges and universities maintained touch with their religious heritages, they encouraged liberal forms of Christianity that emphasized morality but not spiritual conversion or the authority of Scripture. Revivalism meanwhile became more exclusively oriented to popular audiences. In reaction to the secular and liberal trends in higher education, the most successful evangelists were often anti-intellectual.

John Brown, one of the more successful of the many traveling evangelists in the early twentieth century, founded John E. Brown College (soon renamed John Brown University) in this atmosphere. Brown was most interested in vocational training and frankly believed that more conventional collegiate education was likely to lead people astray. Despite its grandiose title of "university," the tiny school, as Ostrander aptly describes it, as it existed in the 1930s looked more like a primitive "utopian community." Students worked for their keep and studied a curriculum that, whatever its merits, was far from warranting accreditation by the usual public standards. Ostrander's history portrays an astonishing transformation. By the end of the twentieth century, John Brown was a well-endowed school, ranked among the top ten of southern liberal arts colleges, chosen for the Templeton Foundation's Honor Roll for Character-Building Colleges, and listed among America's "100 Best College Buys." Despite this remarkable metamorphosis, the college had not forsaken its evangelical heritage. Rather, while continuing its concern for the spiritual welfare of its students, it was dedicated to the challenging task of integrating evangelical Christianity with the highest learning.

It would be misleading to suggest—and Ostrander does not in this notably modest institutional history—that John Brown University was unique in this transformation or in its achievements. Rather, the larger significance of this account is the opposite. The story of John Brown, with some details changed, could be the story of any one of dozens of evangelical colleges in America today. It is the story of a small but significant revolution taking place at the grassroots of American higher education. Many of the better liberal arts colleges in America today are firmly rooted in an evangelical heritage that once was dominated by anti-intellectual sentiments.

Traditions of the scholar are once again at least sometimes seen as important parts of the same Christianity that speaks to the common person. To read this history, then, is not only to learn about John Brown but also to better understand a larger cultural and religious phenomenon.

George M. Marsden

ACKNOWLEDGMENTS

I am indebted to a host of people who encouraged, advised, and prodded me throughout this project. John Brown University President Lee Balzer and former Provost Mel Fratzke supported the project from the start. Writing a history of one's own institution could be potentially awkward, but I am grateful to President Balzer for giving me the freedom to "speak the truth in love," even if that truth may sometimes be unflattering to the present institution. I am also indebted to John Brown Jr. and John Brown III for their willingness to share their experiences and recollections.

Members of the John Brown University archives, in particular Jan Goring, Josh Williams, and Holly Plinsky, were extremely helpful in providing me with access to sources and finding photographs for the book. Several of my students wrote research papers on particular aspects of the history of John Brown University, thereby uncovering material that proved useful for my book. Thanks in particular to Luke Afeman, Cherissa Dees, Josh Hofer, Graham Jones, Ryan Marr, Tammy Miller, A. J. Neufeld, and Travis Vaughn. John Brown University constituents Bill George, Pat Gustavson, and Shirley Thomas provided insightful comments on earlier versions of the manuscript.

This project required several summers of work, for which the Faculty Development Committee of John Brown University, under Cal Piston's leadership, provided generous support in the form of research grants. My in-laws, Paul and Beverly Earhart, provided ideal summer accommodations in Lancaster County, Pennsylvania, in which to write the manuscript, while my parents, Tim and Eileen Ostrander, gave constant encouragement and even demonstrated an interest in reading the manuscript.

Finally, I am grateful to my wife, Lonnie, and children Ryan, Tyler, Rachel, and Anna for allowing me to disappear into my barn office during Saturday morning cartoon time. Now that this project is completed, I look forward to joining them for *SpongeBob Squarepants*.

PART ONE

Starting from Scratch, 1879–1934

Founded in 1919, John Brown University has embodied many of the dynamics at work in twentieth-century American religion and society. It was established by a strident antimodernist at a time when the major Protestant denominations were battling over theological liberalism. In subsequent decades, however, the university distanced itself from the rigid dogmatism of fundamentalism. Founded on the periphery of the American South, John Brown University has been heavily influenced by Christians in the North and West throughout its history. The university was created to combine Christian liberal arts education with an emphasis on specialized vocational training. Yet as American society has evolved from an industrial to an information economy, the university has sought to adapt to change while retaining a distinctive "Head, Heart, Hand" educational philosophy. In all, John Brown University represents one attempt to build a lasting Christian institution amid a changing American society.

CHAPTER ONE

The "Laughing Evangelist"

The story of John Brown University begins with the life of John Brown. Such a statement might seem obvious, but it is not. Many colleges' names simply reflect the influence of a wealthy donor. Cornell University, for example, was named after a rich benefactor, and Harvard University was named after a Puritan minister who donated his books to the college. Others colleges have been named after figureheads who could bring the institution favorable publicity. Bryan College, for instance, was created and named to commemorate a famous fundamentalist after his death. John Brown University, however, grew from evangelist John Brown's vision, leadership, hard work, money, and even his own farm property. One alumnus observed in 1935, "Brown was and is the center of everything in those schools." Therefore, the story of John Brown University must begin with the life of a poor, self-educated southern evangelist.[1]

John Brown's Childhood and Religious Conversion

Ironically, "John Brown of Arkansas," as he came to be known, was not from Arkansas at all, but from Iowa. His father, John Franklin Brown, served in the Civil War, attaining the rank of sergeant in the Union army before returning to Iowa to farm the land. Soon thereafter, John Franklin met and married Julia Ann Brammer, the daughter of a Quaker pioneer family. The couple eventually settled in Center Point, Iowa, a small town in the east central part of the state.[2]

Like many rural farming families, the Browns had several children. John Elward Brown, the fifth of nine children, was born on April 2, 1879. Early in life, John Elward showed an avid devotion to having fun. The Brown family farm boasted a tightrope and a trapeze, and young John soon acquired the nickname "Sport" Brown because of his ability to lead the other children in new and at times mischievous forms of entertainment. He also showed a zeal for music at a young age. He joined his father in singing in the church choir. In school, when the teacher was gone from the room, John sometimes pulled out his harmonica and played while the other children danced. According to one account, the teacher once returned early, and John jumped out the school window to escape her wrath.[3]

Despite John's fun-loving temperament, however, the overriding fact of his boyhood existence was poverty. Later in life, John described his childhood with characteristic humor. "The wolf had a standing engagement to howl at the door," he once quipped. However, one doubts this was so humorous during Brown's childhood. The elder John Brown's body had been weakened in the war, and he was unable to perform the arduous tasks required of a nineteenth-century farmer. A soldier's pension was the family's main source of income, but it was inadequate to support a family the size of the Browns. So at the age of eleven, John Elward quit school to work full time helping to support the family. His first job on a neighboring farm paid four dollars a month. Throughout his adolescent years, John performed a host of low-paying, menial tasks; he worked in a livery stable, sawed wood, helped a merry-go-round crew at a carnival, and worked in a print shop in Center Point. Brown grimly recalled, "I seemed cut out especially for work that a mule could better do. Out of the grind and grime of those rather discouraging days there came little of inspiration or little of promise for the future."[4]

The Brown family observed religious duties in strict Quaker tradition, but as John Elward ranged farther from home in search of work, he also began to stray from the moral precepts of his parents. He established a reputation as a caller for square dances in communities throughout Iowa. As John himself described it later, "I became quite reckless and wayward, left the teachings of a Christian father and mother, and became the leader in worldliness and sinfulness. . . . I used to go miles to call for dances, attend horse races, beer drinkings, and anything that promised fun or a few hours of happiness." While such "vices" might seem tame by modern standards, they became important symbols to Brown and other turn-of-the-century Christians of a secular, worldly lifestyle that must be rejected by true believers. After his conversion John would preach strongly against these sorts of "amusements," and they would be banned from his college.[5]

By the time John was seventeen, he had grown tired of Iowa and was ready to seek new adventures (and, perhaps, greater income). His older brother Ben had purchased a fruit farm in Rogers, Arkansas, and invited him to come along. John eagerly accepted, and in the fall of 1896, John joined his brother in a covered wagon bound for northwest Arkansas. His life in Iowa had come to an abrupt end.[6]

John Brown's childhood was cut short by poverty, but his boyhood experience in Iowa was significant in a number of ways. First, John's parents had an important impact on his later development. The elder John Brown was by all accounts a stern and thoughtful man who taught John the importance of mental self-discipline. Later in life, John Brown used to tell a story to illustrate his father's strong will in quitting smoking: "After a little while he got up and laid that plug of tobacco on the mantle and said, 'Mother, I'm through. I don't intend to ever take another piece of tobacco in my mouth; and more than that, to show you that I can do it, I'm going to leave that plug right there so that I can see it, day after day.' And he did it. He walked the yard, chewed sticks, and ate four or five time a day . . . but from that day to his death, he never put another piece of tobacco into his mouth." This heavy emphasis on willpower—on "mind over matter"—would appear in John's life and writings as well. Anything was possible if one set one's mind and will to it. Later when he founded his college, it would be for ambitious young people who displayed such mental and emotional fortitude—those who had already decided that they would be a success in life and just needed the opportunity to do it.[7]

John's mother had an important influence on him as well. To John, Julia Brown represented the ideal of feminine, motherly virtue. Julia was strict but loving with her children, and despite the family's poverty did her best to make the home as satisfying a place as possible for her family. "My father's house was his kingdom," John recounted. "I have known him to walk eighteen miles at night to reach home rather than wait until the morning to come on the train. I don't believe my mother would have changed places with a queen, for to her, her home was her world." Later in life, John would idealize his mother and have much to say about the need for modern women to leave public life and return to their primary responsibility of managing a home. His inspiration for founding a college would be not only to educate boys to work, but to educate girls "back to motherhood." When his mother's death was imminent, John remarked, "No boy was ever blessed with a greater Mother than I. After God, probably the credit for these schools in very large part belongs to her."[8]

If his parents impacted John Brown's subsequent career and ideas, so too did his rural, agricultural upbringing. Although he eventually spent much of his time in the cities of California, John Brown espoused a distrust of and a distaste for city life. In his worldview (common among conservative Protestants in the nineteenth century), cities were havens of worldliness, immorality, exploitation, and busy-ness, while the country was the source of healthy living and clean morals. He once remarked, "the rushing life is rapidly making Americans a race of mechanical beings, blind to the finer things that have been given us, dead to the magnificent loveliness of the natural world about us." The urbanization of society that was occurring in his lifetime deeply troubled Brown. "The movement cityward in the last fifty years," he once warned, "constitutes one of the gravest menaces of civilization. . . . 'Stay on the farm!' and 'Back to the farm!' must be made still more effective slogans." In fact, Brown founded his college expressly for the young people of the "fields and hills and valleys." "I have no desire to train church workers toward the cities," he would say. His original goal was to train rural young people like himself to return to the farms and countryside of America, for the nation's salvation lay in the country, he believed.[9]

Finally, the experience of poverty and grinding toil never completely left John Brown. Deprived of a formal education by the need to work, John Brown retained throughout his life, even as the founder of a university, a suspicion of book learning. He became educated instead in "the book of human life," as he put it: "While my knowledge of books was limited to the point of actual ignorance, my knowledge of men was limited only by my capacity to learn. I came to know men." Although John Brown would later educate himself as to "the literature of the world," he professed, "if I had to give up today my knowledge of books or my knowledge of men I would surrender my books, and that without a second's hesitation." John Brown succeeded in life not through education but through hard work, and he maintained a veneration of manual labor throughout his life: "The Bible opens with God in His workshop. And he hasn't a white collar on. He's working. . . . Everywhere in the Holy Bible God magnifies industry and honors honest toil." Brown's remarks throughout life expressed an idealization of blue-collar manual workers and farmers—the "producers," he called them—as superior to the overeducated professional classes.[10]

John Brown came to epitomize the American Dream, Horatio Alger–style: the poor boy who made good through hard work and initiative. The college he founded sought to attract and train young people like himself—poor, rural, hard-working young men and women with ambition who could not afford to pay for an education. John Brown's Iowa childhood, therefore, had far-reaching effects not only on his own life but also on the institution he founded.

For John Brown's first half year in Arkansas, life seemed simply more of the same endless days of hard work. As Carl Moneyhon explains in *Arkansas and the New South, 1874–1929,* Arkansas in the late-1890s was just emerging from a prolonged agricultural depression that had afflicted much of the South. In northwest Arkansas, fruit farming and timber emerged as industries that attracted workers from surrounding regions. John first found employment cutting and hauling timbers to be made into railroad ties. Next, he worked at another local industry—a lime kiln. There he spent twelve-hour days breaking up limestone with a sledgehammer and wheelbarrowing it to a kiln for burning into lime, for which he was paid one dollar a day.[11]

All of this changed one evening in May, the date Brown gave for his conversion to Christianity. He later recalled, "on the night of May 15, 1897, I made the decision that has so wonderfully changed my life. I am lost in wonder, and to this day I cannot explain nor do I understand the wonderful workings of God." After a long day of labor, John and some working friends were idling away a cool, wet, dreary evening in a cafe in Rogers, Arkansas, when they heard the bass drum of Ensign J. M. Olson, the local Salvation Army worker, as he made his way down the street summoning down-and-outers to his nightly revival meetings. The group of young men drifted outside to mock the strutting, rotund bass drummer Olson, but for some reason on this night John Brown found himself attracted to Olson. John said to himself, he later explained, "if this man is willing to sing and beat his drum on a night like this, he has something I want." John left his friends and followed Olson to Hoffman Hall, a creaky old building that served as the Salvation Army mission. Olson's preaching found an attentive ear in the young Brown. After attending Olson's meetings for several consecutive nights, Brown finally summoned the courage to go forward and make a public profession of Christian faith.[12]

Brown's public speaking career began almost immediately after his conversion. Since it was commonly known that Olson called on new converts to give their testimonies on the night following their conversion, Brown went home and prepared a speech to give the following night. However, when the time came and Olson called on Brown to give his testimony, he recalled, "I stood up speechless. I just couldn't talk. It was not that I wouldn't. I could not." The next two nights, Brown's stage fright continued, until finally on a Saturday night he stopped under a large tree on the way home and prayed for God to give him the ability to speak in the Sunday service the next morning. Sunday morning came, and John was called upon to pray. "I prayed like a house afire, and could not find a place to stop," Brown recounted. "The next night I did not wait to be called upon. I was the first to testify. I began talking and have been doing it ever since."[13]

For three months after his conversion, Brown continued to pound rocks by day while pounding the Salvation Army drum by night, having taken over Ensign Olson's bass drum duties. Soon John decided to go into full-time Christian service. Ensign Olson recognized John's vigor and potential, but also his complete lack of training, and sent him off to Texas to be trained as a full-time worker for the Salvation Army. John Brown's life as a manual laborer was over, and his life as an evangelist, writer, and educator had begun.[14]

As with his childhood experience in Iowa, certain elements of Brown's conversion story are significant for later developments. First, John Brown's evangelical conversion experience led him to sharply distinguish between simply "clean living" and a living Christian faith.[15] John had grown up in a religious, morally upright family that attended church regularly. And despite his tendency to magnify his youthful rebellion, as many revivalists did, John was a rather sober, hard-working, responsible young man before his conversion. In fact, he occasionally contributed money from his meager earnings to Olson's Salvation Army before his conversion of May 15. Yet Brown dated the beginning of his Christian life to his conversion experience on that May evening, and throughout his life he would implore Americans to testify to a definite conversion experience, even as he railed against immoral behavior. When he founded a college, John Brown would seek only "clean," upright, responsible youths, but he did not necessarily equate such traits with genuine Christianity. During the college year, John Brown sought and often claimed conversions to Christianity from among his "clean-living" student body. For John Brown, spiritual conversion was always essential for Christian living.

A second significant element in Brown's conversion was that it was done through the auspices of the Salvation Army, not one of the mainstream American denominations of the day such as the Baptists or the Methodists. Founded in England by William Booth, an independent evangelist, the Salvation Army spread to America in the 1880s. Although most influenced by Methodist ideas, the Salvation Army in its American form was not aligned with any particular denomination and was one of the first nondenominational Christian organizations. This meant that John Brown was converted to a nondenominational, ecumenical form of Christianity, and though he later joined the Methodist church, Brown was explicitly and adamantly nondenominational throughout his evangelistic career. His college would also be intentionally nondenominational, something that proved to be both an asset and a handicap, as will be seen.[16]

An Evangelist and Fundamentalist, 1899–1919

Upon his return from Texas in the fall of 1897, Brown was sent along with Ensign Olson to establish a Salvation Army outpost in Siloam Springs, a small community on the western border of Arkansas. Fortunately, Brown's earlier life had prepared him for the hardships of a Salvation Army worker on the outskirts of civilization. "The pay was pitiably small, and the preaching perhaps even more pitiable," Brown recalled. "I slept for two weeks in the Salvation Army hall on benches, and lived most of that time on oatmeal." Their headquarters was a dilapidated little building on the hill above the city park that required extensive repairs before it could be used for meetings. Olson and Brown repaired the building themselves, built benches, and cut and hauled firewood to heat the building. Once the mission had been established, Olson returned to Rogers, and Brown was left to carry on the work in Siloam Springs alone. For the next few months, Brown received a crash course in practical Christian ministry. He was simultaneously pastor, evangelist, musician, and custodian, while also doing odd jobs on the side to supplement his meager income. He worked himself into exhaustion, took a few weeks rest, then returned to the job.[17]

Early in 1898, John was transferred to a new post in Denison, Texas. In April, however, the United States declared war on Spain, and John immediately volunteered for the U.S. Army. Because he was only nineteen years old, he needed written consent from his

1. John Brown *(third from right)* plays the banjo at the Siloam Springs Salvation Army in 1898.

parents to be accepted by the army. His mother objected, but John Brown's father, a Civil War veteran himself, gave his son permission to join. Julia Brown's fears about her son's safety proved unwarranted. The Spanish-American War was over in a few months—a "splendid little war," one American called it—and John never made it beyond a sun-baked army boot camp in southern Texas. John's military record, therefore, was hardly glamorous or distinguished. He later remarked that the man who drew military recruiting posters was "a liar." Nonetheless, Brown later cited this record of military service in establishing a number of military schools for boys, schools that would later contribute financial support to John Brown University in Siloam Springs.[18]

After the war, John returned to his Salvation Army post in Siloam Springs, where his energy and optimism earned him the nickname around town of "Happy Brown." John had come to enjoy life in Siloam Springs, but in the fall of 1898 he was transferred to Kansas City. Apparently, Kansas City was not to John's liking. Whether because of the surroundings of the big city or because his new position entailed more office work and less direct contact with people, John resigned from the Salvation Army a few weeks after his service in Kansas City had begun. He decided to return to Siloam Springs and become a professional evangelist.[19]

The train from Kansas City to Siloam Springs stopped in Gravette, Arkansas. While John was standing on the depot platform taking a break from the ride, he was approached by a local pastor who recognized him from his Salvation Army work in Siloam Springs. The man told Brown that he had intended to hold a series of revival meetings but had been unable to find a willing evangelist, and he asked if John would help. John eagerly agreed. The nineteen-year-old former Salvation Army worker hardly fit the part of a professional evangelist. His only coat had lost its buttons, and a lady from the church in Gravette had to sew new buttons on for him. Attendance at the meetings was sparse in this small farming community, and John had to rely on his enthusiasm and sincerity to compensate for the lack of polish in his sermons. The meetings continued for three weeks, and John received $3.65, plus room and board, for his services. Even at that rate, Brown later quipped, "I don't know but that I was slightly overpaid." Nevertheless, Brown's career as a professional "revivalist" had begun, and for the next twenty years he threw himself into the task with his typical energy and enthusiasm.[20]

Revivalism is a movement that promotes periods of spiritual intensity in church life, during which the unconverted come to Christ and Christians are shaken out of their spiritual lethargy. By the beginning of the twentieth century, revivalism had dominated

American religious life for over a century, and it remained especially strong in the South. During the Great Awakening of the mid-1700s, American religion was characterized by periodic bursts of spiritual activity in which a traveling preacher played a key role. The first so-called itinerant evangelist in America was George Whitefield, an Anglican minister who traveled the American colonies during this Great Awakening, preaching outdoors to large crowds and exhorting his audiences to experience the "new birth." In the early nineteenth century, a period known as the Second Great Awakening, revivalism was advanced by the efforts of Charles Finney, a Presbyterian minister and the leading evangelist of his day. Before Finney, American Christians had generally believed that revivals were mysterious, unpredictable events brought about by the sovereignty of God. Finney, however, taught that revivals could be "worked up" through human efforts, not simply "sent down" from God. Finney pioneered "new measures" for bringing about revivals—protracted meetings in a particular locale with a professional evangelist, techniques for the preparation of meetings, an "altar call" by which new converts walked forward at the end of the meeting to proclaim their faith, and the use of emotional appeals in preaching—which became standard fare in American church life.[21]

The premier evangelist of the late nineteenth century was D. L. Moody, a former shoe salesman from Massachusetts who adapted revival methods to the burgeoning cities of America and Great Britain. An uneducated layman who eventually preached to millions, Moody was known for his simple, low-key preaching style, his willingness to work with Christians from all denominations, and his use of business methods in organizing large urban revivals. Moody also pioneered the use of gospel songs during revival meetings, and his musical sidekick Ira Sankey became almost as famous as Moody himself.[22]

Moody died in 1899, the same year that John Brown entered full-time evangelism, and revivalism entered a new phase that one historian has called "Vaudeville Revivalism." The professional evangelist became half preacher and half entertainer, and the annual revival became a feature of a town's life on a par with the circus or the carnival. Evangelists such as Sam Jones, the "Moody of the South," became known for their coarse humor, anti-intellectualism, and aggressive, combative preaching style. "If anyone thinks he can't stand the truth rubbed in a little thicker and faster than he ever had it before, he'd better get out of here," Jones declared in his meetings. "Half of the literary preachers in this town are A.B.'s, Ph.D.'s, D.D.'s, LL.D.'s and A.S.S.'s," was one line sure to spark an enthusiastic response from Jones's audience.[23]

By far the most famous evangelist of the early twentieth century was Billy Sunday, a former baseball player who preached to millions in the largest cities of America—and became quite wealthy in the process. Sunday's flamboyant antics, theatrical poses, and impassioned gestures attracted the attention of the press and made him a household name. One headline in 1904 read "Evangelist Does Great Vaudeville Stunts in Tabernacle Pulpit." Sunday was frequently pictured in cartoons preaching in his shirtsleeves with perspiration pouring off his brow as he "lambasted the devil" with "hot shots at sin," much to his audience's delight. He outdid Sam Jones in colorful speech, once referring to his listeners as "hog-jowled, weasel-eyed, sponge-columned, mushy-fisted, jelly-spined, pussy-footing Christians." In Sunday's campaigns, salvation virtually became equated with decency, patriotism, and manliness. Christian converts "hit the sawdust trail" to shake the hand of the evangelist and sign a decision card. Sunday racked up such decision cards by the thousands—98,264, to be exact, in one ten-week campaign in New York City.[24]

Billy Sunday was not alone, however, during the heyday of Vaudeville Revivalism. A host of professional evangelists traveled the roads of America, almost all of them imitating Sunday's methods to a greater or lesser extent. There were, among others, five called "The Singing Evangelist," three called the "The Boy Evangelist," five called "the Gypsy Evangelist," as well as "The Railroad Evangelist," "The Cowboy Evangelist," and "The Labor Evangelist," and one who simply called himself "the thriller." One observer estimated that in 1911 there were 650 active professional evangelists crisscrossing the country offering their services in the towns and cities of America. One of this 650 was John Brown, whom reporters distinguished as "The Laughing Evangelist."[25]

After his modest beginning in Gravette, John Brown spent several months conducting revivals in small towns across Arkansas, Oklahoma, Missouri, and Iowa. In the spring of 1899 he purchased a tent that could seat about eight hundred people and hired a song leader, Ed Phillips, the "Pilgrim Singer of Texas." Subsisting on the meager freewill offerings that came in, Brown and Phillips conducted revival meetings in towns such as Maysville, Arkansas; Pierce City, Missouri; and Walker, Iowa. They also conducted a revival in Brown's hometown of Center Point, which he deemed a great success. Declared the *Center Point Journal*, "a few years ago, a young man left our town a practically unknown man; today he has the profound admiration of an innumerable host of people." Center Point could now claim as one of its own a professional evangelist. "Sport Brown has become known as Evangelist Brown," wrote one local pastor.[26]

For the next few years, Brown and Phillips traveled the southern plains states conducting revivals in towns such as Sumner, Spiro, Marble Rock, and Washburn. One revival held in Sallisaw, Oklahoma, was more noteworthy than the others. Here John met and fell in love with Juanita Arrington, a last-minute fill-in at the piano for the evening meeting. John continued his busy revival schedule while he courted Juanita. Eventually they were engaged and scheduled a wedding for December 19, 1900. Ed Phillips had become engaged to a girl from Siloam Springs, so the evening of December 19 became the occasion of a double wedding for the revivalist team, first John and Juanita in Sallisaw, Oklahoma, then Ed and his bride a few hours later in Siloam Springs. The wedding only briefly interrupted Brown's revival itinerary, and by January the Browns and the Phillips's were back on the revival circuit, now with two extra musicians to help out in the meetings.[27]

While Brown's reputation as a revivalist slowly grew in the first decade of the twentieth century, he ventured into other areas as well. Despite his busy schedule, John sought to remedy his lack of education by reading literature late into the night. He purchased numerous literary classics, including the complete works of Ralph Waldo Emerson, Mark Twain, Victor Hugo, and James Whitcomb Riley. He became fascinated with the printed page and the medium of writing, and in 1900 he purchased Center Point's weekly newspaper, the *Center Point Herald*. Thereafter, although he was traveling constantly as an evangelist, he doubled as editor and publisher of a newspaper. Within a few years, Brown was issuing the first of many monthly periodicals, publishing books based on his sermons, and even composing songs for hymn books.[28]

Brown's lack of education did not prevent him from taking on publishing work; nor did it keep him from trying his hand at running a college. In 1902, despite only five years of formal schooling, Brown became a college president at the age of twenty-three. Scarritt Collegiate Institute was a small Methodist college located in Neosho, Missouri, just across the Arkansas border, whose only claim to fame was that Will Rogers had studied there. By 1901, when Brown and Phillips conducted a revival campaign in Neosho, the college was on the verge of extinction. Hearing of the dire straits the college was in, Brown and Phillips met with the trustees. Brown offered to take charge of the school and finance its operations if the trustees would repair the buildings. The trustees agreed, and Brown was named president of Scarritt Collegiate Institute in the summer of 1902.[29]

John Brown's first college presidency was brief and unsuccessful. He was able to recall this experience later in life with a chuckle: "I have always had a sense of humor, and an appreciation of the ludicrous. In those days, I never allowed the dignity of my position to blind my eyes to the fact that it was more or less of a joke for me with my limited knowledge to undertake to direct the affairs of a long established, standard college." Brown proposed adding typing, shorthand, and other vocational courses to the Scarritt curriculum, but in general he left the college to govern itself with J. T. Pritchett, the former president, serving as dean of the school. John continued his evangelism, now with the added responsibility of promoting the interests of the college to his audiences. Despite Brown's efforts, the college continued to decline from eighty-four students in 1902 to only a handful of students by the end of 1904. Finally, in January of 1905, he quit Scarritt and moved his wife and two daughters to Siloam Springs. Acceptance of the responsibilities of a college president on top of his evangelistic and publishing activities, he concluded, had been an "unwise experiment." American higher education had made an unfavorable impression on Brown, and he determined to do things differently if he ever got a chance to build his own school.[30]

With Scarritt behind him and a growing family in Siloam Springs, John Brown launched into evangelism with renewed vigor. Ed Phillips had left, and Brown was now joined by C. P. Curry, a noted singer who remained with him until 1916. Attendance at his meetings steadily grew, as did the size of the cities in which he preached. By 1910, Brown and Curry had been in a third of the states, mainly in the central and southern portions of the country. They were now holding revivals in cities such as St. Louis, Kansas City, Louisville, San Antonio, and Houston. At the same time, John was building relationships with businessmen that would become crucial in later years in supporting his fledging college. For example, Jesse Jones, a prominent American businessman who later served in Franklin Roosevelt's New Deal administration, came forward at a 1905 Brown revival in Tyler, Texas. Jones became a loyal and generous supporter of John Brown's schools in ensuing decades.[31]

Early in 1911, Brown took another major step in his career when he conducted a revival campaign in Fresno, California. John Brown and California were a perfect match. Brown's energy and driving ambition found a counterpart in this boom-state populated by transplanted midwesterners and southerners like himself. The Fresno campaign was so successful that Brown and Curry canceled previously made plans and spent the next several months in California. They held rallies in Santa Ana, Redlands, Fullerton, Santa Barbara, and elsewhere. At the end of the summer, Brown and Curry were invited to conduct the main services for the Southern Methodist Assembly in Huntington Beach, California. They drew large crowds and were invited back for the next seven years. The California media gave Brown and Curry rave reviews. "Great day in Santa Ana Religious Circles," headlined the *Santa Ana Daily News*. The *Los Angeles Times* editorialized in 1912, "Brown preaches a message of joy and hope. His smile is itself a cure for long faces."[32]

Brown was so taken by his success in California that in 1913 he sold his house in Siloam Springs and moved his family to California. While he continued to travel to other states for revivals, California dominated his attention for much of the decade. He remarked in 1922, "my work has been confined to California—all but exclusively so—for the past ten years." In 1914, Brown made another key friendship when William Waterhouse, a retired building contractor and the former mayor of Pasadena, was converted at one of his meetings. Waterhouse volunteered to go ahead of the evangelistic team and construct temporary tabernacles for Brown's meetings in towns where there was no suitable church or auditorium space. These tabernacles, a subject of fascination to local media wherever Brown went, could be built in two days using two hundred local volunteers and could seat two thousand people. Waterhouse obtained 40,000 feet of lumber from local yards for approximately two thousand dollars and used it uncut to build a tabernacle 90 feet by 128 feet. After the revivals, the tabernacle was dismantled and the lumber returned to the yards for approximately what it cost originally.[33]

The late 1910s were peak years of activity for John Brown as an evangelist. California continued to be his main area of work, despite the fact that he moved his family back to Siloam Springs in 1915. His revivals in Pasadena in the spring of 1915 were headline events in the growing city and were deemed his most successful meetings to date. Hundreds of people were unable to get into the five-thousand-seat auditorium for his meetings, and at the end of the five-week campaign the *Pasadena Daily News* estimated that four thousand people had walked the aisle. Brown also made evangelistic forays outside of California during these years in cities such as El Paso, Texas, in 1918 and Vancouver, British Columbia, in the summer of 1919.[34]

By the end of the decade, John Brown had established himself as a significant regional figure in American revivalism. It is easy to be misled by headlines into exaggerating the extent of Brown's fame in the early twentieth century. Earlier biographers of John Brown have made much of a claim in the *El Paso Morning Times*, on the eve of Brown's campaign there, that "the name of John Elward Brown has meant in the great southland and the west what R. A. Torrey, Wilbur Chapman, and Billy Sunday have meant to the east and northeast." However, this remark must be taken with a grain of salt, since it was made by Thurston Price, a member of Brown's own evangelistic organization. John Brown was sometimes called the "Billy Sunday of the South," but during the decades of Sunday's fame many of the more than six hundred professional evangelists in America claimed the title of being the "Billy Sunday" of something. There was at least one other claimant to the "Billy Sunday of the South" title, a Methodist evangelist by the name of Burke Culpepper. Another writer in the *El Paso Morning Times* probably put it more accurately when he described John Brown as a well-known preacher, "hardly as big as Mr. Sunday, but he's coming."[35]

In message and preaching style, Brown established himself somewhere between the extremes of Billy Sunday's flashy stunts and D. L. Moody's low-key approach. In many ways, John Brown seemed to share the traits of that flamboyant generation of Vaudeville Revivalists. "He is a born actor," one reporter remarked of Brown, "probably the best that has appeared on that stage for months." In fact, Brown seemed remarkably similar to Billy Sunday in certain respects. Sunday was born and raised in poverty in rural Iowa, just seventeen years before John Brown. Sunday was described by his mother as a boy who "would go after things pell mell" and who "always had an extra supply of energy," a description that could just as easily apply to Brown. Sunday, like Brown, worked a variety of menial jobs before embarking on a professional career, first in baseball and then in revivalism.[36]

In his revival campaigns, Brown preached fiery messages that often resembled Sunday's. One popular theme in Brown's revivals was his denunciation of "amusements." This was expected of revival preachers of the day, and Brown did not disappoint. Under the headline "Pleasures Denounced," the *Los Angeles Tribune* described Brown's address as "less harsh and extreme than the famous sermon of Billy Sunday," but "not one whit less effective." The amusements in question typically centered around that "triumvirate of Satan—drink, cards, dance," but other questionable pursuits came under fire as well, sometimes literally. In one of his campaigns Brown had his audience bring "unclean and suggestive books and papers" to the meeting so that he could kindle a bonfire with them. In Norfolk, Virginia, Brown attracted the media's attention by declaring a "kindly war" on fancy women's hats that obstructed the views of others in the audience. He found it "impossible to preach to flowers, dead birds, and plumes," he remarked.[37]

John Brown could also launch into harsh invective reminiscent of Sam Jones and Billy Sunday. He once referred to "flappers" of the 1920s as "a brainless, purposeless, prayerless, godless, blasphemous, wine-guzzling, gambling, jazz-drunk bunch of social bacchanalians." Like many evangelists of the day who found professional evangelism financially as well as spiritually fulfilling, Brown also had to answer questions about money. During one of his California campaigns, charges circulated that he was a "grafter." In reply, he declared that he had received over $100,000 as an evangelist, but that he had given so much away that a check for $8,000 would cover everything he owned. Other evangelists were not so scrupulous with their finances, thereby giving rise to a popular view of revivalists as con men that would hamper Brown's fund-raising efforts in the 1920s.[38]

Concerning the manner of Brown's preaching, observers seemed divided on the extent to which John Brown copied Billy Sunday's outlandish style. In 1913, the *Los Angeles Tribune* carried an article on Brown showing him in various "action" poses of a revival preacher. During his sermon, the reporter wrote, "He began that remarkable series of gestures, which are as full of force and action as those of a baseball player. . . . His right hand shot up and his voice rose. Then it swept down in what might be called an impassioned arc and his black-shocked head almost disappeared between his shoulders. The tent was ringing with his notes and the electricity of his 'knockout' with his ready right was in the air." Most observers, however, described Brown differently. A Mason City, Iowa, reporter remarked that Brown avoided "the clatter and bang of the ordinary evangelists." When one man said that he was not going to attend Brown's meetings because "Mr. Brown is trying to ape Billy Sunday," the reporter replied, "I have heard Billy Sunday, and only a crazy man will see anything like Billy Sunday in Mr. Brown." A Pasadena reporter concurred: "I remember to have seen an evangelist in an opera house stand on the stage and kick off his overshoes into the flies as he exhorted; Mr. Brown is a gentleman and comports himself as such, and all claptrap is lacking." Concluded one admiring writer, "he is not a pulpit acrobat nor a clerical clown. He indulges in no grotesque posturings."[39]

The dominant impression that John Brown seemed to convey in his meetings was that of a blunt, direct, but cheerful speaker, earning him the nickname "the Laughing Evangelist." Asked to describe his preaching, Brown replied, "you look straight at them and give them all you've got, right in the heart and between the eyes. They like it that way." One Boston reporter observed that Brown's approach "differs considerably from the usual shaking over Hellfire and the sobbing appeal ordinarily employed. It has been said that 'he laughs them on their way to Heaven with the open and breezy air of the Great West.'" In fact, this Boston reporter was closer to the mark when he looked beyond Billy Sunday to New England's own D. L. Moody for a comparison to John Brown. If Brown had any figure that he sought to emulate, it was D. L. Moody and his simple, direct, but positive approach. "While I never saw Mr. Moody," he would later remark, "he was my ideal in evangelistic work." In later years, Brown's resemblance to Moody, an uneducated country boy who founded three schools, became even more apparent.[40]

While Brown clearly enjoyed his growing success as a traveling revivalist, he did not relish the time away from home that such a profession required. Brown's letters to his family reveal something of the anguish it caused him to be away from Juanita and miss so

2. John Brown, the "Laughing Evangelist," circa 1905.

much of his children's lives (by 1919 the Browns had five daughters). "I know that I do better work, and more of it, when I am alone," he wrote from Pasadena, "but I would be perfectly willing to forgo a lot of the work if you folk—all of you—were here." He signed the letter, as with most to his family, "How I miss you all, and how dearly I DO LOVE YOU ALL. Kisses, and prayers for every one of you, Daddy—devotedly." In one hurried but heartfelt letter, Brown poignantly remarked, "life is too short to be away so much." Brown's success as a traveling evangelist was always dampened by the anguish of separation from his family.[41]

During the years that John Brown was making a name for himself as an evangelist, he was also taking strides in another direction that would be important for the formation of his college. He was firmly establishing himself in the subculture of Protestant fundamentalism, a new religious movement of the early twentieth century. In the nineteenth century, northern white Protestants had comprised a generally unified movement that dominated the ideas and institutions of American society. However, by the 1880s Darwin's theory of evolution and scientific criticism of the Bible, coupled with the new social problems generated by industrialization and urbanization, were beginning to divide American Protestants into factions. Some Protestants, viewing the new outlook of modern science as authoritative, sought to reinterpret Christianity to fit the outlook of modern educated Americans. Calling themselves liberal Protestants, they stressed the ethical teachings of Jesus and tended to equate Christianity with a spirit of social service rather than belief in particular doctrines. While never a majority of Protestants, liberals, or "modernists," as they were called in the early twentieth century, occupied influential positions in the seminaries and denominations of the North.[42]

At the same time that liberal Protestantism was taking shape, a movement was forming among conservative Christians, one that would emerge as fundamentalism by the 1910s. While liberals eagerly sought to adapt to the modern world, fundamentalist Christians reacted strongly against such trends. Conservatives from across the denominational spectrum organized themselves to oppose liberal theology in the church and modern cultural developments outside of it. Their task in the church, as they saw it, was to defend the "fundamentals" of the Christian faith such as the infallibility of Scripture, the virgin birth, the resurrection of Christ, the Second Coming of Christ, and other key doctrines. They also believed that American culture, once predominantly Christian, was being wrecked by evolutionary teachings and the new social forces of the city. Uncomfortable with modern developments such as foreign immigration, new forms of music and dress, and the rise of popular entertainment, they often lashed out at a litany of behaviors that they equated with modernism, broadly defined.[43]

Like most revivalists, John Brown fit comfortably into the fundamentalist movement. His 1920 book *The Foundation of God* defended the inspiration of the Bible against liberal critics. "Higher criticism has sent its blighting, withering, damning influences over all the civilized world," Brown charged. Much of the book was devoted to refuting the theory of evolution, but Brown reserved his most intense criticism for liberal Protestants in the mainstream denominations, those "smug professors" who propagate heresy "while wearing the livery of the church and talking the language of heaven." He concluded, "it is not infidelity on the outside that the church needs now to fear but the infidelity on the inside . . . that the church needs to fear—needs to locate—needs to eradicate." Here and elsewhere, Brown demonstrated a fundamentalist outlook by his efforts to combat liberal Protestant ideas.[44]

Brown also shared with other fundamentalists a critical view of many modern behaviors that he considered to be of the devil. Brown's first book, *Sowing and Reaping,* written in 1902, condemned such evils as dancing, alcohol, card-playing, and "Sabbath desecration." By the 1920s, fundamentalists were becoming increasingly alarmed about American culture as the fads associated with the Roaring Twenties became popular. Brown devoted the book *Slime Pits* to spotlighting the "slime pits" in modern culture that threatened to corrupt and destroy America's youth. Alcohol consumption, Sabbath-breaking, "flapperism," calf-length skirts, dance halls, movies, card-playing, popular novels, and tobacco all came under fire. Brown was especially adamant about Sunday observance. He once remarked that "Sunday baseball is a violation of both the laws of God and the laws of man." He took the Lord's Day so seriously that during the 1930s, semesters at John Brown University began on Saturday rather than on Monday so that students would not have to travel in trains on Sunday. Such views may seem extreme by modern standards, but they were fairly typical of conservative Christians in the early twentieth century.[45]

While denouncing modern behaviors, Brown also formed associations with leading fundamentalists of the day, bonds that would tie his school to the fundamentalist—and later evangelical—subculture. As a young evangelist in 1900, John Brown traveled to Chicago to spend a week at Moody Bible Institute, one of the headquarters of American fundamentalism. Here he attended lectures by G. Campbell Morgan, a London minister who was a prominent speaker at fundamentalist Bible conferences and meetings. While at Moody, Brown also acquired a spiritual mentor, Reuben Torrey, the superintendent at Moody Bible Institute in 1900 and one of the leading fundamentalists of the day. Brown valued Torrey's friendship and in later years would capitalize on Torrey's reputation to boost his credibility among other conservatives.[46]

In 1913, Brown established the International Federation of Christian Workers (IFCW), an interdenominational organization for evangelists and missionaries. Although never as prominent as its name suggested, the IFCW did sponsor a summer Bible conference each year in Sulphur Springs, Arkansas. Because fundamentalism was an interdenominational movement, Bible conferences, weeklong events in which Christians would gather at a summer resort setting for meetings and fellowship, were one of the main vehicles by which conservatives from various denominations networked with each other. The most important conferences were at Winona Lake, Indiana (the site of Billy Sunday's summer home), and Montrose, Pennsylvania, where Reuben Torrey presided. However, John Brown managed to attract a number of prominent speakers and musicians to Sulphur Springs over the years. The list of preachers and musicians who participated in Brown's Bible conferences reads like a Who's Who of early-twentieth-century fundamentalism: G. Campbell Morgan; Reuben Torrey; William Bell Riley, the leading Baptist fundamentalist; William Evans of the Moody Bible Institute; Lewis Sperry Chafer of Dallas Theological Seminary; and Homer Rodeheaver, Billy Sunday's song leader. Brown's work in establishing contacts in the conservative evangelical subculture would bear fruit in subsequent years. Although John Brown University did not belong to a Christian denomination, it remained firmly established in a broader religious movement whose influence on American culture surpassed that of any particular denomination.[47]

By 1919, the forty-year-old Brown was a father of four daughters, a successful evangelist, a publisher of Christian literature, and president of the IFCW. Yet he was still as restless and adventurous as ever, and the summer of 1919 would launch him on his most demanding enterprise yet—founding a college.

CHAPTER TWO

Creating a New Kind of College

The inspiration for the founding of a college occurred at John Brown's Vancouver revival campaign in the summer of 1919. This is how he explained it:

> At the close of a six week's tabernacle campaign, I made a call for young men and women who were ready to dedicate themselves to any and all departments of public service, to present themselves at the platform. . . . The response was immediate and amazing. Ninety young people, made up of as fine and as high grade material as is found in any audience or in any city, gathered before my platform. . . . Their ideals were of the highest and their ambitions reached out to every phase of consecrated effort. I found that practically all of these young people required more schooling, and most of them required several years hard effort in the ordinary branches of an English education.
>
> The question arose immediately, where were these young people to go? Out of the ninety not half a dozen of them could finance themselves through school, and most of them hadn't means with which even to start and the question arose at once, 'Where can we go, and how can we get the preparation which we must have in order to serve?'
>
> This scene on a smaller and sometimes larger scale I had witnessed in almost every town and city I had visited in my evangelistic work. With the passing of the years the conviction had deepened in my mind and heart, my work was incomplete. Under God, I was privileged to arouse hundreds of young people to an unselfish dedication of their lives to the public good, and then I had gone away leaving most of them to battle against overwhelming odds and to fail. What was I to do? What should I do?

> On the morning of the 23rd of July, after a restless, sleepless night, the decision came to launch an institution built and dedicated for the specific purpose of helping the boy or the girl who stood absolutely without financial support.
>
> I could not but feel that such an institution as that about which I dreamed, would be the crowning event of my life, and the culminating goal toward which I might, under God, turn all the fruits of years of friendships and favors. . . . I decided to follow the convictions that had gradually come to dominate my life, and without further questioning, and without further delay, I decided to begin to build.[1]

When John Brown stated that he would begin his college "without further delay," he truly meant it. Brown finished up a revival in Long Beach, California, on July 27 and left immediately for Siloam Springs. Realizing that starting a college required substantial funds, he stopped in Texas on the way home to present his plan to Jesse Jones. Jones gave Brown his blessing and pledged financial support. By early August, Brown was back in Siloam Springs making plans to open a college that autumn. A few years earlier, Brown had bought a farm on the western edge of Siloam Springs. This farm now became the campus of Southwestern Collegiate Institute. Brown deeded to the school three hundred acres of land, a two-story home, two barns, twenty dairy cows, seventeen horses and mules, a number of hogs and sheep, farm equipment, a printing plant, and a pre–Civil War log home.[2]

The proposed college had no dormitory or classroom space, however, so Brown contacted William Waterhouse, his tabernacle-building friend, and summoned him to Siloam Springs. When William Waterhouse arrived from California on August 24, Brown informed him that he needed a college building by the end of September. Waterhouse's years of practice throwing together tabernacles now came in handy. In thirty-five days, Waterhouse and a team of volunteers completed—at least enough to be useful—Southwestern Hall, a two-story building 48 feet by 110 feet. For the next thirteen years, the White Building, as it came to be known, served as the all-purpose center of the campus—containing at

3. Southwestern Hall, the first building on campus, was hastily constructed by William Waterhouse, John Brown's tabernacle-building friend from California.

various times dormitories, classrooms, a chapel, offices, a dining room, and a kitchen.[3]

With a building under way, John Brown's publishing and fundamentalist networks became valuable. He immediately began advertising in his periodicals the opening of a college that autumn and summoning students and faculty. Amazingly, within a few weeks, seventy students and a handful of teachers had arrived. On Monday night, September 29, a dedication service was held, and Southwestern Collegiate Institute, a high school academy and two-year junior college, came into existence.[4]

Since some people, including John Brown himself, claimed that his school was unique in American higher education, it might be helpful to pause and consider the historical background, John Brown's philosophy of education, and to what extent Southwestern Collegiate Institute was distinctive in American education. Higher education in nineteenth-century America had been overwhelmingly Christian. Most of the eight hundred or so institutions of higher learning were run by Protestant denominations, mostly Methodist, Baptist, and Presbyterian, and even the public universities reflected Christian standards. University presidents were usually ordained ministers, and well into the 1890s students in many public universities were required to attend daily chapel. The purpose of college was not so much to transmit knowledge as to mold character. Historian Mark Noll has observed, "instructors in the old-time colleges were less like modern professors and more like the guidance counselors in our contemporary high schools who work with the same group of students throughout their academic careers."[5]

The turn of the twentieth century brought dramatic changes to this Protestant system of higher education. Public universities, influenced by new German models of education, underwent a process of professionalization and secularization. The new model of a professor was that of a dispassionate, highly trained, narrowly specialized scholar or scientist. As Noll states, "while professors in the old colleges had taught students, those in the new universities taught subjects." The purpose of university education became that of educating young people for competency in an age of professionalism and technology. Christianity, often seen by scholars as an impediment to rational, open-minded inquiry, was pushed to the margins of the university.[6]

At the same time that public universities were becoming more secular, traditional church-related colleges were becoming more denominational. Before the rise of large public universities, the typical local church-related college served the interests of a broad Christian constituency and drew students from among the surrounding population regardless of denominational affiliation. However, as public universities began drawing students away from local colleges, denominational schools began to focus more on attracting students and finances from their own denominational constituencies statewide and beyond. Many of them were struggling to survive by the turn of the century.[7]

During his brief tenure as president of the Scarritt Collegiate Institute, a Methodist college, John Brown witnessed firsthand some of the problems facing American higher education at the time. His experience there led him to criticize higher education as too expensive, impractical, and doing a disservice to Americans. He recalled:

> Most of those young people were from homes of modest means, and in one instance, to my knowledge, the father of the student had mortgaged the farm to get the boy through school. Education, to these parents, spelled out success for their children; and education, sad to say, for most of these parents, spelled out emancipation from daily toil. . . . It was there in that school that the conviction came that it was a crime, unpardonable, to take millions of boys and girls from the hills and valleys and farms to run them through the standardized courses of a smattering of book theories, allowing these young people to waste the formative period of their lives in indolence or in an exaggerated program of fraternities and athletics and amusements, to at last graduate them and dump them into a specialized and intensified age as unprepared to live and serve as they were when they were babies in their mother's arms.

It was this experience at Scarritt, Brown later claimed, that started him on the road to founding his own college.[8]

As Brown mulled over the difficulties facing education during his years as an evangelist, another problem developed: the infusion of liberal Protestantism into many church-related colleges of the early twentieth century. As Brown and other fundamentalists saw it, liberal Protestantism was corrupting most Christian institutions of higher learning by the early 1900s. Modernism, Brown claimed, "is being pumped into tens of thousands of our students today, and much of this work is being done in the name of Jesus Christ, and from schools that have been built and endowed by praying, self-sacrificing, weeping, suffering saints, who if they could know to what purposes their money is being used, would turn over in their graves." In 1922, Brown quoted T. C. Horton, a prominent fundamentalist, when he proclaimed, "Christian schools were once the pride of our nation. Now, many are the progeny of Satan."[9]

By the 1910s, Brown believed that American education had reached a crisis point on a number of levels. First, Brown argued, higher education failed the nation because it had failed to adapt to the educational needs of a technological society. The nineteenth century educational ideal had been that of one-on-one instruction in the classics and in ethical living. A widely cited remark of the nineteenth century was that the ideal classroom consisted of Mark Hopkins (reputed to be America's best educator) on one end of a log and a student on the other. Brown, however, believed that with the onset of industrialization this educational task had changed. Stated Brown, "one hundred years ago a professor, a boy and a saw-log might have made a university, but not so to-day. There must be added a saw mill that the professor may teach the boy how to make useful boards of that log for the various needs of humanity." Brown claimed that American education was failing in this task. Rather than educating young people to work, Brown claimed, "we are impressing the youth of America with the false idea that education means emancipation from daily toil."[10]

The result, according to Brown, was a disaster not only for the nation but for the students the colleges and universities purportedly served. Ninety percent of the nation's college students were specializing in academic subjects and training toward "non-productive departments of the national life," but there was only room in the white-collar world for 10 percent of these students, he claimed. The key to success in life, Brown believed, was hard work; yet American colleges were leading young people away from the Protestant virtues of discipline and hard work that had made the country great:

> There isn't a man in American life today that is worth three whoops, who did not have to get out and get under. He knows something of the acid test, and something of the flash of steel, and something of the bloody sweat of stern necessity, sacrifice and sometimes suffering. Having achieved success he

> now turns around in his maudlin, sickly, sentimental and damnable pity to say: "Please God, my children will never suffer what I suffered," and in saying that the man does not realize his words are tantamount to "Please God, my children shall be robbed of the same opportunities I had out of which to build success."

Colleges where children were sent to read books without learning the virtues of hard work, Brown believed, were dooming their students to failure in life.[11]

Worse yet, Brown believed, was what students *were* learning in college. With the decline of Christian influences, colleges had become corrupting agents where young people joined fraternities, learned to drink, dance, smoke cigarettes, and devote their time and attention to college athletic contests rather than to studies or work. American colleges, Brown concluded, did "nothing but pump theory into the heads of our youth to turn them out into a nation of specialization, specialized in nothing, unless it is cigarette smoking, athletics, and the Charleston."[12]

America's colleges and universities had failed the nation in another way, Brown believed. They had failed to teach women to value homemaking and to excel in it. While Brown did not rule out altogether the possibility of women assuming public roles, he maintained that God's intended role for most women was that of homemaker. Because American society depended on godly families, Brown argued, "the world needs women who in home and church and social set will stand four-square for Jesus Christ and the highest ideals of motherhood, despite the sneers or ridicules of the little society wart." Brown, therefore, was one of many fundamentalists who expressed alarm at the rise of "flappers"—young women who repudiated Victorian notions of modesty, socialized with men, smoked cigarettes, danced, and exhibited a new frankness about sex. One of the most troubling trends of modern America, Brown claimed, was the rejection of motherhood by millions of "emancipated" women who preferred the company of pets to that of children. Women's colleges were one of the worst culprits in promoting this trend away from motherhood, Brown believed. "Most of our girls are training away from wifehood, motherhood, and home-making, . . . and are entering into competition with men to such an extent that the homelife is actually being threatened." Moreover, the education of women to pursue a man's world was resulting in fewer jobs available to men. By driving Christianity out of education, educating women into men's roles, and educating both men and women away from practical labor, Brown believed, American colleges had failed the nation.[13]

Southwestern Collegiate Institute was John Brown's remedy to these problems in American higher education. First, Southwestern would be wholeheartedly Christian, but not denominational. As in the colleges of the 1800s, daily chapel attendance was required for students and faculty, and students were required to attend church in Siloam Springs on Sunday. Teachers were expected to hold fast to the fundamentals of the Christian faith—"the deity of Christ, the Atonement, and the inspiration and infallibility of the Word of God"—but the school accepted teachers from a variety of denominations. To ensure that his schools would not fall prey to modernism, Brown even considered inserting a "revertible clause" into the school's charter, by which the school property would revert back to the Brown family if the school ever failed to teach the "fundamental truths" of Christianity, but he abandoned this idea on the advice of his friends.[14]

To address the problem of cost in higher education, Brown intended that Southwestern would be "built and dedicated exclusively for boys and girls without means." Not castoffs or misfits, Brown frequently warned, but "clean, honest, industrious boys and girls who are outside the school room today because they haven't had a chance." Those who could afford an education could go elsewhere. His school would specialize in educating young men and women who had ambition but not finances, who otherwise would be left without an opportunity for an education, as Brown had been. At first, Brown had planned on having students pay back their tuition when their schooling was complete, but he feared this would place them under a "burden of debt" immediately upon leaving school. Thus, rules governing the paying of tuition were abandoned, and all students were accepted without price or obligations.[15]

Furthermore, unlike the typical college of the day, Brown's Southwestern College would give students a practical education. To help cover the cost of their education, all students would work four hours a day in some industry of the college, in addition to four hours a day of classroom work. This work would not only help pay for their education, however. It was a key part of Brown's intention to have his students "educating their way toward work" rather than simply "working their way toward an education." Regardless of their future plans, all students would learn a trade and, in the process, learn "the dignity of labor, and the necessity of working right." Boys would work on the school's farm, dairy barn, or carpenter shop, learning more efficient methods of agriculture and building. Others would work in Brown's printing plant, learning all aspects of the publishing trade. Girls would learn the practical tasks of homemaking by working in the kitchen, cannery, or sewing plant. Thus, Brown maintained, "side by side with the high standards of a cultural education there can be placed the high standards of vocational specialization."[16]

Southwestern would also be coeducational, but in a healthy sort of way. Modern universities with their unsupervised system of coeducation, Brown believed, had led to "a heart-breaking holocaust in the realm of morals" in many an instance. However, single-sex education was not the solution. In an age where marriage and motherhood were already on the decline, separating the sexes during the years when they would most naturally find a mate would simply make a bad problem worse. Rather, coeducation "under proper restrictions, supervision and direction" was the best way. Friendships between the sexes would be encouraged, but they "must not be made too prominent in the school and must be kept on the highest and most wholesome levels." After all, Brown reasoned, "where in all the world would young people find a more opportune time or place for coming in contact with that someone who is to play the important part of a life's partner?" Coeducation without immorality was the ideal at Southwestern.[17]

Finally, John Brown wanted a spirit of social equality to pervade his school. The primary problem that Brown perceived in college fraternities and intercollegiate athletics was that they led to social distinctions and elite groups among students. Not only did college athletics waste students' time, he asserted, they gave rise to "a few who occupy the center of the stage, and to whom the entire school's program is made to minister." At Southwestern, while intramural sports would be encouraged, there would be no intercollegiate athletics to rob the precious time of the students and create class distinctions. For the same purpose, John Brown also proposed school uniforms at Southwestern. Part of his rationale was to save students money and to avoid the type of girls' dresses that tended "to work havoc in the imagination of an immature, unformed boy," but the more important reason was to promote a spirit of equality among all of the students. By prohibiting fraternities and intercollegiate athletics and by promoting standardized clothing, John Brown hoped to avoid the elitism and class distinctions that prevailed in American colleges.[18]

Clearly, Brown intended Southwestern to be a total educational experience, not simply a few years of training in academic subjects. In an age before "holistic education" and "seamless curriculum" were buzzwords, John Brown was adamant that "education must be all-inclusive." By modern standards, John Brown's schools might seem more like a Christian boot camp than a Christian college. Southwestern had strict rules regarding conduct, but to some extent, such rules seemed unnecessary. With four hours of classes, daily chapel, four hours of work, meals, two hours of study time in the evening, and lights-out at 10:00, virtually all hours of a student's day were already accounted for. This, in fact, was John Brown's intention. As he saw it, he was preparing young people for responsible living as mature Christian adults, something he believed few other colleges did:

> We are trying to create in the formative period of the child's life just as nearly as possible the attitude toward life, and the habits which are absolutely necessary in home making, and

> successful industry or business when the student shall leave the school-room. To believe that our boys and girls can spend the formative period of their lives in the extremes of amusement, athletics, dress and idleness that characterize many a student body, and then when leaving the school room can as completely change their mode of living as though they were passing from one world to another is to simply believe that the leopard can change his spots or water can reverse itself and run up hill.

He did not state it as such in 1919, but by 1926 John Brown was able to articulate his conception of education as embracing the head (through academic education), the heart (through Christian formation), and the hand (through vocational instruction).[19]

So was this a truly unique form of education in America? Not completely. From a historical perspective, one can see all of the elements of Southwestern Collegiate Institute in existence in certain parts of nineteenth-century education. For example, John Brown's idea of combining practical, affordable education and manual labor was by no means original. Francis Wayland, president of Brown University and one of America's leading educators of the nineteenth century, anticipated John Brown's criticism of strictly academic education decades earlier when he asserted:

> That such a people should be satisfied with the teaching of Greek, Latin, and the elements of mathematics was plainly impossible. Lands were to be surveyed, roads to be constructed, ships to be built and navigated, soil of every kind under every variety of climate were to be cultivated, manufacturers were to be established . . . all the means which science has provided to aid the progress of civilization must be employed if this youthful republic would place itself abreast of the empires of Europe.

In order to make education affordable to as many young people as possible, many Christian colleges of the nineteenth century subsidized the cost of their students' education. Few waived tuition costs altogether as John Brown would try to do, but a number of colleges had very low tuition rates. Also, many western and southern colleges in the 1830s and 1840s provided "manual labor" programs in which students combined academic studies with half a day of work. Dartmouth College was an early leader in promoting the idea that manual labor should be part of a student's education, and Oberlin College, today one of America's most exclusive liberal arts colleges, began as a work-study college.[20]

Public universities during John Brown's lifetime also displayed a trend toward practical education. The land-grant colleges founded in the wake of the Morrill Act of 1862 emphasized as their raison d'être the education of the populace for useful employment in industry and agriculture. Concludes historian Frederick Rudolph concerning late-nineteenth-century higher education, "Vocational and technical education had become a legitimate function of American higher education, and everywhere the idea of going to college was being liberated from the class-bound, classical-bound traditions which for so long had defined the American collegiate experience." Although John Brown may have had some small liberal colleges and denominational schools in mind when he railed against impractical education, the trend in higher education by the early twentieth century was already toward the practical model that he promoted.[21]

Nor was Brown's emphasis on strict rules and character formation unprecedented. As noted earlier, nineteenth-century colleges typically stressed the moral and religious education of the student as well as academic education. In addition to chapel and religious training, elaborate lists of rules governing the students' daily schedule were common. The laws of Union College in 1802, for example, consisted of eleven chapters, each of which contained from seven to twenty-three sections. Moreover, nineteenth-century colleges often expressed John Brown's concerns about athletics and other extracurricular activities. Faculties generally frowned upon most sports contests as inappropriate for college students and possibly even dangerous to their health. Except perhaps for school uniforms, nothing in John Brown's Southwestern Collegiate Institute would have been considered out of the ordinary in nineteenth-century higher education.[22]

If John Brown's college was not unprecedented in American history, it also did not stand alone in the early twentieth century. Berea College, founded in 1869 in Kentucky and still active in the twentieth century, was created to provide a practical Christian college education for underprivileged youths of the southern Appalachian region. Its president stated in 1893 that Berea's purpose was "teaching people how to get a living, and then how to live. Berea College stands with a spade and a spelling book in one hand, and a telescope and a Testament in the other." Closer to Siloam Springs was the School of the Ozarks, founded in 1906 in Point Lookout, Missouri. As John Brown sought to do, the School of the Ozarks, according to its charter, was "for the purpose of providing Christian education for the youth of both sexes, especially those found worthy but who are without sufficient means to procure such training." Moreover, students were required to help pay for their education by performing tasks that developed practical skills for a particular vocation. Southwestern, while unusual for its time, was not unique.[23]

However, Southwestern Collegiate Institute was more than either a throwback to the nineteenth-century college or an imitation of other vocational colleges. Southwestern's true identity in early-twentieth-century higher education is best understood in the context of John Brown's fundamentalist orientation. To combat what they saw as the growing apostasy in America's educational institutions, fundamentalists by the early twentieth century had developed a new type of institution in higher education, the Bible school. The earliest Bible schools date back to the late 1800s. The first of these was begun by A. B. Simpson, founder of the Christian and Missionary Alliance. Next came D. L. Moody's Bible Institute in Chicago in 1886, and in 1889 A. J. Gordon founded what became Gordon College in Boston. Bible schools were created as a response to what fundamentalists perceived to be pressing needs in America and the world. Trained Christian workers were needed to take the gospel to America's teeming cities and around the world, yet traditional church colleges were abandoning the faith. As a result, Bible schools were created to provide a simple, affordable, practical education to Christian young people to prepare them for Christian service. The curriculum was based on the English Bible (no Greek or Hebrew was needed); music and Christian homemaking were also stressed. John Brown often visited the Moody Bible Institute, America's leading Bible school, and his colleagues and mentors in the revivalist world were important figures in the Bible school movement. Most notably, Reuben Torrey, his avowed mentor, was the superintendent of Moody Bible Institute and instrumental in the creation of the Bible Institute of Los Angeles, later Biola University.[24]

When viewed through the lens of the Bible school movement, the resemblance between John Brown's college and those of his fundamentalist colleagues is striking. Bible schools typically attracted older students who did not have the educational background or financial resources to be admitted into traditional colleges. This type of older, more motivated but financially strapped student was typical at John Brown's college as well. Like Southwestern, Bible schools provided affordable education. To this day, in fact, Moody Bible Institute does not charge tuition for its students. Bible schools also focused on practical education, something that John Brown extolled at Southwestern. D. L. Moody complained that frequently a young preacher has learned "nothing about human nature, doesn't know how to rub up to common men and adapt himself to them." His Bible institute sought to educate such students in the practical matters of Christian work. Writes historian Virginia Brereton, of the Bible school outlook, "liberal or general education was considered an unwanted extravagance given the exigencies of the time."[25]

John Brown's college most resembled the Bible schools in its spiritual life. All students were required to take courses in the English Bible, where Southwestern would, like the Bible schools, "condense the long drawn out courses of the average theological seminary" into brief but practical sessions. One of Brown's goals was to outfit "Christian boys and girls seeking special training for the pastorate, the mission fields, and for evangelistic work." Teachers at Southwestern and at Bible schools were chosen more for the quality of their spiritual lives than their intellectual attainments, and Bible schools shared with Southwestern detailed rules regulating students' lives and relations between the sexes. As will be explained later, Bible studies, prayer meetings, and testimony services abounded at Southwestern as at other Bible schools, and John Brown began each school year with a weeklong revival to stoke the spiritual fires.[26]

Of course, Southwestern differed from the typical Bible school in one important way: its emphasis on vocational education. This, however, was to Brown not so much a repudiation of the Bible school ideal as it was an expansion of it. Bible schools focused on education for practical "Christian" work such as missions and evangelism, but John Brown viewed *all* honest work as potentially Christian. "All labor, if it is necessary," John Brown asserted, "is both sacred and divine. There are too many artificial lines running through human society today. There is too much talk about divine work and secular work." For Brown, vocational training was simply another form of Christian work that Bible schools should prepare Christian young people to do.[27]

The other primary difference between Southwestern and the Bible schools was geographical: Bible schools were usually founded in cities in order to help reach the non-Christian urban masses, while John Brown intentionally founded his college in a rural setting. While other Bible schools trained Christian workers in cities, John Brown—perhaps in a veiled reference to Moody Bible Institute—claimed to train pastors and missionaries "far away from the slime and grime of a city life." The purpose of Southwestern was an expanded version of the Bible school's, but the setting was different. A rural, vocational version of the fundamentalist Bible school, therefore, is the best description of John Brown's college at its beginning.[28]

Such was John Brown's vision for his new college. In the fall of 1919, however, the task of making that vision a reality had just begun. One obstacle, of course, was money, so Brown's first step was to build financial stability. After turning over his own bank account to the school, Brown appointed Connely Harrington and O. P. Maxwell, the heads of the two banks in Siloam Springs, as chairman of the executive committee and treasurer, respectively, to supervise income and disbursements. He also created a board of trustees consisting of "prominent men over the United States." It included Jesse Jones, William Waterhouse, and other successful businessmen who had pledged their support to the new school. Actual control of the school, however, remained firmly in Brown's hands. He was president of the board, and his wife, Juanita, and his brother J. Alvin were also members of the board.[29]

Brown did not want the school to depend on a few wealthy men, but on "the thousands of gifts of the thousands." Brown therefore created the Southwestern Loyalty League, whereby with an annual donation of one dollar, a person would receive a year's subscription to the monthly periodical *The Southwestern* while contributing financial support to the school. With characteristic optimism, Brown assured his supporters, "this enterprise is not an experiment, but is an assured success." He confidently predicted that with the support of his readers, Southwestern would soon have five thousand students, and he vowed, "we will build the greatest school in the world." As he had done at Scarritt, Brown planned to maintain his busy speaking schedule and leave the day-to-day running of the school to others. He appointed Charles Rexroad, a decorated World War I veteran and professor of English, as dean of Southwestern to supervise education while he devoted most of his time to evangelism.[30]

Despite Brown's high hopes for the school, securing sufficient funds continued to be a problem. Starting any college requires a significant financial investment, but John Brown was proposing to build a school in which the students did not pay. This would prove to be a daunting task throughout the first decade of the institution. The pages of the college's monthly periodical are replete with urgent appeals for funds from his supporters. As early as September, the first month of the school's existence, Brown was informing his readers that he needed thirty thousand dollars within the next fifteen days. "If my friends fail to respond as I am expecting them to respond," he warned, "then I shall fail and these plans for our boys and girls will fail." By the end of the first semester, only a hefty check from Jesse Jones allowed Southwestern to end 1919 with its bills paid. The next semester, Brown devised a new way to appeal for funds. He calculated that the cost to educate a student at Southwestern amounted to $360 per year, and he appealed to individuals or groups (such as churches or Sunday School classes) to donate annual "scholarships" to cover the cost of one student.[31]

The continuing need for funds drove the most significant development of Southwestern's first school year, the changing of its name. In April 1920, Brown cited pressure by "many of the heavier donors to the Institute" that the school should bear his name. Brown claimed that he had "shrunk from doing this," but he eventually consented and gave his reasons for doing so. One motivation was dissatisfaction with the name "Southwestern." Many felt that it implied a local school, whereas Brown intended his school to have a national constituency. Furthermore, "Southwestern" seemed to many to be too bland and nondistinctive. Two other colleges, Brown discovered, already bore that name. More important, however, was the need to capitalize on Brown's fame as a revivalist in the South and West to raise much-needed funds. As one supporter advised Brown, "your name is the richest asset that the school has. I do not believe the school should be denied it." Naming the school after its founder would ensure that Brown's ideals for the school would continue even after his death and "ensure its constant support." And so in May 1920, Southwestern officially changed its name to John E. Brown College.[32]

In June, a major new source of funding seemed available. A wealthy donor offered to contribute $250,000 toward a $1 million campaign to build new buildings and begin an endowment. John Brown eagerly accepted and rushed to inform his readers of the new campaign. It all came to naught, however. Brown subsequently learned that the college would only receive this gift if it "eliminated, in part or wholly, the high Christian ideals which we had set for the school," so the donation was rejected. Furthermore, in the wake of a financial crisis in America during the summer of 1920, the general response to Brown's $1 million campaign was, he admitted, "pitiably small." The campaign was quickly abandoned. By December of 1920, Brown was urgently asking his constituents for $8,000 in order to finish paying faculty and staff salaries for the previous semester.[33]

One major reason for the college's financial difficulties was its interdenominational character in an age before nondenominational para-church ministries were commonly accepted. Christians in the early twentieth century were accustomed to supporting Christian enterprises through their denominations, and outside agencies were often viewed as a threat by local church ministers. Because fundamentalism was an interdenominational movement, it had to create its own networks and institutions; thus the Bible schools often functioned as virtual denominations. Schools such as Moody Bible Institute created their own publishing houses, Bible conferences, and in the 1920s, radio stations. While increasingly popular among conservatives, they were also viewed with suspicion by traditional church schools in the Methodist, Baptist, and Presbyterian denominations. After all, there were only so many Christian dollars (and students) to go around, and a dollar donated to a Bible school might mean one dollar less in the coffers of the local Methodist college.[34]

As a virtual Bible college, John E. Brown College faced the same sort of opposition. "A few pastors and evangelists," Brown noted in 1921, "have been openly hostile to our work" because money from their church members was, they believed, being diverted from denominational ministries to the college. Some denominational papers were going so far as to instruct members not to support the college because the denomination had educational institutions of its own. Brown, however, adamantly rejected the idea that his fledgling school competed in any way with established denominational schools. Since students who attended John E. Brown College were only those without financial means, they would not have gone to a denominational school anyway, Brown claimed. Concerning money, Brown urged his supporters not to substitute giving to the college for their normal tithe to a local church. "Deal fairly with your own friends," he instructed, "and then, after you have played square with your own church, make whatever of contribution you can to this wonderful work." The impression that some Christians were supporting the college instead of their local church, he noted, has meant that "our beloved school is placed in an unenviable light and is made to suffer."[35]

In order to alleviate the college's financial problems, some of Brown's friends urged him to affiliate his school with a particular denomination. Since Brown was a Methodist, that denomination seemed a natural fit. Brown, however, steadfastly refused to tie his fledgling school to the fate of any particular denomination, whatever financial benefits might accrue. He had built a successful career as an evangelist by appealing to Christians of all denominations, and he felt his school would be best served by doing the same.

> I felt definitely led of God to mold this school after the fashion of my evangelism—non-sectarian and interdenominational. I realized that in doing this I could look to no church board for financial support, but I believed that my thousands of friends, without doing injustice to their denomination, would take delight in contributing from their surplus money, or from their few dollars saved for other than church purposes, the necessary funds for the construction and maintenance of this school.

Brown advocated broad, interdenominational Christianity rooted in certain fundamental truths that all orthodox Christians could agree upon. In retrospect, John Brown's refusal to seek refuge in denominational affiliation seems to have been a wise choice. Such a policy added to the school's financial burdens in its early years, but in the long run, as mainstream denominations declined and denominational loyalties in America weakened, John Brown University's interdenominational character became a strong asset.[36]

For the time being, however, lack of denominational affiliation deprived the school of much-needed funds. After two years of operation, the college continued to subsist primarily on John Brown's own personal funds. Fortunately, Brown's evangelistic career continued to thrive in the early 1920s, with major stints in San Francisco and Chattanooga. Such campaigns brought in not only souls for Christ but much-needed dollars for the school. Nevertheless, in June of 1921 Brown announced his intention to avoid all debt in the future and adopt a more conservative "pay as we go" policy for the school. Such a policy would prove easier to announce than to execute.[37]

Forced to go outside the normal channels of church support, John Brown realized that national publicity was crucial to the school's success. Fortunately, publicity was soon in coming. In the fall of 1919, a lengthy article entitled "The Long Boy from the Lime Kilns" appeared in the *Country Gentleman*. This article idealized John Brown as a Horatio Alger figure who was now providing the same opportunity for success to other poor boys and girls. After years in the public spotlight, Brown was not bashful about promoting the interests of his school. In response to inquiries from one reporter, Brown instructed Robert Leflar, his publishing editor, "it's publicity we want now . . . send him everything we have." In another letter to Leflar, Brown observed, "it looks like we are in position to get some nation-wide publicity . . . and this publicity will be worth thousands of dollars to us." Other articles followed, usually in the same "poor country boy makes good" theme. *Success* magazine entitled its portrayal of John Brown "The Covered Wagon Leads to a Great Institution in the Ozarks," and *Holland's* magazine printed an article entitled "For Bigger and Better Lives." Brown soon tired of this typical treatment of his life and college ("I wish they would get away from tracking entirely the original *Country Gentleman* article," he complained to Leflar). But, he acknowledged, "we are getting publicity." Brown was clearly exaggerating when he claimed that "probably no school in American history has received such widespread publicity," but nonetheless the attention given to the young college was remarkable given its size and location. Unfortunately, publicity at times seemed to compound money problems rather than alleviate them by increasing the demand to take in more students. Brown observed in 1924, "the nation-wide publicity has brought very little, if any, financial help; but it has brought an avalanche of appeal from struggling fathers and mothers of discouraged, yet hopeful, sons and daughters."[38]

Despite constant struggles to secure funding, John E. Brown College continued to grow. In the summer of 1920, the cornerstone was laid for the first permanent brick building on campus, a boys' dormitory that would become J. Alvin Brown Hall. Because part of the vocational curriculum at the college included construction, this building, like most buildings in the school's early history, was built mostly by students. The opening of the 1920–21 school year came with a student population nearly doubled to 150; by the third year attendance increased to 200 full-time students. Boys wore striped overalls, while the girls wore standard blue dresses made in the school's sewing plant. Since Southwestern Hall was already bursting at the seams, new teachers took up residence in John Brown's own home. Other teachers and staff packed into the home of J. Alvin, who had become the business manager of the school, and some even stayed in the pre–Civil War log cabin on campus.[39]

The growing college was dependent on supporters for more than finances. In order to provide a library, John Brown issued a plea for constituents to donate used books to the school. To build a college band, Brown requested used instruments from his constituents. This created some difficulty for his evangelistic services when some California supporters, instead of sending supplies to Siloam Springs, showed up at Brown's meeting with an assortment of musical instruments (including an unidentifiable "big horn") for Brown to take back to the college with him. Because of such generosity, however, the school was able to continue through the lean early years.[40]

By the summer of 1922, J. Alvin Brown Hall had been completed, and John Brown was ready to announce construction of a second major building project, a girls dormitory. Because California had always been central to Brown's evangelistic career and Californians had done the most to support his school, Brown announced his intention to make this a building done in Californian architectural style and funded with donations from California. The building, Brown boasted, would be "the best constructed and the most beautiful building in our part of the country . . . It will stand for ages to come." On July 6, a groundbreaking

4. California Residence Hall, named in honor of John Brown's West Coast donors, is dedicated in 1927.

ceremony was held, and G. Campbell Morgan, the special speaker for the event, himself contributed $500 toward the new building. Brown, whose optimism sometimes got the best of him, announced a plan to use the building to house female students during the school year, then convert it into "a high grade summer hotel" when Siloam Springs became a fashionable summer resort. Because of frequent stoppages in construction due to lack of funds, building on the new structure proceeded in fits and starts, but California Hall was finally completed in 1927.[41]

Vocational programs continued to expand as well. By 1924, the college included an automobile repair shop, plumbing, carpentry, blacksmith and electrical shops, a brush factory, a furniture factory, a canning department, and "the largest publishing plant in northwest Arkansas." The farm expanded to cover five hundred acres, and the college dairy barn boasted twenty-eight Jersey cows. Because student vocational work provided so many of the needs of the college (the Jersey cows, for example, furnished the college with $500 worth of milk each month), Brown was able to claim that he could educate each student for only $100 a year. "Nowhere in the world," Brown declared, "will a little money go as far in the building of character and the training of mind as here in this school." Moreover, Brown had managed to build an endowment of $100,000 for the college.[42]

By the end of the 1923–24 school year, John E. Brown College was a modest success. The student body had grown to over 200, and the college seemed to be achieving the purpose its founder had set for it of educating poor, ambitious rural young people in the John Brown mold. For example, the *Ozark American* told the story of Jimmie Clayton, a student at the college in 1924. Clayton grew up in a poor farming family where the demands of hard work tended to crowd out education. Unable to afford college, Jimmie's future seemed bleak, and "several bad habits were developed." One day, however, a traveling evangelist visiting the community rekindled Clayton's religious fervor and his ambition to make something of himself. Soon thereafter, Jimmie came across a pamphlet describing John E. Brown College, "A School Where Every Student Works His Way." By the end of September, Jimmie was in Siloam Springs walking toward the college. "As the buildings came into view," the article concluded, "there went up a prayer of thanksgiving for the place where his dreams would come true." John E. Brown College had buildings, but, more important, it had a sense of identity in the world of American higher education.[43]

CHAPTER THREE

From John E. Brown College to John Brown University

John E. Brown College had survived its fragile early years, but its financial situation was still precarious in the spring of 1924. Construction on the California building was suspended due to lack of funds, and the college still was not functioning on a debt-free, pay-as-you-go basis, as Brown had intended it to do. Many supporters were shocked and alarmed, therefore, to learn in May 1924 that John Brown had bought an entire city in order to build a new university. Actually, the news was not as dramatic as some newspaper headlines made it seem. The "city" was Sulphur Springs, Arkansas, a small town of about one thousand people thirty miles north of Siloam Springs; and Brown had only purchased part of the town, albeit a major portion. Nevertheless, Brown's attempt to create and maintain two institutions of higher education produced a time of turmoil and instability for John E. Brown College.[1]

Years of Turmoil, 1924–28

By the spring of 1924, John Brown had decided to open a school with the same work-study philosophy as John E. Brown College, but to run it on a tuition basis for children whose parents could pay for an education. He initially planned to build this new school in Siloam Springs, but in March he was approached by Storm Whaley, the president of the Bank of Sulphur Springs, with a proposition. Years earlier, a group of investors, hoping to take advantage of the natural springs in the town, had built hotels in order to establish a health spa at Sulphur Springs. The venture did not work out, and the investors wanted to unload their properties. Whaley asked Brown to purchase their holdings, valued at $250,000, according to Brown. He offered to buy them for $100,000 with only $500 down. The owners, desperate to sell, agreed to his terms. Thus, Brown acquired for his new school three hotels, forty business lots, 360 residential lots, a city park, springs, and a lake. In May, John Brown announced his purchase and his plans to leave John E. Brown College in Siloam Springs and build John Brown University thirty miles to the north in Sulphur Springs.[2]

In addition to receiving a good deal on the Sulphur Springs property, John Brown's decision to move to Sulphur Springs was motivated by tensions that had developed between himself and the town of Siloam Springs. At the founding of the college in 1919, the Siloam Springs community seemed to enthusiastically support the new institution. However, by 1924 relations between the college and the town had cooled considerably. Explaining his decision to leave for Sulphur Springs in the Siloam Springs newspaper, Brown asserted that certain influential men in the town "have repeatedly gone out of their way to interfere with my work and to cast reflection upon it." Criticism of the college, he claimed, was even sent to donors in California to persuade them withhold their support of the school. Furthermore, Brown complained, soon after the founding of the college, a building was erected nearby to be used as a dance hall, something that Brown detested having near his college. Ultimately, John Brown's complaint was that Siloam Springs was not progressive and forward-thinking enough. The town was controlled by a "machine" of a few powerful men who retarded progress and initiative. While neighboring communities like Springdale and Fayetteville were growing rapidly, he asserted, "Siloam Springs has practically been at a standstill for years." As a result, Brown planned not only to begin a new university elsewhere; he also moved the International Federation of Christian Workers, his summer Bible conference, and his own family to Sulphur Springs. While the college would remain in Siloam Springs for the time being, it appeared in 1924 that John Brown's days in the town were numbered.[3]

In September 1924, John Brown University at Sulphur Springs opened its doors to one hundred students. Brown envisioned the college as a place for his wealthier supporters to send their children to receive a college education and also learn the virtues of hard work. The university boasted many of the recreational features of America's best colleges, including swimming, golf, tennis, and horseback riding while offering well-equipped dormitories, classrooms, and laboratories in the former hotels. However, unlike most universities, this one would be "jazzless"; that is, the corrupt amusements available to college students on most American campuses would be strictly banned. Students would pay $500 per year, and in keeping with John Brown's spiritual and vocational ideals, each student would spend one hour a day in chapel and one hour a day working at a trade. Brown assembled a faculty with first-rate academic degrees and appointed as dean Dr. T. Marshall Morsey, a graduate of Princeton Theological Seminary. Other professors boasted degrees from schools such as Cornell, Stanford, and the University of Chicago. With typical optimism, Brown asserted that "the school is being made an accredited school at once" and predicted that it would be "swamped with students" by its second academic year.[4]

John Brown now managed, in addition to his revival schedule, the presidency of two colleges, the editorship of a daily newspaper and a monthly magazine, and the presidency of the IFCW. He had always been a whirlwind of activity, but was especially so in 1924. At one point during a 1924 evangelistic crusade in Knoxville, Tennessee, a frazzled Brown wrote to Robert Leflar, "I have three secretaries now working in my room. I have the scholarship campaign, the California building campaign, the band concert tour, an awfully heavy correspondence, magazine work, and am speaking on an average of three to five times a day." John Brown clearly threw all of his energy into his enterprises, and he expected the same tireless commitment in his workers. Once while on a campaign in California, he wrote a sharp reprimand to one of his teachers at John E. Brown College who had, he learned, "taken some liberties in the matter of going to town at night." Brown wrote, "your job requires constant attention, and every ounce of energy you can throw into it. . . . We must learn to be on the job every second."[5]

Such driving of himself and his employees allowed John

Brown's institutions to thrive despite limited funding, but it also could result in the loss of some quality workers over the years. At one point in the spring of 1924, Robert Leflar, director of Brown's publishing plant, expressed his frustration to Brown after the latter had increased his responsibilities: "There comes a time when one more straw will break even a camel's back, and I'm afraid that I'll have to respectfully decline any more additions to my work just now. . . . As soon as the days get to be 36 hours long, or a device is invented by the use of which men can do without rest, I will be more than glad to take on more work. Until then, though, eighteen hours a day is the best I can do." A few months later, Leflar left Siloam Springs. He eventually graduated from Harvard Law School and went on to become dean of the University of Arkansas Law School.[6]

Brown's tireless energy and unbounded optimism convinced him that he could successfully run two colleges at the same time. The venture in Sulphur Springs, however, turned out to be a failure. A number of Brown's friends warned him that at a time when John E. Brown College was struggling, starting a separate university was an unwise decision. Brown, accustomed to success, disregarded such warnings. "The longer I live the more thoroughly convinced I become that it is unjust to our friends and a reflection on God when we take the visions which God sends us, and the plans which God makes for us, to have them passed on by fallible, erring, though sympathetic men." This time, however, Brown would discover that he was the fallible one. The years of trying to maintain two separate colleges in two different towns would be the most difficult ones in the early history of John Brown's schools.[7]

One problem, as always, was money. John Brown now had a host of new facilities in Sulphur Springs to pay off, as well as two separate faculties and staffs to pay. Despite his hopes, the Sulphur Springs school never was able to turn a profit. Donations lagged due to the departure of a number of supporters over the founding of a second university. John Brown was forced to raise even more money from his evangelistic campaigns, and this at a time when professional evangelism was falling into disfavor with the American public. By the mid-1920s, the era of large citywide crusades was in decline; it would not revive again until the advent of Billy Graham in the late 1940s. Professional evangelists acquired a reputation in the American consciousness as showmen and hucksters. Billy Sunday's career declined in the 1920s amid criticisms of his handling of finances. It was generally known that his free-will offerings had totaled over a million dollars by 1918. Although he donated much of his earnings to charity in response to criticism, Sunday also defended his lavish lifestyle made possible through soul-winning. In 1927, Sinclair Lewis wrote a best-selling novel, *Elmer Gantry*, which depicted a corrupt evangelist who made a fortune through his tent revivals.[8]

The mid-1920s, therefore, was a poor time to be raising money through old-fashioned revivals; yet John Brown continued to depend on his evangelism income to help support the schools. In 1926, Brown himself fell prey to the criticism of being a "grafter." The previous year, using royalties from sales of his books, John Brown had built a stately, spacious home for his family in Sulphur Springs. Although he planned only a modest home, a number of additions were included before the house was completed. As a result, Brown explained, "When the work was done we found that the home was so much larger and so much more expensive than planned that I realized at once that the house would become a 'point of attack' for that certain group that always seeks for something to criticize. . . . One of my evangelistic friends insisted that the home could not be produced for less than $40,000." So, in order to avoid criticism—and to help pay off some of the college's debts—Brown put his new home up for sale and moved his family back to Siloam Springs. Not until 1933 would the Brown family purchase a home of their own.[9]

Another source of the school's financial difficulty continued to be the college's nondenominational status. By 1925, battles between fundamentalists and modernists raged in America's major denominations, and fundamentalists were losing most of them. In the late 1920s, many fundamentalists would leave the mainstream denominations to form new ones. Denominational pastors thus viewed fundamentalist institutions such as Bible schools with increasing suspicion. Some conservative supporters of John E. Brown College, unhappy with the theological drift of their own denominations, were sending their money to Brown instead of to their own congregations, thereby causing further opposition to Brown from denominational ministers. One man, Brown learned in 1925, made a donation to the college and then informed his pastor that that was his tithe for the month. The result, exclaimed Brown, "probably cost the school ten dollars for every dollar the man was giving." In an age of denominational conflicts, funds for an interdenominational institution such as John E. Brown College remained difficult to come by.[10]

Such exigencies led Brown to make changes both to his college and to his speaking schedule. The college's financial policy was revised in 1925. From now on, students would be asked to pay back the cost of their education—calculated now at $150 per year—after their graduation. At the founding in 1919, Brown had considered this approach but rejected it in order to graduate students free of financial obligations. Now, however, discretion proved the better part of valor, and Brown figured that after a few years, money from graduates would provide a healthy stream of income to help free the school from dependence on him. Besides, he reasoned, students would value their education more, and learn responsibility, if they were required to pay for it. In the meantime, Brown undertook a $250,000 subscription campaign to build up a "Loan Fund" to pay for the needy students currently at the college. To do so, Brown reduced his evangelistic schedule in order to "take to the field with the story of my schools." In 1926, Brown lectured in more than one hundred cities and towns in the South and Midwest, explaining what he saw as a crisis in American education and his proposed solution. The tour seemed successful, as Brown was able to speak to a number of prominent people, including an address to the combined House and Senate of the State of Oklahoma.[11]

In addition to finances, another problem with the Siloam Springs/Sulphur Springs arrangement was complexity and duplication of effort. For the 1925–26 school year, John Brown announced that the two schools would no longer be kept separate, as had been originally intended, but would be partially consolidated. The result was a system Byzantine in complexity. In order to reduce staff, music, art, and Bible teachers from Sulphur Springs would spend two days a week teaching at the college in Siloam Springs. Since the John E. Brown College continued to function as a two-year junior college, graduates from there would have the option of transferring to Sulphur Springs for the last two years of college. Also, the university in Sulphur Springs would now be operated partially on the college's work-study model. Students who could afford it would continue to pay full tuition and room and board and work only one hour a day, as originally planned. Other students at the university, however, could pay $250 per year (half the full amount) and work two hours a day to help subsidize the cost of their education. John Brown now had two semi-independent colleges with three different payment plans on his hands.[12]

One reason for this change in policy at Sulphur Springs was a lack of student interest in the university. By 1926, Brown discovered that many supporters who had praised his idea of a vocational university for paying students were not actually willing to send their own children there. In a public statement to his supporters, Brown could not mask his disappointment with them. "Nine out of ten of the parents who have money—whatever their talk about wanting their children to work—are only 'talking through their hat.'" When push comes to shove, Brown complained, "most parents today who have money are going to educate their boys and girls to idleness." Lacking a sufficient number of paying students, Brown tried to salvage his university at Sulphur Springs by accepting work-study students as well.[13]

Further weakening the Sulphur Springs university was the fact that the professionally trained faculty that Brown had assembled—including Dean Morsey, who lasted only two years—never fully accepted Brown's "educating to work" ideal. When he was away conducting revivals, Brown later claimed, Morsey and other members of the faculty would emphasize classroom work to the detriment of the vocational program. They made "a joke and a farce" of his vocational program at Sulphur Springs, and some of them, Brown claimed, were even "making fun of the Siloam ideal." The bitterness that Brown, who never had the opportunity for a university education, felt toward these "dyed in the wool school men," as he called them, was readily apparent.[14]

What finally convinced John Brown to abandon his dream of a vocational university at Sulphur Springs was the failure to achieve accreditation as a four-year college. Brown realized that he would never generate sufficient student interest in the university unless it were fully accredited by an academic body. In early 1926, therefore, Brown invited Dr. J. D. Ellif of the University of Missouri to visit Sulphur Springs to point out what would be necessary to achieve accreditation by the North Central Association of Colleges and Secondary Schools. Ellif's report was sobering. The conditions for accreditation included a new library, a standard laboratory, more students, more credentialed teachers, and an endowment of at least half a million dollars. Brown finally realized that he could not build a university at Sulphur Springs and a junior college at Siloam Springs at the same time. Making this attempt, Brown concluded, "would involve a five year program that would have killed, dead beyond recovery, the school at Siloam Springs." Ellif's report, coming in the wake of financial difficulty, declining student interest, and faculty unrest, convinced Brown to abandon—for the time being, at least—his dream of creating a Christian vocational university. He informed his supporters, "We have decided that the cost of establishing an accredited university would not bring to the young people whom we are seeking to serve, results that would justify the cost."[15]

Brown still had plans for Sulphur Springs, however. In the spring of 1926, Brown announced another reorganization of his schools. Now both Siloam Springs and Sulphur Springs would be high school academies and junior colleges for students who could not pay for school. Students would borrow the $150 per year cost of education and pay it back after graduation. Siloam Springs would become an all-boys school, while Sulphur Springs would become an all-girls school. Whereas earlier Brown had trumpeted the

5. A group of female students at the Sulphur Springs campus in 1928.

virtues of supervised coeducation, he now changed his mind, professedly due to concerns about a rise in immorality associated with the 1920s and the age of flappers. "Under the peculiar conditions of this day and age," he concluded, "a complete separation of sexes is better." The 1926–27 school year, therefore, opened with two all-work colleges, one male and one female. The new plan apparently was not popular among students who had become used to socializing with members of the opposite sex. Brown admitted in September that it would "probably be difficult to find anyone here in these schools" who was "delighted in the present program." Nonetheless, he avowed, "we have settled definitely the plans for these schools."[16]

Brown might have solved, for the time being, the problems in his schools, but in 1927, a more serious crisis arose in Sulphur Springs which threatened to destroy Brown's educational efforts altogether. Brown had clashed with some powerful men in Siloam Springs, but a more serious controversy arose between Brown and some leading residents of Sulphur Springs. A strong-willed, outspoken man, Brown had always sparked his share of criticism, and early on in Sulphur Springs he managed to create enemies. One of Brown's purchases in Sulphur Springs was the city park in the middle of town. Apparently, this park had been sponsoring activities on Sunday, and so one of the first things Brown did when he bought his property in the spring of 1924 was to close the park to all "desecrations" of the Holy Day. The move angered some of the townspeople. In response, some leading men of the city scheduled a carnival on the outskirts of town during Brown's summer Bible conference. According to Brown, "they had the county seeded down with bills announcing HORSE RACES, BASEBALL and a CARNIVAL in Sulphur Springs on Sunday." Brown publicly accused certain men of deliberately doing this to embarrass him in front of his Bible conference visitors.[17]

Brown also provoked the wrath of some denominational loyalists in Sulphur Springs. Believing that Christians in the town were too attached to their particular denominations, Brown created a nondenominational community church for John Brown University students, faculty, and whatever townspeople chose to attend. This move angered a number of traditionalists in town who, according to Brown, "began a constant flow of circulars, letters to church papers, letters to ministers, leaflets, etc." full of erroneous and misleading charges against Brown and his school.[18]

By the spring of 1927, relations between Brown and the community reached their nadir. Certain townspeople composed a letter full of what Brown claimed were "lies and accusations." With the aid of the local postmaster, these men acquired Brown's entire mailing list and sent the letter to his constituents. They accused Brown of exercising a tyranny over his school in Sulphur Springs and of having expelled more than one hundred students. More serious, in the age of Elmer Gantry, his enemies accused Brown of financial improprieties: Brown had valued his large, expensive home in Sulphur Springs at only eight hundred dollars in order to avoid paying taxes on it, they claimed.[19]

Such an attack could be life-threatening to a religious institution in America. As Nathan Hatch and other historians have observed, American religion has always functioned as essentially a "free market" economy. Without a government-established church in America, religious entrepreneurs, as with economic entrepreneurs, created a "product" and then sought to acquire a share of the American religious market that would buy into that product. There were always plenty of alternatives vying for support, and as American Christians chose where to devote their attention—and money—old enterprises died and new ones arose continuously. The religious free market dictated who survived and who did not. This was especially true in a nondenominational movement like fundamentalism. Without a denominational board to certify him, Brown's institutions were completely dependent on his personal reputation among his supporters. If they perceived that he or his institutions were not credible, they could easily shift their resources to another religious entrepreneur eager for their support.[20]

Recognizing the danger that the Sulphur Springs controversy posed to his institutions, John Brown wrote a lengthy pamphlet defending himself. The school at Sulphur Springs had expelled only one student during its years of existence, not one hundred, as his critics claimed. Brown never devalued his house for tax purposes. In fact, he asserted, no taxes were paid on the house at all, since it was deeded to the school, a nonprofit organization. In addition to answering charges, Brown sought to reaffirm his credibility to his audience. Lacking a denominational board or any external governing organization, he did so in the best way possible for a fundamentalist—by citing the testimony of public figures in the fundamentalist world. A number of prominent men in Sulphur Springs and Siloam Springs, including the mayors of each town, wrote letters expressing their faith in Brown. More important for his California constituents, however, Reuben Torrey came to Brown's aid. Torrey spent two weeks with Brown in Sulphur Springs, inspected the books and business affairs of the school and issued a public letter stating his conviction that the operation was sound and trustworthy. Brown gratefully published Torrey's letter of approval in his monthly periodical. A year after the controversy, when another highly regarded figure in fundamentalism, Boston minister J. C. Massee, visited Brown's Bible conference in Sulphur Springs, Brown eagerly printed Massee's assessment for his supporters: "Not a single word of criticism has reached me during the eight days of my stay." Brown's aggressive response to attacks kept his schools alive at this critical time.[21]

His schools may have survived the attacks on his credibility, but they remained too complicated and costly. In April 1927 Brown announced a new set of changes to the system: Siloam Springs would become a four-year nonaccredited college, with girls from Sulphur Springs eligible to finish their last two years of college training at the Siloam Springs campus. Brown's brief experiment in single-sex education was already beginning to revert to the previous setup. In the meantime, thirty girls from the Sulphur Springs campus had already been transferred to Siloam Springs due to lack of space. Furthermore, the schools had developed additional vocational programs, so that by 1927 there existed, among other things, a furniture shop, a motor company, a brush factory, two farms, a laundry shop, an art department, a dress factory, printing presses, an electrical department, a radio repair shop, and a stationery shop, all spread out between the Siloam Springs and Sulphur Springs campuses. The two separate schools and expanded vocational programs required additional funds, and Brown's pay-back system had yet to kick in. In May 1927, Brown exclaimed, "with two schools, and three faculties, and additional Bible teachers, and two large student bodies, my income from evangelism does not begin to meet the needs of these schools."[22]

Unfortunately, other funds were not arriving in very large quantities. Whether related to the damaging letters from his Sulphur Springs critics or not, the fact is that Brown found it increasingly difficult to raise money to meet the rising demands of his schools. In July, Brown began his monthly periodical with an article entitled, "Will Our Schools Live?" It was a fair question to ask at the time. That fall, Brown announced a Christmas campaign to raise $50,000 for student scholarships. By December, the campaign had raised only $10,000, and Brown was faced with raising $20,000 immediately or sending one hundred students home the next year. All building projects were stopped, and Brown pledged to take no more students in the coming year who were not previously underwritten with a $150 scholarship by some donor. The 1927–28 school proved to be, by Brown's own admission, "one of the hardest years, generally speaking, of school history." Brown's predictions of having five thousand students now seemed a pipe dream as he struggled to maintain the 275 students that he had. Brown admitted, "I have lost all desire to build the 'Largest Schools' in the world, and have turned time, attention, and effort to building the best schools." Clearly, the revised arrangements at Sulphur Springs and Siloam Springs were still not working out.[23]

By the end of the 1927–28 school year, Brown had had enough of trying to sustain two colleges in two different towns. In July 1928 he announced that the schools would be consolidated on one campus in Siloam Springs. The attempt to maintain a separate school in Sulphur Springs, he recognized, "has confused our friends and caused us financial loss." Moving all operations to Siloam Springs would save about $25,000 a year in costs, he estimated. Equally important, it would allow him to remove his college from the "poisonous atmosphere" and controversies in Sulphur Springs, a situation that had cost him "many heartaches and sleepless nights." In August 1928, Brown informed the people of Sulphur Springs in the town's newspaper, "I want to wash my mind and heart and hands of the whole unpleasant business." Brown was removing his college from Sulphur Springs but not leaving the city altogether. He planned to turn the Sulphur Springs campus into a summer resort, "The Ozark Health and Recreational Center," the profits from which would go directly toward the support of the Siloam Springs college.[24]

The 1928–29 school year thus began with the entire John Brown student body together on one campus for the first time since before Brown's Sulphur Springs venture began. The previous four years had been filled with changing policies, criticism, and financial difficulties. "Every school must pass through an uncertain beginning period, and must be subjected to all sorts of skepticism, fears, doubts, and unfounded rumors," Brown observed in 1927. John Brown's school had certainly experienced its share, some of it inevitable, some of it of Brown's own making. Overall, it is difficult to disagree with the assessment of Clyde Kilby, the college's registrar during these years, that "the one great handicap of the John Brown Schools" was "our inability to establish excellence in one place, then maintain it while going on to the next." However, whether Brown knew it or not, the worst was over. John E. Brown College had survived, and the next six years would see it develop into the Christian university that Brown had tried and failed to establish in Sulphur Springs.[25]

Building a Christian University, 1929–34

John E. Brown College was a long way from university status in 1929. Over the next six years, however, John E. Brown College progressed toward this goal. Three major trends characterized the college during these years and pushed it toward recognition as a university: increased financial stability, more direct leadership by its president, and improvements to the college's programs and facilities.

At the beginning of 1929, the college's financial situation was still precarious, but it was improving. Brown's supporters reacted favorably to his announcement that he was consolidating his schools at Siloam Springs, and donations increased. In January, Brown announced that while affairs were still tight, "financially speaking we are probably in the best condition we have been in in two or three years." Finances continued to improve in ensuing years, despite the onset of the greatest economic crisis America had ever faced. In October 1929, Brown announced the start of a Ten Year Jubilee campaign to clear the college of all debts. His timing could not have been worse. On October 29, the stock crash known as Black Monday occurred, inaugurating the Great Depression that would dominate America for the next decade. Millions of Americans lost their jobs, and during the peak of the depression, one-third of America's workforce was unemployed. John E. Brown College, like many institutions, had its share of struggles during the crisis. In the fall of 1930, Arkansas banks were forced to call in loans in order to avoid collapse. Brown went to his supporters to announce that he needed $20,000 immediately to pay back loans the college had taken from some local banks. People responded, and the crisis was averted.[26]

Financially, 1932 was the most difficult year of this period for the school. The college was forced to reduce faculty and staff salaries by 10 to 25 percent, and all building projects on campus ground to a halt for lack of funds. In October, Brown instructed Richard Hodges, the business director of the school, to pare down expenses to a minimum: "There is no improvement in a business way, at least financially, and I want us to rigidly adhere to the idea of 'cash on the barrelhead' for everything we buy." Nonetheless, even during the darkest days of the depression, Brown sought to put a bright face on the crisis. During one of many "emergency calls" for funds during these years, Brown assured his supporters, "If these institutions can keep their doors open in a dark hour like this, with state schools and church schools facing serious reductions or shortening of terms and with some actually closing, our schools will have proven themselves and forever established themselves."[27]

Brown's optimism eventually proved to be well-founded. Despite the troubles, the college continued to meet its financial obligations, retain students, and even expand its physical plant. In August 1933, Brown could boast that during the financial depression, John E. Brown College had faithfully made payments on its bonds and bills. "While other institutions, considered immovable and unshakable, have crashed to earth," he asserted, "our schools have maintained their paper at par." While still by no means prosperous, the college's financial future at least seemed stable.[28]

While shoring up the school's finances, John Brown also began taking a more active leadership role in the day-to-day operations of the college during these years. The year 1928 had been successful for Brown as an evangelist. He began with a revival campaign at the famous Tremont Temple in Boston. The Boston media seemed fascinated with this flamboyant country boy from the "Great West" and his distinctive name. One reporter remarked, "John Brown's body occupied the pulpit in Tremont Temple today, and this particular John Brown gave no indication whatever of having been 'a-mouldering in the grave.'" According to Brown, those in the know in Boston claimed that no greater meetings had been held in Tremont Temple since the days of D. L. Moody.[29]

After 1928, however, Brown's evangelistic meetings dropped off sharply, and he began devoting more of his time to personally directing the affairs of the college. The difficulties in Sulphur Springs had taught Brown the danger of relying on others, especially academically trained educators, to faithfully employ his educational ideals. In 1931, Brown explained this change of strategy. In the early years of the school, Brown had devoted most of his time to evangelism and left others to administer the college. The result, he claimed, had been "en epidemic of resignations or discharges." By 1928, however, Brown had come to the conviction that if God had called him to found this school, God would provide the wisdom and strength to directly govern it. Hence, asserted Brown, "I have taken full charge, top to bottom, and have made it my business to employ all workers and direct all workers." In 1932, Brown took over not only day-to-day administration but also personally supervised religious education at the college. He took over direction of the Bible department and taught one course each semester.[30]

The fact that Brown was able to spend more time on campus and yet see improvements to the college's finances can be attributed to the emergence of radio technology. Radio became crucial to the college's progress because it enabled Brown to continue his evangelistic work and widen the college's constituency while traveling less. American revivalists have always been innovators in finding ways to capture a wider audience. In the eighteenth century, George Whitefield acquired the nickname of "the divine dramatist" because he used the techniques of the stage and applied them to open-air evangelism. By the late-1800s, D. L. Moody was speaking to large audiences in huge, cavernous buildings. By the 1920s, evangelists recognized the potential of radio to reach even more listeners with the gospel, and many of them, Brown included, established radio ministries.[31]

With itinerant evangelism in decline by the late 1920s, Brown began to place great hopes in the possibilities of radio. Because of the influx of modernism into the traditional churches, Brown declared, evangelism was dying out and the Protestant churches were in decay. However, he said, God had raised up the medium of radio to allow the gospel to be preached. He concluded, "I have come to believe that the greatest field in America today for preaching the gospel is over the radio." Brown's folksy preaching style and his simple evangelistic message made radio an ideal medium for him, as he himself recognized. "I have been blessed with a radio voice," he noted, "and God has graciously granted me the type of message to build a great radio audience." In 1928, Brown purchased his first radio station, KFPW, and moved it from its original site in Cartersville, Missouri, to Siloam Springs. He sold the station a year later because its power output was inadequate, but his venture into radio had begun and would continue. Three years later, Brown bought radio time on KMPC in Beverly Hills, California, and began broadcasting a daily radio program called "God's Half Hour." By 1932, it was also being broadcast in Fort Worth, Texas.[32]

Brown recognized that radio had other uses besides evangelism;

it allowed him to maintain contact with donors and expand the potential financial base for John E. Brown College. Brown once quipped that his first radio station, KFPW, stood for "Kind Friends Please Write." His daily radio program, "God's Half Hour," Brown claimed in 1933, had "put tens of thousands of dollars in gifts and wills and property and loans into our schools," and he predicted even more benefits in the future. Over the years, radio would become an important tool in widening the college's ministry, constituency, and support base.[33]

While stabilizing its finances and coming under more direct control of its founder, John E. Brown College also improved its programs and facilities in the years leading up to state recognition. Concerning its admissions policy, the college gradually became more like conventional colleges by increasing the financial responsibilities of the students and decreasing the work-study aspect of the college. Some of John Brown's supporters expressed displeasure that his school only allowed poor children. One donor complained to Brown in early 1930 that "you build exactly the type of school I would like to have my children in, and then because I am a man of moderate circumstances you bar my children from the privileges of the school." This was, of course, the type of parent that Brown had started his university in Sulphur Springs for, but few had actually responded. Now, Brown officially opened up the Siloam Springs college to children of middle-class parents, though on a limited basis.[34]

In 1930, John E. Brown College announced a new payment plan that signaled its first steps toward the type of pay arrangement that had existed earlier at Sulphur Springs. The college's scholarship fund had been used up to cover existing students, so Brown announced in August that he would accept only new students whose parents could pay a tuition of $120. Such an amount seems rather small, but this was the first time that Brown had asked some students at the Siloam Springs campus to pay up front for their education. The next year, the trend toward paying students continued. All students would continue to work four hours a day to cover their room and board, but tuition (calculated to be $300 per year at this point) would be paid for in three different ways. The neediest students, the ones that John E. Brown College had been originally established to serve, would continue to pay no money up front for their education but would pay back $150 per year of their tuition after graduation. A second group of students would be accepted on a half-pay, half-loan basis: They would pay $150 up front and borrow $150 from the school's loan fund to be repaid after graduation. A third group, "which of course is very limited," Brown assured his supporters, would pay the full $300 up front.[35]

By 1932, it seemed that opening up the college to "students coming from homes of the well to do" had been a success. Brown announced in September 1932, "this limited test has proved so entirely satisfactory that the program is being enlarged upon for the coming year." Under a new payment plan to go into effect in 1933, all students would be charged $450 annually for room and board and tuition, payable according to three schedules. Most students would pay $100 up front and pay back the rest of the amount after graduation. Others would pay $150 up front, while students from wealthier homes would pay $350 up front.[36]

These changes were significant in a couple of ways. First, John E. Brown College was proposing to reduce its vocational character and expand the academic component. Under the new plan, the amount of hours a day that students spent in vocational work would vary depending on their financial contribution. Students who paid only $100 would work four hours a day and students paying $150 up front would work three hours a day. Those paying $350 up front would be allowed to specialize in academic rather than vocational departments and work only two hours a day. This would allow them to devote extra time for academic studies. Thus, vocational specialization at John E. Brown College would be simply an option, not a requirement. Students could specialize in either academic or vocational studies.[37]

More important, the college had now become a pay school for all of its students. Even the poorest students were required to contribute $100 up front to the cost of their education. In announcing these changes, Brown was careful to reaffirm the original purpose of his college. "This does not mean," he reassured his supporters, "that we are changing in the least our original plan of education, . . . nor does it mean that we are changing our high ideal of serving the boy or girl who must have financial help." However, while still committed to providing affordable education for needy young people, Brown's views on this matter had changed somewhat from his original plan. "It is my conviction," he stated in 1933, "that every student should be compelled to make some contribution to his education." Affordable education, not free education, was now the stated purpose of John E. Brown College.[38]

As the college evolved toward more pay and less vocational work, the size of the student body expanded slightly, from 275 students in 1927–28 to 300 students in 1931–32. As students increased, so too did the number of professors, up to forty full-time faculty by 1933.[39] The college's facilities also grew, despite occasional building stoppages due to lack of funds. Because construction work was done by the students, building programs could often continue even in the face of economic depression and low financial support. In 1927, the California building was dedicated and joined J. Alvin Brown Hall as the second large permanent structure on campus. J. Alvin continued to house male students, as well to serve as living space for some of the faculty and working space for the campus printing plant. The California building, named in honor of the university's donors in that state, served as a women's dormitory, campus kitchen and dining room, office space, and living quarters for teachers. Other buildings followed in the wake of the California dedication. The alumni building, completed in 1931, housed the campus electrical and power plant, a bakery, a canning factory, a laundry and pressing department, a dress factory, a typing department, and science laboratories. An engineering building soon followed and contained classroom space, an electrical shop, and an automotive shop. In 1931, Helen Brown Hodges, John Brown's youngest daughter, died after a brief illness. This tragedy became the occasion for the construction of the Helen Brown Hodges Memorial Building, which served as the main classroom building, the library, and the campus auditorium, as well as housing for administrative offices.

6. John Brown University's printing press in the 1930s. Such industries were intended to provide vocational education for students and generate revenue for the university.

John E. Brown College was slowly expanding, both in terms of students and facilities.[40]

In 1932, John Brown announced that he was ready to establish in Siloam Springs what he had failed to create in Sulphur Springs: a four-year, degree-granting university. Because of his low opinion of American higher education, Brown was ambivalent about pursuing recognition by the "educational machine," as he called it.

"Everything would be gained and practically nothing lost," he asserted, "if everything that is classed under the head of 'standard curriculum' and 'credits' and 'degrees' could be swept from the school room and swept from the minds of our modern youth." Nevertheless, Brown pursued university status for both practical and ideological reasons. Employers wanted young people with degrees, he realized, so part of providing a practical, useful education in modern America included giving students a college degree that would help them get a job. This would also help the college financially, the pragmatic Brown noted. Students who graduated with college degrees would have more earning power, and thus be better able to quickly pay back their financial obligations to the college.[41]

The other reason for seeking recognition as a university was more ideological. Students who transferred away from John E. Brown College to finish their four-year degree somewhere else, Brown believed, risked losing their religious faith in an educational system dominated by "evolution and atheism." In many instances, he claimed, "there has been a malicious attempt to laugh these students out of their faith in God and their unquestioned faith in the integrity of the Word of God." Enabling students to finish a college degree at Siloam Springs would help protect them from attacks on their faith. Thus, Brown declared, "we stand ready, man to man, to stand the test of the most rigid examination the state may wish to subject us to, and on our merits we shall ask and receive full authority to grant any and all degrees justified by the work done."[42]

In the spring of 1934, the Arkansas State Board of Education examined the college and approved its program. On June 11, John Brown traveled to Little Rock and received an unrestricted charter for the "John Brown University" to offer degrees in the arts and sciences. The next day, Brown held up the charter in chapel, to thunderous applause from faculty and students. On July 14, a dedication service was held on campus to raise the flag on the new John Brown University, formerly John E. Brown College. Brown's close friend Robert "Fighting Bob" Shuler arrived from Los Angeles to give the dedication address. A couple of months later, John Brown University officially opened its doors to the largest number of students in school history. Fifteen years after Southwestern Collegiate Institute began, John Brown's dream of creating a "Christian university" was fulfilled.[43]

After it was announced that John E. Brown College was recognized as a state-chartered university, John Brown received a mildly critical letter from a supporter. Noting that Brown's publications were often filled with mistakes and misspellings, one reader advised that, as Brown put it, "with the beginning of a university program, our publications should be more carefully edited." Brown penned an interesting response. After stating that he wrote most of his articles during hectic revival campaigns and rarely had time to proofread them, Brown remarked, "All of this, of course, raises an issue, . . . whether we should give to the world the best we have, regardless of the perfection or imperfection of it, trusting God to use it to the vast appreciative and often unreached masses, or whether we should think only of the intellectuals and withhold our product until we are ready to speak the language of perfection." Such a remark typified John Brown's approach to life and helps explain the occasionally erratic nature of the first fifteen years of John Brown University's existence. Brown was a man of action, not deliberation. "Ever since I entered public life," he remarked, "there has been a voice with its insistent demand that I produce, produce, produce!" Sensing a need for a new type of higher education, Brown acted—just as he wrote—immediately and at times seemingly impulsively. "We might have written a better editorial had we written fewer editorials," he observed. "We might have built a better school if we had built more slowly." But the urgency of the day demanded action, Brown believed, and so he acted. When an attempt failed, as in Sulphur Springs, Brown frankly acknowledged it and went on to something else, usually with better success the next time. What separated Brown from most Christians was not necessarily greater genius or deeper spirituality but the courage to act, to produce, even if that meant risking failure. The final product could always be improved upon or refined later, but John Brown University is indebted to its founder for having the energy, faithfulness, and courage to act where others may have simply deliberated.[44]

PART TWO

Achieving Permanence, 1935–1962

By the 1930s, John Brown University resembled in many ways the utopian religious communities of the nineteenth century that dotted the American landscape. As historian Bruce Shelley describes them, "each was the lengthened shadow of some charismatic leader or self-conscious innovator. The leader's vision of utopia created the community, and his or her firm will imposed order." The danger in such communities, of course, is that their founders do not live forever. Unable to sustain a life and vision apart from their founders, the nineteenth-century communities were prone to extinction. Shelley observes, "in most cases, when the charismatic leader passed on, the community drifted toward death." How would John Brown University avoid a similar fate when its founder passed away? This was the most serious challenge facing the university. The history of John Brown University during the middle decades of the twentieth century can best be understood as an attempt to become a nationally respected Christian university in its own right, one that could outlive its founder and achieve permanence.[1]

CHAPTER FOUR

College Life in the Early Years

Like the nineteenth-century utopian communities, the John Brown University community in its early years of existence truly was the lengthened shadow of the founder. John Brown's persona and ideology shaped every facet of the university, even the daily lives of the students. At this point, therefore, it may be helpful to step back and ask the question, What was it like to be a John E. Brown College/John Brown University student in the 1920s and 1930s?

To answer this question, one must first examine who it was that made up the student body. Brown sought to educate primarily poor children, but he claimed that his college was exclusive in other areas, both mentally and physically. "We want students above the average in mentality," he wrote in 1923, "clean of body and clean of character. Our students must stand erect, without the handicap of physical infirmities." The school, he adamantly maintained, was not for "the miss-fits, the laggards, the cast-outs, the unfortunates, the backward, the halting, the unpromising." Apparently, though, this strict standard was not always followed. In 1927, Brown admitted the college had "slipped" in that "we have permitted friends in the field to send us their own sons and daughters or to send us boys and girls in whom they were interested," not all of whom measured up to Brown's high standards. The sending of below-average students, however, Brown claimed, only brought "embarrassment to the student," since they typically were not able to meet the requirements of the school.[1]

The same gap between stated intentions and realities existed geographically as well. Having a strong rural orientation himself, Brown claimed early on that his college was for rural young people. "We do not want boys and girls from the cities who come to us from the shadow of great schools," he remarked. "We do want the boys and girls from the mountains, hills, and valleys." One reason for this stated rural preference was that the college was originally intended for young people who had no other educational alternatives, and Brown believed that the cities already had plenty of schools and ministries devoted to underprivileged urban young people. Furthermore, Brown believed that city kids were unable to adapt to his college's strict regimen and emphasis on hard work: "It is worse than useless to try to assimilate and adjust the average city boy or girl into such a program as we have here," he declared. "Boys from the streets, trained in the atmosphere of the moving picture show and knowing no restraint positively will not make good here."[2]

One of the ironies of John Brown's life is that while he professed a strong preference for the country, he spent much of his life in the cities of southern California. The same paradox existed at his college. While Brown originally claimed to having built his college for local rural young people, that group was never the college's sole constituency. Even in the first decade, a national, and eventually international, student body came to inhabit the Siloam Springs campus. By 1925, the college claimed that its two hundred students originated from twenty different states, from New York to California. J. Ellis Williams, a student in the late 1920s who wrote a memoir of his college experience, claimed that "California is in the center of the sun at J.E.B.C." Williams may have been a bit biased, since he hailed from California himself. Most of the students in the 1920s and 1930s seem to have come from the states surrounding Siloam Springs, most notably Texas; but from the earliest years an inordinately large number of the college's students came from California and returned there after graduation. Of the thirty-five members of the first four-year class in 1935, thirteen ended up in California, while only six stayed in Arkansas. Remarked John Brown, "I did not realize so many former students were scattered throughout southern California." Such a heavy California presence was attributable to the fact that Brown's evangelistic crusades were a main source of the college's constituency, both in donors and in students. Williams observed, "the major part of the student body came in response to the call of God, having felt the divine call directly through Brother Brown in his great evangelistic career."[3]

The institution also came to have an international flavor in its early years due to the presence of missionary kids. Because of its financial policy and its strong Christian ethos, the college was an ideal place for children of foreign missionaries, and by the late 1920s such students gave a multinational character to the college. The cover of the college monthly magazine for November 1928 showed a group of ten "M.K." students from Africa. Such students apparently did well at the college. Of the twelve students on the honor roll in March 1929, six hailed from Africa.[4]

Californians and missionary kids were not likely to end up as rural farmers or manual laborers after graduation, and this fact points to another irony concerning the university's student body in the early years. While John E. Brown College/John Brown University claimed to be training more efficient farmers and skilled laborers, it seemed to have a "white-collar" effect on its students. While valuing manual labor at the college, most graduates went on to enter service and information industries rather than blue-collar trades. Registrar Clyde Kilby, perusing the college's graduation statistics in 1928, noted "the contrasting percentages between the number of pupils wanting mechanical or farm training and the actual number of graduating pupils turned out for that work." Of the fifteen graduates from the college in 1928, only three intended to go into mechanical or farm work. Most planned to teach or enter Christian ministry. J. Ellis Williams illustrates this trend. Williams hailed from California and appreciated the college because, he declared, "it puts me in the 'new aristocracy of the common people.'" Yet Williams went on from John E. Brown College to earn two advanced degrees and become a pastor, not a skilled laborer. A perusal of alumni updates in the 1920s and 1930s reveals this same trend. Most alumni, and certainly the ones spotlighted by the college itself, were in professions such as teaching or pastoral work, not in manual labor. A 1927 article entitled "From Former

Students" referred to its alumni as "the ministers, doctors, lawyers, teachers, and all other workers." A typical John E. Brown College success story of the 1920s narrated the career of L. G. Chalmers, a poor boy at the college who earned his college tuition as a janitor on campus. Chalmers eventually became not a professional cleaner, as the college's "education to work" ideals might suggest, but the postmaster of Siloam Springs. As colleges often do, John Brown University, even in its early years when it purported to be a vocational college, seemed to produce graduates intent on careers in the "information" world, not the world of skilled labor.[5]

One other fact about the student makeup in the early years of the college must be noted: it was white, and intentionally so. Belief in Anglo-Saxon racial supremacy was virtually an unquestioned assumption among early-twentieth-century white Americans. The leading biology textbook used in public high schools informed students that the Caucasian race was "the highest type of all." Feminists of the day such as Margaret Sanger championed birth control for its eugenic effect in lowering birth rates among what they perceived to be lower races. Not surprisingly, such racial views also emerged among fundamentalists. Alarmed by the decline of white Anglo-Saxon Protestant hegemony in modern America, and borrowing from the racial theories prevalent in America at the time, some fundamentalists identified the rising influence of non-Anglos as one of the alarming trends of the 1920s. William Bell Riley, for example, a leading fundamentalist and a frequent visitor to John Brown's Bible conference, was an outspoken anti-Semite who warned of a Jewish conspiracy in America.[6]

As a patriotic fundamentalist, John Brown was not immune to such tendencies. During a 1922 crusade in Chattanooga, Tennessee, members of the Ku Klux Klan came forward at one of Brown's services and contributed one hundred dollars in appreciation for the work he was doing in their city and in Arkansas. And while Brown never endorsed the Klan, his revivals implicitly sanctioned the Jim Crow system that characterized the era. When conducting revivals in southern cities he typically set aside one Sunday morning service for African Americans. Furthermore, fundamentalist xenophobia and racist rhetoric did sometimes appear in Brown's writings. One reason for Brown's expressed intention to return American women to motherhood was that white Anglo-Saxon Americans were in danger of "race annihilation" because "the best blood and the best brain of America is not reproducing." He speculated that a Jewish conspiracy lay behind the immoral movies and songs being produced, and that foreign immigration endangered America's morals. Reflecting the events of the first wave of anticommunism in 1919, Brown suggested that suspicious foreigners be "shipped back to the land from which they come."[7]

Unlike some fundamentalists, Brown's use of racial rhetoric was never very prominent. One has to search the sources diligently to find examples such as those given above. Nevertheless, it is undeniable that early-twentieth-century white racial views did play some role in the founding of John E. Brown College. John Brown cited "experts" who claimed that one of the last remaining "seedbeds of pure Anglo-Saxon blood left" was in the Ozark mountain region. His ambition at John E. Brown College, he claimed, was "to build here in the Ozarks a school that will house thousands of these wonderful descendants of pure Anglo-Saxon stock." That the college was originally intended as a "white" school was made clear by Brown's comments about Booker T. Washington's Tuskegee Institute, a famous vocational school for black Americans. Brown expressed support for this black college but went on to describe his college as a white counterpart to Washington's—established, he said, for "sons and daughters of our own race." John E. Brown College in its early years, like most educational institutions of the day, reflected the racial segregation of American society. Though nonwhite students would appear at the college by the 1940s, it was intentionally white in its first two decades.[8]

Among the students at John E. Brown College/John Brown University, a strong sense of solidarity and equality existed. Because all students shared tasks and engaged in manual labor, the college exhibited strong democratic ideals from the founder on down. John Brown was known on campus as "Brother Brown," and he personally greeted new students on campus. Uniforms were required and fraternities were prohibited so that no sense of distinctions or rank would beset the student body. One student, Harry Huey, recounted that to "break down false dignity right from the start," a tradition developed whereby new students were picked up at the Siloam Springs train station in the college truck by older students and driven to the college. When it introduced different pay plans, the college was careful not to let this create social distinctions among the students. Claimed Huey, "all students are treated just alike, regardless of the plan they're on. No one knows the other's system, or cares." As a poor working boy who had achieved cultural prominence, John Brown sought to prevent social distinctions from influencing his college.[9]

Just as the school's students were expected to differ from the average college student of the 1920s and 1930s, so too did the university seek teachers who differed from the norm. Because he sought to educate for character in addition to occupational skill, John Brown looked for traits in his teachers that hearkened back to nineteenth-century models. Personal zeal and spiritual commitment, more than advanced credentials, were the desired qualities in teachers. In 1924, Brown issued a call for teachers who had a four-year college degree and who demonstrated "the proper attitudes in life." Because the college paid teachers very little, John Brown sought personnel from among Christians who were considering missionary service. "There is scarcely a member of our force," he warned applicants, "who is not serving our school at more or less of sacrifice." Most teachers, he declared, "are practically giving their time as a missionary enterprise." In addition to low salaries, teachers had no homes of their own; they lived in campus housing like the students did, or in Brown's own home.[10]

As the college pursued degree-granting status in the 1930s, the standards for its teachers changed slightly. By 1934, Brown was still seeking teachers with a "missionary spirit," but also ones with master's degrees. Nevertheless, he maintained, the final criteria for judging teachers should not be numbers of degrees but "a knowledge of God and a knowledge of youth, . . . that first of all young life may find anchorage, spiritually and morally." Because of the emphasis on character formation, close personal interaction between teachers and students was a strong part of the college's program. Even meals were shared by students and faculty, though a glass partition separated the two groups to provide teachers with some respite from college meal-time banter.[11]

If one were to visit John Brown University in the 1920s and 1930s, the first feature that would most likely strike the modern observer would be the primitive nature of the facilities. Students testified to having to haul coal on winter days before a heating plant was built and to shivering in classrooms whose temperature hovered just above the freezing mark. Not until 1928 did the college make its first efforts at creating an attractive campus, and even that produced limited results. Flowerbeds and borders were dug, but the cows that wandered the campus apparently took a liking to trampling the new plants, much to the amusement of the students. By 1933, plans were still afoot to attempt to beautify the campus. All rocks and sticks were to be removed "to make it possible to mow the campus all over."[12]

Inside the buildings, conditions were just as rough. In addition to freezing temperatures, poor sanitation was a common problem. In a letter to Richard Hodges, the school superintendent, Brown confessed, "the one outstanding criticism from California has always been that our school lacks cleanliness." The boys' dormitory was the worst offender. Brown complained to Hodges about "the tongue lashing which I got over the fact of the bedbugs." Apparently, one student had to be sent home because he contracted illness from bedbugs in the boys' dormitory. An exasperated Brown gave up on having the boys themselves clean their rooms. He instructed Hodges to hire "some good woman who will just live in the rooms of those boys, and fight dirt until those rooms will pass the most rigid inspection." Apparently, this solution was not completely effective in repairing the image of the boys' dorm. Months later, Brown lamented that a woman had considered sending her son to Siloam Springs but changed her mind after touring the boys' dormitory. Observed Brown, "it seems that the toilets up there killed her off."[13]

Aside from appearances, another element that would strike the modern observer of John Brown University in the early years would be the rigidly prescribed lifestyle of the students. As noted before, rules and requirements were strict and plentiful in the college's first decade. Liquor, tobacco, card-playing, dancing, and obscene language were prohibited, but so too were "objectionable habits," "boisterous conversation," and "painting" (makeup) for women. Time as well as behavior was rigidly controlled. Students awoke at 5:45 A.M., ate breakfast at 6:15, and were kept busy with classes and work throughout the day. Each night students had study hall from 7:00 to 9:00 P.M., "with five minutes intermission at 8 o'clock for 'stretching.'" In addition, students were insulated as much as possible from contact with the outside world. Students had to receive special permission to venture off campus, and unsanctioned visits to town could result in expulsion. When it was learned that some male students were visiting a Siloam Springs café, the university instructed the local police to apprehend the offending students until a university official could pick them up. Asserted Brown, "all recreation, social life, home life, and school life are supervised and directed by the John Brown Schools organization."[14]

The deliberate insularity of the university existed for a couple of reasons. First, the university sought to be a truly self-sustaining community where students' vocational training could have a practical application. With student industries providing for virtually every physical need of the campus, from buildings to furniture to food to clothes, the college could keep its costs to a minimum and train students in practical industries at the same time. One student described J.E.B.C. as "a self-contained little city, . . . one of those places that could build a fence around itself, and live." A more important reason for the college's isolation, however, was the defensive, siege mentality of American fundamentalism of that era. Since American culture had become a place of evil and danger, Brown and his constituents believed, it was best to keep fundamentalist children away from it as much as possible. "Since there is no contact with other towns and cities in the matter of amusements, athletics, etc.," Brown reassured parents, "our schools are relieved of one of the serious problems which many schools face in the matter of discipline." Isolation from the outside world was considered an asset in the early years of the college.[15]

As is the case today, one attempting to establish rules governing lifestyle and behavior in the 1920s and 1930s could expect to receive criticism from both sides of the fence. Some of Brown's constituents complained that he did not go far enough in outlawing immoral practices. One woman wrote to Brown complaining that he allowed "immoral dress" on the tennis courts because women were allowed to wear silk leg stockings, not just cotton. Brown replied that he refused to "become fanatical" and maintained that silk stockings were acceptable for his female students. Many students, however, while most likely obeying the rules, may have found them a bit on the strict side. Alumnus J. Ellis Williams, who strongly supported Brown and the college, nevertheless criticized "the iron-clad discipline that prevailed and which I thought too severe, as it tended to weed out students." Even Paul White, the dean of the college in 1929, remarked, "we often wonder if there are too many 'don'ts' in the program at John Brown College." Nonetheless, John Brown proudly declared at the school's ten-year anniversary in 1929 that there had been "no deaths, no arrests, and no proved cases of immorality," and he repeated this declaration again in 1939. Such was vindication to him that a rigid behavioral policy was a wise one.[16]

That is not to say that the John Brown University student's life was a joyless existence. Although leisure time was obviously limited, students did find ways to have a good time and were encouraged to do so—in carefully prescribed ways—by school authorities. In 1924, recreational time consisted merely of a "weekly play-hour" for students. Time for recreation increased throughout the 1920s, however. By 1929, tennis had become the craze at the college, and according to the school newspaper, "hardly an hour of the day passes that the courts are not being played upon." As mentioned earlier, intercollegiate athletics were banned at the college. Brown believed that they led to social distinctions among students, took time and attention away from studies, and gave occasion for drinking, dancing, and other immoral behaviors among the student body. He vowed never to build an athletic stadium at John Brown University or pay a coach more than a teacher. Nevertheless, Brown wanted his students to exercise and encouraged participatory sports at the college. Basketball and baseball games were held regularly between teams of different classes and departments, and occasionally a team from the college would travel to play a local high school or college. In 1921, the college made a brief attempt to play the most popular college sport of the day—football. The result was not a positive one.

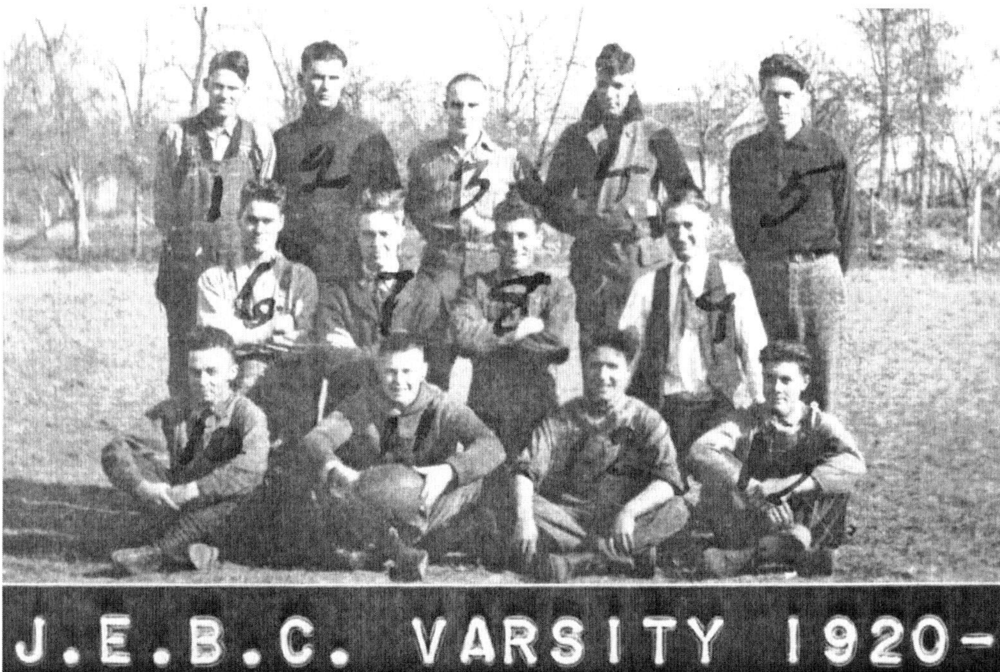

7. The short-lived John E. Brown College football team.

With little time for practice, the team was defeated by Siloam Springs High School, and a number of John E. Brown College players were injured. Football was dropped from that point on.[17]

The recreational ideals of John Brown were best realized in intramural athletics, in which all students could participate, rather than in intercollegiate athletics. Saturday was typically a normal class/workday for the students, but in 1927, the college began setting aside certain Saturdays as "Intramural Days." On these days, the college was divided up into teams for competition in baseball, basketball, and track and field, with all students participating. The purpose of these events was not only to give students exercise and fun but to reinforce the college's emphasis on character and sportsmanship. One student observed, "on Intramural Day our school is put to a test to see if she is a good sport."[18]

Students looked to other areas than sports for amusement as well. Hikes and picnics to Dripping Springs and other local attractions were common. Musical and literary events also held a prominent place in campus life. The college boasted a vibrant literary society, a poet laureate, and a college band that gave a weekly concert on Saturday night. Often as part of Intramural Day, an after-dinner speech contest would be held, with students voting to determine the winner. Overall, the impression one gets of student life in the 1920s and 1930s is not that of repressed, joyless fundamentalist robots but students who worked as hard at having fun as they did in the classroom and the workshop, albeit with little free time to do so.[19]

Of course, part of the attraction of college life was not only playing games but meeting members of the opposite sex. John Brown's brief attempt at separating the sexes into a Sulphur Springs and a Siloam Springs campus apparently was not appreciated by the students themselves. J. Ellis Williams declared that the day that the female students returned to the Siloam Springs campus in 1928 was considered by the boys to be a "red letter day in the history of the John Brown schools." The girls "swarmed around our college like bees around a hive." One night each week, the evening study hours were converted to the social hour instead. This was when the "big dates of the week," as Harry Huey called them, occurred. Immorality was a constant fear for Brown and school administrators, so contact between the sexes was closely supervised, and dates were chaperoned by faculty. Nonetheless, John Brown University was not prudish about relationships between the sexes. In one instance, the school paper good-naturedly reported on the visit to

8. "Social hour" in the 1920s—a weekly event at which closely chaperoned dates occurred.

campus of "Nab's blonde," an off-campus girl that one of the more sought-after male students was dating. The event, wrote the paper, "sent hearts crashing on the rocks, broke up all work at the print shop and sent Nab's temperature to the blazing point." The visit also ignited "a general feeling of resentment in feminine hearts" around the campus. One of Brown's purposes in creating a coeducational college was to encourage marriage among students, and by the looks of alumni reports in the 1920s and 1930s, he seems to have succeeded well in that regard. Sometimes, the close interaction between faculty and students could itself be an encouragement in this area. In 1929, the school magazine proudly announced the marriage between a female student and the head of the college's construction department.[20]

Amid classes, work, and recreation, a fervent piety typical of fundamentalist institutions pervaded the campus. An hour-long daily chapel service was required for all students, but many also participated in a voluntary, student-led Saturday night prayer meeting. This informal event consisted of singing, prayer requests, testimonies, and Scripture reading. By the mid-1920s, a tradition had been established of beginning each school year with an eight-day revival, often led by John Brown himself. In the 1931 opening revival, Brown claimed, "more than one hundred young people volunteered for definite Christian service."[21]

John Brown University had a strong evangelistic thrust in the early years. Because the university did not require a statement of Christian faith from its students, some came as non-Christians. These students could expect to experience heavy pressure to convert to Christianity. On Saturday night prayer meetings, Harry Huey noted, "special interest is paid to the welfare of the students on the Hill, especially those who are not Christians. Hardly one prayer meeting is held but that some soul finds his Saviour." One primary purpose of the year-opening revival was to evangelize the non-Christian students. During the 1926 revival, groups of Christian students met in the dormitory each evening "to pray for those of their number who were not converted." Such methods often met with reportedly successful results. During the 1932 revival, Brown claimed, "every student, not yet a Christian, made a decisive stand for Christ." As a result of this revival, Brown claimed that the college was a "one hundred percent Christian school."[22]

Because of the insular nature of the college, religious activity was one of the few means by which students encountered the surrounding community. In 1929, the Junior Federation, a campus ministry group, was created with the involvement of about one third of the student body. Members of the Junior Federation organized into teams of four and went out to minister in areas surrounding the campus. They sang, visited the sick, organized and taught Sunday Schools, conducted revival services, and held Bible study classes. Some of the male pastoral students practiced their preaching skills by filling empty pulpits in local churches.[23]

In the early years of John Brown University, attending church on Sunday morning was one of the few times that students would be in the Siloam Springs community. Students were required to attend one of four different denominational churches in town. By the early thirties, this changed. In 1932 the college began holding its own interdenominational Sunday School and church services on campus. The response was favorable, and the next year the Christian Fellowship was born, providing students and faculty with a Sunday church on campus. One reason for the birth of the Christian Fellowship, according to Brown, was parents' concerns about the orthodoxy of the Siloam Springs churches. "Our assurances as to a lack of modernism in the churches of Siloam Springs," he claimed, "were not sufficient." Another factor was Brown's increasing disenchantment with Protestant denominations in America, which he believed had become overly divisive. "There is a death struggle on today," he asserted, "between denominationalism and a wider, higher, spiritual democracy in Christian thought." For years, the Christian Fellowship provided college students and staff with a nondenominational alternative to the local churches of Siloam Springs.[24]

If life at John Brown University revolved around religion, it also revolved around the person of John Brown. Indeed, nothing better illustrates the extent to which the university was the lengthened shadow of its founder than the reverence given to John Brown personally. In the 1920s and 1930s, students typically gathered on the steps of Brown's home to bid him farewell when he left for speaking tours, and they would stay up until midnight just to welcome him home. Edith Fessenden, a student in the early years, recounted, "when he came home, the whole place took on a different atmosphere. How dearly we all loved him!" For some, admiration for the founder seemed to verge on cultlike adulation. J. Ellis

Williams called Brown's return to campus "the occasion of great rejoicing. . . . We would go almost hysterical with delight." Williams composed a poem "John Brown: The Man and His Message," which contained such memorable quartets as

> His thoughts like lightning flash,
> His words like thunder crash;
> His deeds are mighty, his work is great—
> Helping the race to a higher, nobler fate.
>
> John Brown is God's man,
> Made by God according to plan;
> Of his kind there's an awful dearth,
> And as I see him, he's the greatest on earth.

Williams sent this poem to Brown and asked that Brown publish it in his magazine. Brown wrote Williams back claiming to be unworthy of such lofty praise—but published the poem nonetheless.[25]

Undoubtedly, not everyone idolized John Brown to the extent that Williams did, but Brown did seem to possess an exalted status that was potentially dangerous to his university. William Ringenberg, a historian of higher education in America, has noted the propensity toward authoritarian leadership styles among fundamentalist colleges. One such danger of these schools, as Ringenberg observed concerning Bob Jones University, is the stifling of academic inquiry or even questioning the wishes of the founder. In 1953, a number of top figures at Bob Jones University resigned, charging the founder-president with demanding that "the tiniest facet of his thought be considered red letter gospel." Another danger of colleges dominated by a founder, Ringenberg noted, is that like the utopian communities of the nineteenth century, they often find it difficult to survive when the founder is no longer around.[26]

By all accounts, John Brown harbored a domineering personality. He could deal harshly with critics, as opponents in Sulphur Springs and Siloam Springs had discovered. He named the university after himself and named buildings after members of his family.

When he started a private girls boarding school, he named it after his mother, Julia. He even started a summer youth camp and named it "Buddy Brown Camp" after his son, John Jr.

Yet despite Brown's domineering personality, his university avoided the dangers often associated with dependence on an authoritarian founder. This was partly due to the strong devotion to the Bible among fundamentalists, which inhibited unquestioned devotion to a particular leader. This healthy biblicism among Brown's constituents was demonstrated in 1932, when Brown announced that students would begin reading his own books in Bible classes. Rumors began circulating that John Brown was substituting his books of sermons for the Bible as the text book for Bible classes. Brown was alarmed at the damage to his school and reputation that such rumors could do. His books, Brown wrote, were to be "simply a background for their studies, and where the teachings of my books contradict the Word of God, if they do, then throw my book to one side and study with the Bible." A week later, Brown completed his recantation to his supporters. He declared, "If ever there was a time when we needed to lay aside man-made Bibles and copyrighted systems to go straight to the Book, it is now!" As a result, he informed his readers, "I am making the request that the authorized version of the Word of God be carried into our classrooms and that there be no textbook but the Bible." A strong Protestant reliance on the authority of Scripture gave Brown's fundamentalist supporters the right to question him and limit his religious authority.[27]

In addition to fundamentalist devotion to Scripture, Brown himself served as a healthy check on his authority. While he could be proud and domineering at times, Brown's own humble beginnings gave him an ability to laugh at himself and not take himself too seriously. As noted earlier, Brown readily acknowledged his presidency at Scarritt Collegiate Institute for what it was, a sign that the school was in its death throes. Brown also liked to tell a story about his early days of evangelism, when he bought a Prince Albert coat in order to look respectable:

> I felt exceedingly well-dressed. When the time came for my sermon, though, I felt ill at ease. Then it was that I realized I had come to depend upon my trouser pockets as a place to dispose of my hands. Now, when I tried to find the pockets, I could not. My hands felt too heavy hanging by my side; nor did I feel at all at ease with them behind my back. Growing desperate, I finally opened that coat, pushed back the tail, and dug my hands into my trouser pockets as deep as they would go. From then on I preached the rest of my sermon with confidence, and I never wore the coat again!

Such self-effacing humor served Brown well as a college president and prevented his institution from becoming a fundamentalist personality cult. Students and faculty referred to him as "Brother Brown," and he eagerly socialized with students when he was on campus, addressing them as equals. It is a credit to Brown that his institution would gradually grow independent of him in ensuing decades.[28]

CHAPTER FIVE

Foundations for Growth

Whatever John Brown's personal status may have been in the 1930s, the new John Brown University was still struggling as an institution and would continue to do so for much of its early life. Institutional histories often convey the impression of steady growth from the founding to the present, but that was not really the case at John Brown University. Even after recognition as a university, the institution struggled for years with poor academic achievement, inadequate facilities, low enrollment, and even the threat of bankruptcy. The struggles continued throughout the 1940s, but by the end of that decade the foundation had been laid for a more stable future.

Struggling to Survive, 1935–49

In some ways, the years leading up to World War II were a time of progress at John Brown University. One area in which fundamentalists in general advanced was the radio industry. The decade of the 1930s witnessed a renewed interest in evangelism on the part of conservatives. Though the traditional revivalism of Moody and Sunday seemed to have grown stale by the 1930s, as historian Joel Carpenter notes, "in the hands of some creative local practitioners, revivalism was undergoing extensive remodeling." An important part of that remodeling was the growth of religious radio empires across the nation. The commercial radio industry was booming in the 1930s despite the hardships of the depression. Between 1930 and 1939 the number of radio sets in America exploded from nine million to forty-four million, covering 86 percent of American households by decade's end. Fundamentalists eagerly adapted to this phenomenon. Increasingly marginalized from the elite channels of discussion in American life, they used

9. A student worker at radio station KUOA.

their populist style to take their message directly to the American people via radio, apparently with much success. A reader's poll conducted by the *Kansas City Star* in 1932 reported that the most popular radio program in the city was the Central Bible Church's

Morning Bible Hour, which outpolled nationally syndicated broadcasts such as *Amos and Andy* and the *Lucky Strike* program.[1]

Like other fundamentalist empire-builders, John Brown rode the radio wave of the 1930s. In addition to his California stations, Brown acquired KUOA from the Fulbright Corporation of Fayetteville, Arkansas, in the spring of 1935. He moved it to Siloam Springs to serve as the radio voice of John Brown University. As had sometimes occurred in the past, Brown's reach tended to exceed his grasp. Eager to take his voice to the entire continent, Brown briefly acquired time on a powerful radio station just across the border from Eagle Pass, Texas, XEPN. Brown dreamed of a "People's Station of the Nation," operating twenty-four hours a day and broadcasting wholesome programming across the United States and into Canada and South America. When such a lofty goal did not materialize at XEPN, Brown abandoned this effort and concentrated his radio efforts on California and northwest Arkansas. KUOA's main contribution to John Brown University was to expand the vocational programs available to its students, since the radio station would be largely student-run. In 1939, a college of music was added to the academic, bible, and vocational colleges. Courses in radio work were interwoven with the college of music, and majors in the college of music were required to work in the radio station KUOA. Meanwhile, within the vocational college, the mechanics department evolved into the Division of Engineering, offering diplomas in electrical engineering, mechanical engineering, and construction management.[2]

John Brown University also advanced in the area of state accreditation in the 1930s. Although John Brown University had received its state charter in 1934, the University of Arkansas still did not accept credits received at John Brown University. According to John Brown, the registrar of the University of Arkansas believed that there should be only one accredited university in the state and thus he refused to recognize John Brown University. To remedy this situation, John Brown capitalized on his connections with powerful men. He and his good friend Jesse Jones met with Carl Bailey, the governor of Arkansas, to discuss the problem. Jones, who at that time was serving in President Roosevelt's cabinet, put his weight behind Brown's school, and soon thereafter Governor Bailey sent a delegation headed by the state commissioner of education to John Brown University to examine its program. By 1940, the University of Arkansas agreed to accept credits earned at John Brown University on the same basis as from any other accredited college or university. John Brown University had achieved state accreditation.[3]

Such an achievement might indicate that John Brown University was making great strides academically, and in fact university publications sometimes gave this impression. The *John Brown University Bulletin* advertised the Academic College as "an excellent liberal arts college" and the university as a whole as one with the "highest standards of academic work." The reality, however, often failed to match the rhetoric. As John Panage, professor of English at John Brown University during the 1930s and 1940s, remembered it, "we stressed religious, vocational training. The academic, scientific, and cultural side of education was striving for survival."[4]

One fact that mitigated against a quality academic program was the continued rudimentary nature of university facilities and personnel. Dorothy Woodland, a chemistry professor during these years, recalled using feed sacks for towels and empty jars for beakers in her science laboratories. Because of a shortage of quality facilities, academic courses were often housed in close proximity to vocational facilities, which could make for some difficult learning situations. The student newspaper noted the problem of students sitting in math class with power saws ripping boards in the woodshop next door. The professor would time her remarks for the quiet intervals in between the ripping of the wood. Clyde Kilby recalled having no books available for his English class and using the spring from a screen door as equipment in his physics class. Moreover, John Brown's desire to pare his staff to the bone often resulted in a lack of trained personnel in positions of leadership. Kilby enrolled at John Brown University in the late 1920s as a freshman, but because he had worked with John Brown's evangelistic team, Brown also appointed him the college registrar. Ralph Kennedy, a student at John Brown University in the early 1940s and later a communications professor at the university, recalled a similar phenomenon. He worked in the broadcasting department but soon thereafter was named dean of the Academic College. Kennedy remarked in retrospect, "you did some things you weren't qualified for." Sometimes John Brown's own lack of experience in higher education had a disruptive effect. As registrar, Kilby found it difficult to establish an academic calendar because periodically John Brown would arrive on campus from California and declare a day off from classes to celebrate.[5]

Also preventing progress as an academic institution was the makeup of the John Brown University student body in the 1930s and 1940s. Although John Brown repeatedly protested that his university was not simply a school for poor boys and girls, most students who attended continued to be those from underprivileged backgrounds with little exposure to academic life. Ralph Kennedy observed concerning the university students in the 1940s that though there were a few wealthy students, "by and large, the students came to JBU because they couldn't afford to go anywhere else." As such, manners at John Brown University were sometimes less refined than at most colleges. In 1937, the home economics department, noting with disapproval the eating habits of the students, distributed rules of etiquette to be observed in the dining room. John Brown once found it necessary to devote part of his chapel address to scolding students for shooting squirrels on campus.[6]

Sometimes these traits affected the academic climate as well. In 1938, the faculty decried the lack of basic English skills among many of the students and began a campaign to improve on it. One paper would be secured from each student each month for examination by a special committee, and students beyond the freshman level found deficient in writing would be required to take corrective work. Such efforts to improve students' academic performance continued throughout these decades. Even the campus newspaper, the *Threefold Advocate*, got into the act by advising students "How to

Pass an Exam." This editorial sagely advised students to "take notes" in class and study those notes before the exam. Evidently, the student body in general was not particularly inclined toward high scholastic achievement.[7]

Nor was the university itself effectively organized to excel as an institution of higher education. At this time, the Siloam Springs campus still housed both a college and a high school, the Brown Academy. In 1937, John Brown converted the Julia Brown School for Children in Sulphur Springs into a high school and moved the high school students there, but a fire at this school required that the students be moved back to the Siloam Springs campus in 1940. The overlap between high school and college sometimes spilled over into the classroom. When the Arkansas State Committee on education visited John Brown University in the late 1930s, one weakness it observed was the teaching at the junior and senior level. A system of rote memory of textbook material that characterized high school and freshman classes was being employed at the higher levels as well, with a lack of independent thought and research required on the part of the student. Moreover, the schedule itself was not conducive to rigorous academics. As we have seen, the daily schedule for students provided for only two hours of study, from 7:00 to 9:00 P.M. A 1948 issue of the *Threefold Advocate*, noting the large number of students being cited for low grades, speculated that one source of the problem was the host of extracurricular activities that crowded out studies and recommended that the university do more to "provide time for study without other competition." Clearly, a host of factors contributed to the university's lack of progress in academics.[8]

Such weaknesses, however, did not prevent John Brown from pursuing his highest goal for the university, recognition by the North Central Association of Colleges and Secondary Schools. Accreditation by the State of Arkansas was one thing, but if John Brown University was to be recognized as a national university, it would have to become accredited by a national body such as North Central. Back in 1926, NCA had sent a representative to John Brown's college in Sulphur Springs, and the ensuing critical report had been one factor that led him to close down the school. Brown's efforts on behalf of John Brown University in the 1930s fared no better. In the early 1930s, against the advice of Clyde Kilby, Brown traveled to Chicago to meet personally with the NCA Board of Accreditation in Chicago. According to Kilby, the result was a disaster. The board peppered Brown with academic questions that he was unprepared to answer, and at one point a member of the board asked, "Are you really the president?" Such treatment by the academic establishment must have been especially galling to the self-educated evangelist who had been forced to leave school at the age of eleven.[9]

Nonetheless, John Brown University doggedly continued to pursue NCA accreditation. In 1946, a team of NCA inspectors visited the Siloam Springs campus and explained that for the university to receive serious consideration for accreditation, the high school would have to be separated from the college. A year later, high school students were once again transferred from Siloam Springs to a newly renovated facility in Sulphur Springs. In 1947, Brown once again optimistically announced his plan to invite representatives from NCA to visit the university in preparation for accreditation. Indeed, Roger Cox, dean of the faculty, informed the faculty in October that John Brown University had received favorable recognition from North Central and that "the necessary forms for us to complete are already on the way." This proved to be one of several premature announcements concerning accreditation. A few months later, John Brown traveled to Chicago and withdrew the school's application. Once again, he realized that John Brown University was still a long way from national accreditation.[10]

If progress at John Brown University in the 1930s and 1940s was slow in academics, it was also painfully slow in the area of enrollment. The university grew slowly but steadily in the 1930s, from approximately 300 students in 1930 to about 450 students in 1937, including both college and high school students.[11] Encouraged by steady growth during the depression, John Brown expanded the university's staff and facilities in the late 1930s. In addition to adding a radio department, the university hired new instructors to teach Bible, business, home economics, and music. A new water treatment plant was built, new equipment was acquired for the mechanical department, the science labs were modernized, the library was expanded, more farm land was purchased, and a university hospital was established. In October of 1936, the university broke ground for a combined recreation hall and physical education building that would also house an auditorium; the building was completed within the year. In 1938, Brown learned that the federal government, in preparation for a possible war with Germany, would finance organizations that offered pilot training to their students. Within a year, an aviation department was up and running at John Brown University, complete with two airplanes, an airplane hanger, airfield, shop, and a flight instructor.[12]

The growth of the college infrastructure, however, was not matched by the growth of the student body. The United States entered World War II in 1941, and the ensuing draft depleted the male college student population at John Brown University and elsewhere. At one point during the war, there were only eleven men enrolled in the university. The later war years saw an increase in numbers, but even by 1945 there were still only 104 college students in Siloam Springs, with twice as many women as men. With the return of veterans to college after the war, the student population returned to its prewar level, but the anticipated boom in students never materialized. While many colleges and universities swelled with thousands of new students under the GI Bill, the college population at John Brown University grew to only about 300, where it remained throughout the 1940s and 1950s.[13]

This phenomenon perplexed and troubled John Brown, who had once predicted that five thousand students would flock to his college. "Why does the John Brown University still have vacancies?" he asked in the fall of 1947. Publicly, he speculated that the school's geographical isolation prevented growth. While he had purposefully built his university "far from the contaminating influence of a city," an unanticipated side effect of this, he surmised, was that "few of these youngsters know of our university." Privately, Brown pondered another reason: too many employees sitting in

10. The John Brown University airport. A testament to the founder's patriotic and entrepreneurial spirit, the airport was built on the eve of World War II to provide government-funded flight training to prospective pilots.

their offices rather than beating the bushes for more students. In a 1947 staff letter, Brown wrote, "it is either reduce our staff by half or plan an active organization through which we can fill these schools—AND I MEAN FILL THESE SCHOOLS." A couple of years later, Brown explained to his supporters that it was the balance of diverse emphases that kept the university from growing. Had he chosen to abandon vocational education, he claimed, "I am sure we could have an academic college with a strong Bible department of at least three thousand students." On the other hand, he asserted, had he dropped the emphasis on religion and academics, "there could be built in these beautiful Ozarks one of the great trade schools of the nation." It was the commitment to emphasizing all three areas—religion, academics, and vocational training—that made growth come more slowly. Thus, Brown had come to conclude by the late 1940s that "John Brown University can never be a great school in the matter of numbers." He would have to focus on quality rather than quantity.[14]

The expanding facilities of the university coupled with a stagnant student population meant that finances continued to be a problem in the 1930s and 1940s. By 1939, John Brown University was charging all students $225 per semester for tuition, room, and board. Because many prospective students could not afford that, the university continued to raise money to support the loan fund that had been established back in 1925. Students agreed to make payments of at least 10 percent of their income after graduation to pay back the loan, plus 6 percent interest. Of course, part of the purpose of vocational programs in the early years of the university had been to reduce the cost of education so that more students could afford to attend. By the 1940s, however, it was becoming clear that the vocational program was an added expense to the university, not an economic asset. With programs in radio, engineering, machine shops, and the like, Brown observed, "it is costing more money to train the boys' hands than to train the head." With the student population dependent on the loan fund and with expensive vocational programs to support, John Brown University remained heavily dependent on outside income to stay afloat.[15]

John Brown constantly was on the lookout for other economic ventures that could help support the university financially. For a time, the university owned a chain of gas stations and a hotel in southern California. Most notably, in 1937 Brown acquired two private boarding schools in California. He bought a girls' high school in Glendora and renamed it the Brown School for Girls. He purchased the San Diego Army and Navy Academy for Boys and renamed it the Brown Military Academy. These schools charged students about $1,000 per year, with the profits going toward the support of John Brown University in Siloam Springs.[16]

Eventually, the California schools made a solid financial contribution to the university, but in the meantime the properties had to be paid off. In addition, John Brown University had overextended itself in expanding and upgrading the Siloam Springs facilities during the Depression years. The result was a financial crisis that nearly spelled the end of the university. Throughout the 1930s, John Brown University had issued bonds at inflated levels of interest—sometimes as high as 10 percent—to finance its student loan fund and expansion programs. With the acquisition of the California schools, John Brown assumed even more debt, and in the meantime interest rates had fallen to as low as 2 percent, making interest payments on the old bonds unmanageable. In 1939, financial difficulties led Brown to lay off a number of employees and to cut salaries at the university by 10 percent. By 1941, the university had accumulated $1.75 million in debt, and some bondholders in California threatened to take the university to bankruptcy court to force payment of the principal on the bonds. To prevent this, the university was forced to file a petition with the federal court for financial reorganization and ask its bondholders for at least sixty days of grace.[17]

The ensuing year was a trying one for the university and its founder. Not only was Brown forced to cede control of the university to the federal court during the period of reorganization, but most of the bondholders of the university were personal friends who "in many instances not alone accepted Christ under my ministry, but saw their children likewise won to Christ." Under depression-era reorganization laws, institutions were legally permitted to reduce their obligations on the original debts. Brown, however, refused this escape clause. Doing so would go against the ethical standards that Brown had set for himself and his institution. "Frankly," he told his bondholders, "I would rather call it a day in this great work and end the journey of the school with the marvelous work already accomplished than see the high standards of the school sacrificed and its reputation for honesty lost." It would also make it more difficult, Brown realized, to raise money from donors in the future if his organization survived.[18]

By early 1942, the financial reorganization of the university was successfully accomplished. All the assets of the various John Brown Schools were merged into the John Brown University, new bonds were issued to cover the old bonds at one 100 percent value, and interest on the bonds was reduced to 4 percent. In a show of support for the university, many of the owners of the bonds donated their holdings to the university.[19]

The reorganization not only put the university's financial house in better order, but it marked an important turning point in the life of John Brown University. From this point on, Brown began to concern himself with the question of how John Brown University could become a permanent institution and survive his own departure. In the free enterprise world of American religion, organizations that achieved permanence had to somehow separate themselves from dependence on the personal charisma—and fundraising abilities—of their founder.

Of course, Brown realized that John Brown University had to change its financial habits. In the midst of the debt crisis, Brown vowed to his supporters that he would begin pursuing a more responsible fiscal policy for the university. The threats of bankruptcy suits, he vowed, "will prove the stepping stones to not alone a greater school, but a school that never again can be jeopardized from that source." From this point on, Brown devoted himself to building an endowment fund that would place the university on a firmer foundation in the future.[20]

Achieving permanence involved more than just finances, however. The deeper issue concerned leadership. How could the university begin to function independently of its founder? Since the founding of John E. Brown College, there had existed a board of trustees that theoretically functioned as the governing body of the school. But this was a board in name only. It generally consisted of John Brown University employees and family members that deferred to the founder. "It really wasn't independent," Ralph

Kennedy recalled. "They did what he told them to. You knew that he was very much in charge." Even the faculty displayed a marked reverence for the founder, according to Kennedy. In the 1940s, campuswide prayer meetings were held on Wednesday evenings and were usually sparsely attended by the faculty. However, Kennedy remarked, "if you went and saw a lot of cars and people, you knew Dr. Brown was there. And you had better go. He knew where everyone was even though he wasn't here all the time." The university would have to be weaned from its complete dependence on John Brown.[21]

Another problem concerning leadership was the extent to which Brown's relatives pervaded the organization. John Brown University had always been run essentially as a family business. Brown's wife, Juanita, was a member of the original board of trustees, and his brother Alvin was business officer of the school and later head of the California schools in the 1940s. At one point, Brown estimated that he had nearly forty relatives working in the various departments of the organization. This led to numerous quarrels and incompetence within the organization. "Some of the worst messes we had," Brown observed, "came from the fact that there were too many of the family connections tied up in a school program for which none of them were really prepared." This produced a system of family patronage rather than promotion based on merit, with negative effects for the university. "Only school men can run schools," Brown remarked, and outside evaluators had constantly criticized the fact that the university had "a group of boys trained by our Business department ruling over teachers with doctor's degrees and trying to direct the activities of University work." By the 1940s, Brown had come to believe that "there was no future to our school unless an entirely new program could be brought into existence.[22]

In the wake of the debt crisis of the early 1940s, therefore, Brown began easing relatives out of the organization and seeking to train competent people to take positions of leadership within the university. These included men like Roger Cox, Stewart Springfield, and Robert Jackson—bright young graduates of the university who were encouraged to obtain their doctorates to qualify them for academic leadership. "The time has come," Brown realized in 1944, "to begin to build a leadership that is outstanding educationally, religious, and financially, and for the first time I can do that without the embarrassment of feeling that I am hurting somebody's feelings or repudiating someone who has helped me build these schools." A new generation of men distinguished by their abilities rather than their relation to John Brown was being trained to assume leadership.[23]

Of course, this brought up a crucial question: the future role of Brown's son. John Brown Jr. was born in 1921, attended John Brown University, and graduated in 1942. With the onset of World War II, he joined the navy as a pilot. Thus, he was serving in the Pacific theater as John Brown pondered the school's future in 1944. Back in 1922, a university newsletter cover photo of John Brown Sr. and his son bore the caption "President Brown and his Successor." In 1944, however, John Brown seemed open to other possibilities. In a letter to Juanita, he wrote, "I am sure Buddy will want to go on with me in the school work so far as I may feel he should go, yet knowing his love for cattle and horses I am not inclined to believe that regardless of his feeling he should assume responsibility in education. In other words, all that is in the hands of God." The question was not so much his son's ability as his single-minded intention to running a university. "Buddy is not a school man," John Brown remarked, "but he has got good business judgment, and I believe he could carry on my work if his heart leads him that way." At any rate, that would have to be settled after the war. "When Buddy returns," Brown concluded, "he and I will have a lot of conferences as to just what he wants to do."[24]

As it turned out, the conferences were unnecessary. During his service in the Pacific theater, John Brown Jr. decided that after the war, he would commit himself to serving God at John Brown University. When he returned, John Brown Jr. rejoined the school, and in 1946 he was appointed vice president of John Brown University. This was clearly in preparation for assuming the presidency, although the running of the institution still centered around

11. John and Juanita Brown at the 1945 groundbreaking ceremony for the Cathedral of the Ozarks.

John Brown Sr. In March 1947, for example, the mechanical building burned to the ground. John Brown Sr. was in San Diego at the time, which meant that the vice president theoretically was in charge of the school. John Brown Jr.'s first response, however, was to telephone his father with the news, after which, John Brown Sr. stated, "I started giving orders." John Brown Sr. directed the rebuilding efforts from San Diego until he could return home. For the time being, John Brown Jr.'s authority was more symbolic than real.[25]

By the late 1940s, therefore, steps were being taken to prepare for a stable future beyond the life of John Brown Sr. Physically, this process was exemplified by the beginning of work on the cathedral group, a collection of buildings that eventually would form the center of the campus. In 1945, ground was broken on the first stage, the cathedral building itself, although it would not be completed until 1957. The two other buildings in this complex, a library and a science laboratory building, were begun in ensuing years. Together, these three buildings would become the center of academic life in future decades and symbolize the university's commitment to Head (the library), Heart (the cathedral), and Hand (the science building).[26]

At the same time, steps were taken to enable the university to function as a self-governing unit. For the professors, this meant the formation of a faculty organization in 1946. This body, consisting of all full-time faculty members, met twice a month and was empowered to determine university policy concerning admissions requirements, curriculum, requirements for graduation, the academic calendar, and other school matters. However, this did not necessarily create a fully independent faculty body. According to the organization's constitution, the president of the university served as the president of the faculty organization and presided over the monthly meetings. Nonetheless, the creation of a faculty organization did mark a step in the direction of a independent, self-governing academic community.[27]

John Brown University students also gained a measure of self-governance. In February 1949, a joint student-faculty committee was created to discuss and take action on problems arising on campus. By the next fall, this body had developed into a student council made up of representatives elected by fellow students. The council not only addressed matters pertaining to students but also participated in the rewriting of the student handbook in 1949. The days of complete control by the founder were coming to an end.[28]

12. John Brown Jr. succeeded his father as president of the university in 1948.

The board of trustees also began taking steps toward functioning as an independent board. Accreditation by North Central required that all John Brown University teachers and direct employees be removed from the board, and action in this regard was taken in 1947. Thus, John Brown could state in June of 1947, "the John Brown Schools as a whole are owned and operated by a self-perpetuating Board of approximately nineteen people." In ensuing years, successful alumni who shared the ideals of the university were added to the Board. In 1949, for example, five new members were added to the board, including John Storm, a sales manager for the Sinclair Oil Company, and Lewis Leflar, a general agent for the Bankers Life Insurance Company of Nebraska.[29]

Another important step was taken in 1948 when John Brown Jr. was elected by the board to take his father's place as president of John Brown University. Though this position was largely ceremonial for the time being (John Brown Sr. remained on as chairman of the board), it nonetheless marked another step toward moving outside the shadow of the founder. At the time, John Brown Jr. was only twenty-six years old, which made him the youngest university president in the nation. Such a fact was deemed newsworthy by *Time* magazine, which included a short article on the event. Although John Brown Sr. had interpreted his youthful presidency at Scarritt Collegiate Institute as a sign of the institution's weakness, John Brown University apparently took pride in the youthfulness of its new president. The *John Brown University Bulletin* ran copies of articles on the event from secular newspapers, and when *Newsweek* erroneously named a Rollins College president as the nation's youngest, the university's director of publicity wrote a letter correcting the magazine on its error. As for advanced degrees, an honorary doctorate for John Brown Jr. was awarded from Biola University in 1952.[30]

By 1949, therefore, the foundation had been laid for an institution that would outlive John Brown Sr. Financially, affairs remained precarious. In an effort to build a larger endowment for the university, John Brown acquired another California school, the Southern California Military Academy, in February 1947. Later in that year, Brown again announced his intention to operate John Brown University on a debt-free, cash basis if his supporters could contribute another $80,000 to close out old balances, after which the school would no longer send out "crisis appeals." The attempt was unsuccessful, and in 1949 one loyal supporter complained to John Brown that his monthly publication was back to "begging as usual." Institutionally, however, the structures were in place to carry the university beyond the influence of its founder. An independent board of trustees had been established, and John Brown Jr. was serving as president of the university. To help govern the university, an executive committee had been assembled consisting of Storm Whaley, head of the John Brown University radio stations; Robert Jackson, executive vice president; Roger Cox, academic dean; Joe Smith, business officer; Stewart Springfield, superintendent of industries; and Marion Snider, the university auditor. The faculty organization was functioning, and a student council was in place. John Brown University was not yet financially secure, but it was preparing for a stable future.[31]

From Fundamentalism to Evangelicalism

Amid the structural changes to the university in the 1940s, a less apparent but equally important development was occurring. John Brown University was negotiating the transition from a fundamentalist to an evangelical institution. To understand this process, we must step back briefly and consider changes in American religion in the mid-twentieth century.

Having lost the battles in the 1920s to control the major Protestant denominations and re-Christianize American culture, fundamentalists of the 1930s were becoming increasingly marginalized in American life. The experience of Donald Grey Barnhouse, a Presbyterian fundamentalist leader from Philadelphia, epitomized this trend. In the early 1930s, Barnhouse was gaining popularity as an outspoken opponent of modernism and as a radio preacher. In 1932, however, he was censured by his presbytery for criticizing fellow Presbyterians, and a few months later his radio broadcast was taken off the air by the CBS network. Like other fundamentalist broadcasters, his program had fallen victim to a new policy against airing religious programming that was "sectarian" and "controversial." Only programs sponsored by the liberal-dominated National Council of Churches (NCC) would be aired. Fundamentalists were beginning to feel alienated from mainstream American culture.[32]

Fundamentalists of the 1930s, therefore, experienced a situation similar to the dilemma that the Puritans had faced three hundred years earlier. The Puritans had wanted to reform the English church and nation, but as historian Joel Carpenter notes, "they were increasingly disillusioned about ever being able to carry that agenda forward." Some Puritans thus broke completely with the English church and formed separate sects. Others, such as the Puritans who came to America, sought to remain part of the Church of England but break with it geographically. For fundamentalists of the 1930s and 1940s, the issue was similar: How much separation should be maintained from a corrupt church and culture? How does one reform the culture while maintaining one's own purity? Carpenter writes, "the question of how to take a separated stance brought fundamentalists some fierce internal conflicts and fragmentation. . . . Lack of consensus on these issues charged the atmosphere within the movement for years to come."[33]

By the 1940s, two main positions were emerging within the fundamentalist movement. Militant fundamentalists maintained an ideal of complete separation from mainline Protestant denominations. Led by Carl McIntire, a Presbyterian fundamentalist from Pennsylvania, the strict separationists founded the American Council of Christian Churches (ACCC) in 1941. The organization was created to oppose the NCC that represented the mainline denominations in America, organizations that McIntire and other fundamentalists believed had gone liberal. Membership in the ACCC was thus forbidden to churches that had any affiliation with the NCC. McIntire declared, "the line of separation would have to be clear."[34]

Other fundamentalists believed that a less strident, more inclusive form of conservative religion should be advanced. Led by J. Elwin Wright, a New England evangelist, a group of fundamentalist leaders met in St. Louis in 1942 to create the National Association of Evangelicals (NAE). While the NAE opposed liberalism, it nonetheless allowed congregations that were affiliated with the NCC to join the NAE as well. Thus, the proper degree of separatism became the main difference between the NAE and the ACCC. Another major difference was that the NAE not only sought to reform mainline Protestantism, but it also criticized what it perceived to be weakness in fundamentalism itself. NAE president Harold Ockenga declared, "a terrible indictment may be laid against fundamentalism because of its failures, divisions, and controversies."[35]

By the late 1940s, then, two parties had emerged within the conservative Protestant subculture. The "fundamentalist" label more properly belonged to those who retained the strict behavioral standards of traditional fundamentalism and advocated complete separation from mainline Protestant denominations. In time, Bob Jones University in Greenville, South Carolina, would epitomize this party. Those associated with the NAE came to use the label "evangelical" more self-consciously to distinguish themselves from fundamentalists. While theologically almost identical to fundamentalists, evangelicals saw themselves as a spiritual and intellectual renewal movement within conservative Protestantism, and they sought to be more engaged with American culture than the previous generation of fundamentalists had been. They founded such organizations as Fuller Theological Seminary in 1947 and the Evangelical Theological Society in 1949 to raise up a new generation of Christian thinkers.[36]

So where did John Brown University fit into these developments? Although John Brown Sr. displayed some marks of the old-line fundamentalism, he and his university clearly merged into the evangelical wing in the 1940s. One attribute that Brown shared with the fundamentalists, of course, was an intense concern for behavioral guidelines. The strict schedule and rules at John Brown University remained virtually unchanged in the 1930s and 1940s. Lights out remained at 10:00 P.M., and card-playing, tobacco, alcohol, and movie attendance were strictly prohibited. Saturday evening was "the highlight of the week, socially." A play or musical program was presented, and couples were allowed to socialize in the lobby of the California building or stroll around campus. The festivities ended promptly at 9:30. Some relaxation occurred in the rules for venturing off campus. Beginning in 1942, students were allowed to go to town on Saturday afternoon (girls had to go in groups of three), but student ownership of automobiles by was still prohibited.[37]

Nothing better illustrated John Brown Sr.'s fundamentalist inclination than his celebrated fight to ban alcohol in Benton County. One of the historic tensions in the fundamentalist movement has been its attitude toward American culture. Fundamentalists' belief in an imminent Second Coming of Christ and their sense of rejection by mainstream America led them to separate from American culture. However, as Carpenter observes, "haunted by the 'Christian America' of their memory and imagination, fundamentalists could not shake the proprietary responsibility they felt for their nation's character." John Brown shared this impulse to re-Christianize American culture wherever possible, even if only in Benton County. Furthermore, opposition to liquor had long been a trait of revivalists, beginning with Charles Finney in the 1820s. As John Brown declared, "the evangelism of Sam Jones, George Stewart and Billy Sunday had much to do with the issue of liquor, and there wasn't any question about it. They largely created the Volstead Act which drove liquor out of the nation." For Brown, therefore, banning alcohol in Benton County was part of his identity as an old-fashioned revivalist in America.[38]

National prohibition was repealed in 1933, after which states and counties could decide by local option whether to go "dry." In 1944, John Brown petitioned the Benton County government for a local option vote, and the county became dry. The liquor merchants were outraged, and when the GI's returned from World War II a new petition drive was started to repeal the prohibition ordinance. The belief among the "wets" was that John Brown had cleverly orchestrated the dry ordinance while beer-guzzling soldiers were off fighting the war. The vote for repeal was set for November 1947. John Brown Sr. and the university community led the dry campaign in the months preceding the election. Brown gave a "Bread or Booze" speech in every town in the county, and 25,000 flyers printed by the university press were dropped over the county by airplanes from the university aviation program. Hearkening back to his confrontational evangelistic campaigns of the 1920s, Brown called his campaign a "fight" and a "crusade." The result was a landslide victory. Sixty-one percent of the county's voters sustained the dry ordinance, and forty of the forty-four county precincts voted dry. The results were even more decisive in Siloam Springs, where 945 of 1,546 voters cast their votes with John Brown and the prohibitionists. John Brown, the fighting fundamentalist, had won again.[39]

However, as we have seen in the 1920s, John Brown often exhibited an impatience with theological hair-splitting, and he possessed an ecumenical impulse that led him to start his college as an interdenominational institution. These traits placed John Brown University firmly in the "evangelical" camp in the 1940s despite the founder's anti-liquor crusade. In the early years of the school, John Brown University sought to remain steadfastly Christian but to "ride no hobbies," as the founder put it. This trait continued in ensuing decades. A doctrinal statement, for example, was considered by fundamentalist institutions to be an essential component to prevent a slide into liberalism; yet John Brown University did not adopt one while John Brown Sr. was alive. Earl Smith, professor in the Bible department from 1937 to 1961, expressed the university's ideal of being broadly Christian. Smith maintained that John Brown University was committed to the Christian faith, but not

13. John Brown Sr. leads the Benton County dry campaign in 1947.

"committed to any system of theology," such as Calvinism, Arminianism, Pentecostalism, Dispensationalism, or the like. There had been professors at the university, Smith claimed, who had been premillennialists, postmillennialists, and amillennialists, as well as from a variety of denominations. Such an ideal sharply contrasted with the end-times dogmatism and separatist philosophy characteristic of much of 1940s fundamentalism.[40]

John Brown's initial interview of Stuart Schimpf, who became the campus pastor in 1945, best revealed the founder's lack of concern with theological details. Schimpf recalled the interview:

> Do you believe the Bible is inspired?
> Yes.
> Do you believe Jesus Christ is the Son of God?
> Yes.
> That he died for our sins?
> Yes.
> Rose again the third day?
> Yes.
> Believe in the new birth?
> Yes.
> That he's coming again?
> Yes.
> —and that was about it.

Schimpf himself expressed the university's nonseparatist stance in 1947 when that issue was increasingly dividing conservatives. Commending the decision by the Conservative Baptist Fellowship not to separate from the Northern Baptist Convention, Schimpf stated, "better to be on the inside of an organization, fighting for the right, than to be on the outside throwing stones and letting the main body go to seed."[41]

One event that helped steer John Brown University into the evangelical camp was the founder's involvement with a new evangelical organization of the 1940s, Youth for Christ. In 1943, a New York City musician and evangelist named Jack Wyrtzen began holding area-wide evangelistic youth rallies. These "Youth for Christ" rallies spread to other cities, most notably Chicago, where

Torrey Johnson began holding rallies in the city's Orchestra Hall in 1944. A small book written by Johnson and his partner Bob Cook, *Reaching Youth for Christ*, sold fifteen thousand copies within the year. Later that year, a twenty-five-year-old pastor named Billy Graham resigned from his small Chicago church to become a full-time evangelist with the new organization.[42]

The idea of youth evangelism seems rather conventional today, but in the 1940s Youth for Christ represented a radical departure from old-time revivalism. Notes Joel Carpenter, "their kind of revivalism was more daring and innovative than their predecessors'. . . . Youth for Christ wed born-again religion to the style as well as the media of the entertainment industry." The appeal of Youth for Christ was its use of modern entertainment techniques. Meetings featured updated gospel music, often led by musicians with experience in dance bands or as disc jockeys. Tight-harmony girls' trios abounded, as did swing-style instrumentals. Rally directors used split-second timing, "punchy" announcements, brief rehearsed testimonies, and messages with current-events "lead-ins" to capture the interest of young people. All of this was anathema to separatist fundamentalists. Carpenter observes, "from a fundamentalist perspective, the rally leaders were borrowing from the very dens of the devil—Hollywood and Radio City—to accomplish the Lord's purposes."[43]

With his zeal for innovation, John Brown—the "Laughing Evangelist" of the 1920s—was a natural fit for Youth for Christ. In the mid-1940s, Brown resumed his evangelistic career, this time as a traveling evangelist with Youth for Christ, participating in youth rallies in some fifty cities. The fact that the aging evangelist was in his sixties did not seem to diminish his appeal to young people. John Brown University even adopted a new slogan in the 1940s seeking to capitalize on the organization's popularity, "Training Youth for Christian Living." The "Youth for Christ" in the middle of the slogan was highlighted in bold capital letters. John Brown University hosted several Youth for Christ rallies in the 1940s, and in 1949 Jack Wyrtzen himself visited Siloam Springs to participate in a rally.[44]

As a result of these developments, John Brown University consciously aligned itself with the inclusive, reformist evangelical wing of conservative Protestantism. In 1947, John Brown Sr. began describing the university as "evangelical and evangelistic." A year later, Brown described his school as "interdenominational and definitely evangelical." The university had always been evangelistic and interdenominational, but in the context of the 1940s, the explicit use of the term *evangelical* was sending a clear signal as to which faction of conservative Protestantism John Brown University belonged. Separatist fundamentalism was being rejected.[45]

The end of the 1940s, therefore, saw John Brown University in a satisfactory, if not completely positive, condition. While still poor as colleges go, the university had survived the debt crisis and was building an endowment that would provide greater financial security in the future. While still dependent on the energy, charisma, and fund-raising ability of its founder, the university had created a functional system of governance that could survive the absence of John Brown Sr. And while it was not growing by leaps and bounds, the university had aligned itself with a subculture—evangelical Protestantism—that would experience phenomenal growth in the coming decades. In sum, the components were in place for future growth.

CHAPTER SIX

Emerging from the Founder's Shadow

Although John Brown Sr. was sixty-nine years old when he relinquished the presidency to his son in 1948, he gave no sign of decreasing his control of the university—a fact that the new president readily acknowledged. Responding to letters of congratulations from friends of the university, John Brown Jr. was careful to point out, as he did to Frank Sewell of Liberty National Bank in Oklahoma, "Dad still has the last word and has by no means retired." As to rumors among the student body that changes in university policy were in the making, the new president assured the students that "the policy of the present administration is to maintain the old policies and traditions, to move toward the dream that my father has had for many years in regard to the school. No one should get the idea that Dr. Brown will not be in everything that concerns the university." For the time being, John Brown University was still John Brown Sr.'s school.[1]

The Last Years of the Founder, 1950–56

During these last years of his life, John Brown Sr. continued to steer the university toward the evangelical wing of conservative Protestantism. One seeming anomaly in this arena continued to be his intense concern for certain moral strictures. In this regard, John Brown seemed to be a throwback to the Billy Sunday–style revivalism of the 1920s. Granted, Billy Graham had engaged in some "Slime Pits"–type preaching in the 1940s, but by the 1950s Graham and other new-generation revivalists had moved away from such concerns. Brown, however, continued to battle against what he saw as the two greatest evils of American society in the 1950s, cigarettes and liquor. One of his last books, *Death in the Pot,* was devoted to detailing the damaging effects of cigarettes and alcohol on the physical and moral health of America's young people.[2]

Brown's latent fundamentalism in this regard sparked a public controversy at one of his radio stations. In 1951, Brown purchased radio station KOME in Tulsa, Oklahoma, a local affiliate of the Mutual Broadcasting System. The problem, for Brown, was that Mutual carried beer and cigarette advertisements on its programs. Brown informed the Mutual Broadcasting System that KOME would continue to air its programs but would not carry cigarette and beer advertising. Mutual responded with an ultimatum that KOME must carry all advertisements or lose its affiliation with the Mutual Broadcasting System. Brown's fighting fundamentalist—and populist—instincts were aroused. Brown canceled his affiliation with Mutual and vowed that KOME would survive without the support of this New York City–based corporation. For Brown, KOME was the righteous David doing battle against the wealthy, corrupt Goliaths of corporate America. "No industries in America are backed with as much money today as cigarettes and beer," he declared, "and we have every reason to believe the fight is on to close the mouth of John Brown in Oklahoma and to force KOME back into the usual channels of cigarette and beer advertising."[3]

Brown vowed to fight back. "Thank God I am not a quitter and with the support of a few thousand friends we can win this fight," he remarked. Without the support of Mutual, the station struggled financially throughout the 1950s, but Brown claimed victory against the corporations. His battle against the large corporations had earned the station national attention, he claimed: "Probably no radio station in America has attracted more widespread interest and discussion than Radio Station KOME." The station converted to broadcasting classical music, adopting the slogan "Tulsa's Good Music Station," and became a symbol to Brown and his supporters of opposition to the destructive forces in American culture. "KOME can be a radio station," he declared in 1953, "the example of which and the influence of which may do much to stop the

Atlantic tide of agencies that today are corrupting our children and destroying our homes." In 1955, Brown told his supporters that "we are winning the fight," but privately he acknowledged that the station was losing money. In 1958, long after the Mutual Broadcasting System controversy subsided, KOME was sold.[4]

Although the founder continued to battle beer and cigarettes in the public arena, at John Brown University the rigorous moral atmosphere eased somewhat in the early 1950s. One result of the student council's participation in revising the student handbook was that ties were no longer required for men in the dining hall (although T-shirts and sweatshirts were still prohibited). Having students help make the rules did not always result in loosening of restrictions, however. In 1950, the student council attempted to ban singing in the dining room and to appoint a dining hall "host" to maintain discipline. After widespread student protest, the new proposals were abandoned.[5]

Overall, the changes in regulations seemed to favor men more than women. Beginning in 1951, male students in the dormitories were allowed to stay up as late as necessary to study, though "absolute quiet" was to be observed after 7:30 P.M. No mention was made of a change in policy for women. By 1954, cars were allowed for certain qualified men "for business only," but they were not allowed for women. Also in the 1950s, a tradition developed in which all the male students quit shaving in February in preparation for the annual beard contest held on Engineers Day in late March. Prizes were awarded in such categories as Most Photogenic, Most Unique, Straggliest, and The One Who Tried the Hardest. No opposition was voiced by the administration.[6]

Restrictions concerning venturing off campus began to lessen in the 1950s as well, at least in practice. A prominent student claimed that it was difficult to attract new students to John Brown University because of the strict rules, and faculty members seemed to agree. Special permission was needed to leave campus, but faculty members, who were responsible for enforcing university rules, increasingly granted students permission to visit town for "coffee or hamburgers." Allowing greater ease in leaving campus was one way to create a healthy student morale which faculty members were willing to support.[7]

Theologically, the university continued to steer a moderate evangelical course in the 1950s. As differences between fundamentalists and evangelicals became more pronounced, some evangelical colleges faced accusations from hard-liners that they were going liberal. One such school, John Brown Sr. observed, was "split wide open during the past year on the charge that one of their outstanding and popular teachers was charged with modernism." John Brown University itself faced similar accusations from "neck-chewing fundamentalists," as Brown called them. The executive vice president of the university in the late 1940s and early 1950s, Robert Ferm, exhibited strong fundamentalist tendencies. With his support, some "fire eating students," in Brown's words, began accusing certain professors and students of liberalism. The campus atmosphere was tense, and John Brown Jr., still in his twenties, was inexperienced in dealing with such a crisis. By the fall of 1951, John Brown Sr., who was away managing the prep schools in California, decided that it was time for some housecleaning. He returned to Siloam Springs, fired Ferm, abolished the office of executive vice president, and temporarily resumed complete control of the university. John Brown Sr. quickly squelched any rumors of modernism at John Brown University. While acknowledging that some professors would not endorse fundamentalism, he said, "I would gladly pay a thousand dollars a head for every modernist uncovered on the teaching staff of John Brown University." Some students loyal to Ferm transferred to Bob Jones University, and the controversy ended.[8]

In 1953, another brief controversy arose when campus pastor Stuart Schimpf read from the nonfundamentalist-approved New Revised Standard Version of the Bible in chapel. Some students and a professor made a fuss, but John Brown Sr. supported the young pastor and the controversy quickly died down. In that same year, Torrey Johnson, founder of Youth for Christ, visited the campus and published a glowing endorsement of the work being done at John Brown University.[9]

Increasing laxity in rules and a moderate evangelical stance did not entail a decline in religiosity on campus, however. Religion was riding a wave of popularity in America in the cold war years, often mixed with a strong dose of patriotism. In 1949, Billy Graham had begun a revival campaign in Los Angeles, California, that captured the attention of the mainstream media. Graham became a national celebrity in the 1950s, and religious revival swept through America. In November 1949, the *Threefold Advocate* reported that revival had hit the John Brown University campus and spread to other colleges, with students "confessing their failings and wrongs and reconsecrating their lives to Christ."[10]

In the wake of the controversy surrounding Vice President Ferm in 1951, John Brown Sr. renewed his attention to religious revival on campus. Apparently, the tradition of beginning the school year with a series of evangelistic services had waned, and the founder was determined to restore it. In October, he led a week of evangelistic services on campus that resulted, he claimed, in "the conversion or rededication of our entire student body and staff." A number of students committed themselves to full-time Christian work. Out of the entire student body, Brown reported, "only four students failed to stand as definitely surrendered to Christ." John Brown once again boasted of a college virtually 100 percent Christian. Religion also remained a prominent part of the curriculum at John Brown University. Despite the fact that outside inspectors recommended the university decrease its Bible requirements, in 1955 all students were still required to take a two-hour course in biblical studies each semester of study.[11]

One side effect of John Brown University's alignment with evangelicalism was a gradual parting of ways with an institution that at one point in time could have been considered virtually a sister school, Bob Jones University. Throughout much of their histories, these two universities were alike in more ways than just their names. The founders themselves seemed like mirror images of each other. Born just four years after John Brown in 1883, Bob Jones also grew up as a poor farm boy. Like John Brown, Jones became a traveling evangelist in the early 1900s, patterning himself after Sam

Jones and Billy Sunday. Both men were also Methodists, Brown a northern Methodist and Jones, who hailed from Alabama, a southern Methodist. Descriptions of Bob Jones paralleled those of John Brown. Jones could "preach the devil out of people," but he was also known as a warm and approachable "people person" with a generous sense of humor.[12]

The institutions the two men founded also seemed remarkably similar. Founding his university in 1926, Bob Jones resembled Brown in his lofty ambitions for the school, endeavoring to build "the greatest interdenominational, orthodox educational center in the world," one that would educate "the whole person." Like Brown, Jones used his evangelistic rallies and contacts to raise money for his college, and the college housed a farm that sold vegetables and dairy products. Of course, Bob Jones University resembled John Brown University in the imposition of strict rules, and Bob Jones discontinued intercollegiate sports because, he believed, athletics "was not conducive to the spiritual welfare of the students." Even the dynastic system of the two institutions was similar. Bob Jones Sr. named his son, Bob Jones Jr., president of the university in 1947, a year before John Brown Sr. did the same.[13]

It is not surprising, therefore, that the two men struck up a friendship. According to Bob Jones Sr., they first met as fellow traveling evangelists in 1908. Jones was traveling through St. Joseph, Missouri, to a meeting, and John Brown happened to be preaching in St. Joseph at the time. Jones attended the meeting and was impressed with Brown's abilities. Their paths crossed often on the evangelistic circuit. Their friendship and the similarities of their institutions apparently sparked a quid pro quo system for honorary degree-granting. In 1937, John Brown received an honorary doctor's degree from Bob Jones University. In 1941, Brown returned the favor, awarding honorary degrees to both Bob Jones Sr. and Bob Jones Jr. Ten years later, it was Bob Jones's turn again; campus pastor Stuart Schimpf was awarded a doctor of divinity degree, given "in absentia" from Bob Jones University, on the campus of John Brown University.[14]

In the 1940s, Bob Jones University seemed to be following John

Brown University into the more moderate evangelical wing of conservative Protestantism. In 1944, Bob Jones Sr. attended the annual conference of the National Association of Evangelicals and wrote an article praising the organization. Three years later, Bob Jones Jr. was elected to the NAE's board of administration. By the late 1940s, however, things were beginning to change. Joel Carpenter notes that militant, separatist fundamentalism was on the rise in the late 1940s, especially in the South, where Bob Jones University was located. Bob Jones became increasingly uneasy with the NAE's willingness to engage mainstream Protestants and the desire by evangelicals to interact with secular scholarship.[15]

Throughout the 1950s, as John Brown University steered a moderate course, Bob Jones University became increasingly separatist and critical of other conservatives who were not sufficiently pure. In 1958, Bob Jones University broke ties with Moody Bible Institute, the flagship institution in conservative Protestantism. Bob Jones Jr. condemned Moody as "no longer willing to 'contend for the Faith' or align itself with those who condemn compromise." Two years later, Bob Jones University severed ties with Youth for Christ, declaring the organization "sold out to compromise." By the end of the decade, Bob Jones University regarded the evangelical movement as having sold out the gospel. An evangelical, Bob Jones Jr. quipped, was "someone who says to a liberal, 'I'll call you a Christian if you'll call me a scholar.'" John Brown University and Bob Jones University had clearly come to occupy different parts of the conservative Protestant spectrum.[16]

Given the similarities between the institutions and their founders, a question naturally arises: Why did John Brown University go evangelical and Bob Jones University go fundamentalist? Joel Carpenter has pondered this question for conservatives in general and concluded that the deciding factors seemed to be other than theological. "The critical catalysts for separatism," he states, "seemed to be personal factors more than more general patterns of belief or social standing." The theory seems to hold true for John Brown University and Bob Jones University.[17]

One difference between John Brown and Bob Jones was geographical. Bob Jones was a southerner who grew up in rural Alabama in the post–Civil War years, a time when, as one historian has remarked, "sentimentality for the defeated Confederacy reigned." Perhaps the southern ideal of devotion to the Lost Cause of the Confederacy helped influence Bob Jones Sr. to view his college as a solitary island of righteousness in a corrupt world. Moreover, some geographical dynamics seem to have been at work in the 1940s and 1950s. The evangelical movement of the mid-twentieth century, centered in Chicago and New England, was largely a Yankee phenomenon that bypassed many southern conservatives. In 1949, the NAE refused an invitation by Jones to hold its annual conference in the university's home of Greenville, South Carolina. This perceived snub was exacerbated when word spread that evangelicals at Wheaton College near Chicago were criticizing the conservative educational philosophy of Bob Jones University as being anti-intellectual. Such tensions probably contributed to the rise of separatism at the university.[18]

Although John Brown founded his university in Arkansas, he was a midwesterner by birth, and his primary orientation throughout his life was to the north and the west. Brown's closest allies were evangelicals like Bob Shuler in Los Angeles and Chicago-based evangelicals such as Torrey Johnson and staff at the Moody Bible Institute. Stuart Schimpf recalled accompanying John Brown to Chicago for a Youth for Christ rally. In the course of the weekend, Brown introduced Schimpf to Youth for Christ founders Torrey Johnson and Bob Cook, Moody Memorial Church senior pastor Harry Ironside, and Moody Bible Institute president Will Houghton. Despite his friendship with Bob Jones Sr., Brown moved in different circles, and these personal networks helped steer him and his university away from militant separatism.[19]

Another important difference between John Brown University and Bob Jones University was the personalities of the second-generation leaders at each institution. Bob Jones Jr. was by all accounts even more militant and pugnacious than his father. It was the younger Jones who led the university into militant separatism in the 1950s. "If it were possible to be more fundamental than the fundamentals," he once remarked, "that is what we would be." John Brown Jr., on the other hand, was more conciliatory by nature and less inclined than his father to engage in confrontational battles. He continued to lead the university along a more moderate path.[20]

Whatever the reasons, during the last years of John Brown Sr. the resurgence of fundamentalist separatism bypassed John Brown University despite the founder's continued fight against alcohol and cigarettes. Religiously, John Brown University remained as evangelical as ever. On other fronts, virtually all developments at the university were shaped by one overriding goal: to secure accreditation by the North Central Association of Colleges and Secondary Schools. In 1952, John Brown Sr. declared, "it would electrify our friends across the nation, justify thirty years of school building here in tears, prayers and sometimes blood if the word should be flashed out to the nation that the John Brown University has been recognized by the highest accrediting agency in the United States." In that year, another NCA official visited the campus and detailed what still had to be accomplished before that goal could be met: more stable finances, better facilities, and above all, improved academic quality. The university progressed in all of these areas in the 1950s.[21]

Finances improved, but not as rapidly as the university would have liked. The founder continued to solicit funds not only for the ongoing operation of the university but to build up the endowment to the NCA minimum level—a million dollar investment yielding 5 percent dividends. For John Brown University, that endowment took the form of prep schools in California and Sulphur Springs, radio stations, and a publishing house, not stocks and bonds. By 1953, Brown claimed much progress along this front. The California properties would be paid off in full by 1954, he predicted, and with that the goal of a million dollar endowment would be accomplished. He proclaimed, "the old challenge of the early days of our University, 'When John Brown dies, who is going to ring the doorbells and raise the money for the operation of that school?' has had an answer."[22]

Financial difficulties remained, however. For one thing, the satellite enterprises did not perform at the level Brown expected. He had tried for decades to make Sulphur Springs profitable; most recently in the 1940s it had become a coeducational high school, the Brown Military Academy of the Ozarks. In 1951, Brown finally gave up and moved the students there back to the Siloam Springs campus once again. When it became apparent that John Brown University could never become accredited by North Central while it continued to house a high school, the students were dispersed among the California schools. The Sulphur Springs property was sold to Wycliffe Bible Translators to be used as a summer complex for the missionary organization.[23]

Although Brown claimed that by 1951 the California schools had contributed half a million dollars to John Brown University, privately he complained that the schools were costing too much money to run. A 1952 audit of the California schools was "terribly disappointing." The California schools had to produce a minimum of $100,000 a year in profit, but due to high overhead, the surplus for the previous year had been only about $32,000. John Brown Sr. left Siloam Springs to return once again to California to take over direct control of the prep schools. "All requisitions are to pass over my desk," he announced. Apparently, things did not improve sufficiently. The next year, Brown hired an outside expert to audit the schools' books and Brown personally visited all the California offices to see how staffing could be reduced. High overhead in the California enterprises continued to impede financial growth from that source.[24]

Another problem that exasperated John Brown Sr. was lawyers and family members who contested the wills of benefactors of the university. Such litigation resulted in numerous lawsuits and legal expenses that the university could ill afford. For example, in 1953 Murray Sells, chairman of the Sells Petroleum Corporation of Gladewater, Texas, and a longtime friend of John Brown Sr., died, leaving John Brown University a 20 percent interest in his corporation. Because some of Sells' heirs contested the will, the bequest was not granted to the university until years of legal wrangling had occurred.[25]

In addition to slow progress on the endowment, John Brown University, as it had throughout much of its history, struggled with low cash flow. By 1956, the cost to attend John Brown University was announced as $100 per month, or $800 per academic year.[26] This was considerably lower than the national average of $1,500 per year but still represented an increase over previous years. However, because many students attended through the Student Loan Fund rather than paying up front, actual tuition revenue was quite low. Moreover, because students typically came from lower income brackets, collecting on debts was a constant problem. In 1951, Brown reprimanded his staff and demanded that they have students pay their bills; accounts should not accumulate beyond a thirty-day period. "There are to be no more bad accounts in our schools," he warned. Half a year later, Brown urged his staff once again to be firm on payment of past-dues. "Apparently some of our units are not enforcing the rules," he remarked.[27]

Finally, securing the donations of supporters continued to be difficult for the university. In 1941, Brown had begun a "Master Builders" program in which friends of the university would pledge and give a definite amount of financial support each year. While more than ten thousand supporters signed on in the first year, by the end of the decade the Master Builders still had not become a significant source of revenue. A study of the finances for 1948 revealed that of a quarter of a million dollars in outside revenues, 90 percent came from investments made by John Brown Sr. in the name of the university and only 10 percent came from donations. For the 1957 calendar year, donations from university alumni totaled a meager eight thousand dollars.[28]

Thus, the university continued to struggle with debt, and functioning on a cash basis remained an unfulfilled goal. A friend of the university once exclaimed to John Brown, "You've been in a crisis with that school ever since you started." Brown remarked, "I'm inclined to think the man was right." In 1951, Brown announced once again his intention to run the university on a debt-free, cash basis. Doing so required cutting spending to the bone once again. In August, Brown informed his staff, "We have to pay cash if we are to live up to the new pledge we have made. . . . There should be an everlasting effort to reduce the number of salaries in these different centers and to cut to the bone our buying." Apparently, not all employees were getting the message. A follow-up letter was more adamant: "Here are some orders, AND I MEAN ORDERS: . . . Unless it is a blood necessity, do not buy."[29]

One source of tension during this period was that the goal of operating on a cash basis collided with the goal of NCA accreditation, which required further improvements to the university's facilities. The latter goal tended to trump the former. The two most urgent projects needed to secure accreditation were the completion of the cathedral, begun in 1945, and the building of a library. Work on the cathedral, which had stopped for lack of funds in the late 1940s, was resumed in 1951 even though this meant borrowing more money. By the end of 1953, the rear section of the cathedral was completed and available for use as a radio station and classrooms; building of the actual auditorium would have to wait for more funds. Also, work was begun on the library in 1952 and completed in 1956. With its completion, the university cleared a crucial hurdle for accreditation by NCA.[30]

Thus, the buildings went up, but the debt remained. For the spring 1955 semester, John Brown Sr. issued a simple order to university staff: "Stop buying." All purchasing was to be suspended for the next six months. After thirty-five years of struggling to keep the university afloat financially, the strain was clearly wearing on him. "Some day, please God, we will get out of debt," he exclaimed.[31]

As the university slowly progressed in finances and facilities, it made significant strides in the most important area for NCA accreditation: academic quality. One necessary improvement constantly pointed out by NCA was a stronger faculty. As we have seen, John Brown University was rather generous in the awarding of honorary degrees, even among its own staff. Each spring, the founder would submit a list of names of friends of the university to be awarded honorary degrees, which the faculty would duly approve. One year the university even awarded John Brown Sr.'s

106-year-old aunt an honorary degree in home economics. NCA officials informed the university that honorary degrees for faculty members should be clearly distinguished as such, and that real graduate degrees should continue to be pursued by professors. Clear criteria for advancement in rank for professors was established in 1956. Economic conditions for faculty members also improved in the 1950s. A North Central visitor in 1952 noted that a high percentage of faculty members were now able to purchase their own homes, whereas in earlier years professors typically lived in campus housing. Faculty salaries remained much lower than those of the average university, but improvements were being made. Professors received an across-the-board 10 percent cost of living increase in 1954, and another 10 percent increase followed in 1956. Although at least one faculty member resigned during these years because of low pay, on the whole faculty loyalty remained high despite the possibility of better financial conditions elsewhere.[32]

Standards for student performance improved in the 1950s as well. Most notably, steps were taken to improve liberal arts education at the university. English skills among John Brown University students continued to be a matter of concern, and in 1953 the faculty took action to improve the situation. After much discussion, in 1954 an English proficiency exam was developed that all students had to pass before attaining senior standing at the university. One area of concern to NCA officials had been the lack of a comprehensive general education curriculum at John Brown University. Throughout the 1930s and 1940s, beyond some basic requirements in Bible and English, the various departments had apparently decided for themselves the prescribed curriculum for their majors. In 1952, the faculty launched an extensive effort to create a clear, systematic, integrated program of general education that could be applied across the university. New courses were developed in history and math, others were revised, and a permanent General Education Committee was created.[33]

In all, John Brown University seemed to be taking the nature of liberal arts education more seriously by the early 1950s. This did not come naturally to John Brown University. Like most evangelists, John Brown Sr. tended to see the world in terms of clear contrasts. His sermons and books often bore dichotomized titles such as "Money: Blessing or Curse?" and *One World: Is It of God or Satan?* However, not all the characteristics of the gospel tabernacle transfer well to the academy. Liberal arts education seeks to promote an appreciation of tensions, multiple perspectives, and complexities, not just punchy slogans and simple contrasts. John Brown University professors in the 1950s seemed to be recognizing this fact. While its fundamentalist counterpart, Bob Jones University, centered its educational philosophy on indoctrination ("we teach the student what to believe," Bob Jones III once explained), some John Brown University professors were pursuing a more complex approach. Roger Cox, academic dean in the early 1940s and professor of mathematics in the 1950s, described the goal of education at the university as to "communicate a Christian view of the content, while maintaining completeness and objectivity." The John Brown University professor "maintains an open mind. . . . He is not frightened by new or unorthodox ideas, but will examine them objectively. He stimulates interaction with students."[34]

Two professors in particular helped prod the university toward academic respectability during these years. Both were "outsiders" who, despite their initial discomfort with the place, ended up devoting a good part of their lives to the institution. John Panage grew up on the Mediterranean island of Cyprus and left for America at the age of twenty to further his education. After graduate work in English at Princeton and the University of Minnesota, Panage accepted a teaching position at John Brown University. His arrival in Siloam Springs in 1939 left him unimpressed; the only new building in town, he observed, was the three-year-old post office. Panage was drafted into the U.S. Army during World War II but returned to John Brown University after the war, where he taught English until his retirement in 1974.[35]

In his diary, Panage lamented the state of academic life at the university. "Our students are not consumed with the thirst and hunger for learning," he wrote. "Most of them do not know how to read. Our standards are too low for a college." He urged other faculty members to get students "to think for themselves rather than memorize." After attending a workshop on college teaching at the University of Michigan, Panage observed, "spoon feeding is dangerous but is widely practiced everywhere." Nevertheless, Panage did his utmost to inspire a devotion to learning. He typically employed a short "sales talk" to arouse an interest in reading among his pupils. Apparently, he was fairly successful; students commonly named Panage as their favorite teacher at John Brown University.[36]

Another professor who promoted quality academics at John Brown University was Dorothy Woodland, professor of chemistry. Woodland grew up in Ohio, completed her Ph.D. in chemistry at Ohio State University, and taught at Wellesley College in Massachusetts in the 1930s. A former classmate of hers, Mabel Oiesen, directed the John Brown University Cathedral Choir and urged Woodland to come to John Brown University. In 1944 she accepted a position. Woodland's first impression of the campus was that it was "dreadful." The science department was on the second floor above the laundry, and "a steam engine outside the window competed raucously with the morning's laundry." Nonetheless, like Panage she devoted herself to the university until her retirement in 1974. In 1947, she became the first female dean at the university until she returned to teaching full time in the 1950s. She devoted much of her time in the 1950s toward securing accreditation by NCA.[37]

Like Panage, Woodland desired to make John Brown University more rigorous academically. In a speech entitled "The Climate of Learning," she argued that the goal of the university should be to foster intellectual growth in its students, to produce a mind "free and restless in its desire to experience, comprehend, and use reality." Students come to the university content with their "little minds"; professors need to "find out what can be done to stir them out of this content—to arouse enthusiasm for the life of the mind." This entailed more selectivity on the part of the university, Woodland believed. She remarked in 1956, "I think we ought not to spend our time on the students who have very limited ability. It seems to me that most of our time should go to those who can do

14. Science professor Dorothy Woodland, one of the most influential academic figures in the university's history.

college work." Not surprisingly, Woodland advocated for the creation of an honors program in the early 1960s.[38]

At a time when evangelicals still viewed science with a wary eye, Woodland told her students that "there need be nothing found in science in opposition to or capable of undermining belief in God and in Christ." Instead, she encouraged students to approach the created world with boldness and confidence: "What right have we to nourish cringing, cowardly minds which dare not face the handiwork of God? If we truly trust God, there is no fact discoverable in this physical world of which we need to be afraid." Professors like Panage and Woodland played important roles in building a respectable academic program at John Brown University.[39]

While John Brown University progressed in a number of areas in the 1950s, enrollment failed to budge from the three-hundred-student level. One reason for lack of numerical growth was student attrition. Because incoming students were often poorly qualified academically and struggling financially, dropout rates were high. In the fall of 1952, for example, a Student Mortality Study revealed that 40 percent of the previous year's freshman class failed to return for their sophomore year. Another problem was that in the 1950s John Brown Sr. gave up his Youth for Christ evangelism to directly administer the schools in Siloam Springs and California. Not only had Brown's speaking schedule converted souls; the students at Brown's Youth for Christ rallies formed a natural pool of prospective students. Now Brown, who was in his seventies, spent his time behind a desk, and the university employed no fieldworkers to replace him as traveling spokespersons.[40]

Instead, other recruiting techniques were employed. To give the university public exposure in the absence of John Brown's evangelism, the Cathedral Choir toured the nation and sang on the radio. In 1954 a men's quartet began hitting the summer Bible conference circuit. Other strategies were also employed. The university sought to capitalize on an upsurge in patriotism during the cold war of the 1950s with the slogan "Serving the Nation under Two Flags" (the Christian and the American). With the onset of the Korean War in 1950, John Brown University promoted itself as a place where prospective soldiers could receive the mechanical training needed in a modern army. Pragmatic inducements were also used. John Brown Sr. claimed that, because John Brown University supplemented academic training with specialized vocational programs, its graduates earned more money than those of other colleges. He thus reported the testimony of a woman who, comparing John Brown University alumni to those of another college, remarked, "the John Brown University alumni nearly all drove fine, new automobiles, while those of the other school drove considerably older cars."[41]

Because of the university's reputation as a vocational school, men continued to outnumber women in the student body. Another recruiting strategy, therefore, was to market the university toward women interested in pursuing careers in radio, teaching, business, or clerical work. As one promotion put it in 1954, "daughters will come out of John Brown University prepared not only in mind and body, but with their hands, to take care of themselves as independent, American young women." However, although a variety of majors were open to women, training for homemaking remained the emphasis at the university. All female students, regardless of major, were required to take four to six hours of courses in home economics, and it remained the largest major for female students. John Brown Sr. once quipped, "all who finish work in our Home Economics department will be guaranteed a position or a husband, or both."[42]

Despite these various appeals, enrollment growth remained

sluggish. In 1954, John Brown Sr. appealed to his supporters to "help us fill this school with its growing equipment to reasonable capacity in the matter of students." Specifically, the university sought one hundred more paying students for the coming year.[43]

Like so much else at John Brown University in the 1950s, enrollment was ultimately related to accreditation. All sorts of innovative appeals could be made, but without national accreditation students would never be drawn to the university in large numbers. A pastor in California once told John Brown Sr., "I could put a hundred students in your university of the highest and finest type, if you were accredited." The promise of increased enrollment thus further motivated the university to achieve accreditation by North Central. In February 1952, Brown announced that the university was ready to apply for accreditation. The *Threefold Advocate* announced the summer of 1955 as "the expected date when John Brown University will be accredited with North Central." Once again, the prediction was premature. The year came and went without accreditation.[44]

John Brown University would eventually become accredited by North Central, but the founder would not live to see that accomplishment. By the mid-1950s, John Brown Sr. was scaling back his activities on behalf of the university. He had left the Siloam Springs campus in 1952, and John Brown Jr. was assuming more control. In 1954, John Brown Sr. bolstered his successor in the pages of the *John Brown University Bulletin*. The magazine published an article by Gordon Palmer, a well-known pastor and longtime supporter of the university, in which Palmer praised the work of the younger Brown: "What I saw myself convinced me that John Brown, Jr. has his feet on the ground as has his Dad. . . . Young John has the consecration, the vision, the preparation and training to carry on efficiently in the footsteps of his loyal and wonderful father." A subsequent issue published a collection of "Tributes to Our President" that extolled the abilities and accomplishments of John Brown Jr. Clearly, the way was being paved for a complete transfer of leadership.[45]

In 1956, some wealthy supporters of the university provided John Brown Sr. with a lovely home on the Pacific coast in San

Diego. However, retirement was not on the seventy-seven-year-old Brown's mind. While the university was securely in John Brown Jr.'s hands, John Brown Sr. planned to maintain strict control over the California enterprises. A peeved Brown wrote to his son in March complaining that some workers in California believed that "I am about on my last legs and somebody has got to take over my work here on the Coast to lengthen out my flickering lamp of life." However, he declared, "I never felt physically stronger, mentally clearer, and have no thought, unless God calls me, that the supervision and direction of this work will pass to anybody's hands for the next five years."[46]

God was to call him sooner than he expected. On January 12, 1957, John Brown Sr. fell on the stairs of his San Diego home, breaking his hip. Doctors repaired his hip, but a month later, while Brown was recuperating at home, a blood clot developed that ended his life. The years of struggling to create and maintain a university were finally over. "I sometimes think possibly the family and the world has expected too much of me," he once confided to his wife.

> The climb has been a long, terribly hard one for me, and I have had to fight off and fight back inherited tendencies, and mental limitations, and tragic lack of education, until while I haven't accomplished much, I look back over it now and realize that it was nothing but the grace of God that kept me in certain dark hours from throwing everything to the wind and plunging overboard, and certainly God had kept me, for I have had nothing within myself that was deserving of being kept.

Building a university from scratch had been a long, difficult struggle. Yet despite his limitations and self-doubts, John Brown Sr. established an institution that was at its healthiest when he died and was poised to become stronger after his death than it had been during his life.[47]

Years of Transition and Triumph, 1957–62

Soon after his father's death, John Brown Jr. remarked to a friend, "We certainly miss the wisdom and guiding hand of Dad."

While the founder was certainly missed, his absence also allowed John Brown University to make some important changes that would strengthen the institution and further enable it to achieve permanence as a nationally recognized Christian university. Like any institution continuing on after its founder's death, John Brown University sought to balance faithfulness to the founder's ideals with adaptation to new realities.[48]

The clearest indication that John Brown Sr. was no longer around was the rapid emergence of intercollegiate athletics at the university. Throughout the 1940s and 1950s, John Brown Sr. had remained opposed to intercollegiate athletics. Students continued to participate in a vigorous intramural program, but the university continued to ban intercollegiate athletics. By the mid-1950s the time was ripe for a change. The campus newspaper claimed that "student indifference " was growing concerning the customary social activities. President John Brown Jr. believed that intramural sports were no longer drawing the campus together as they had in previous years and that a college sports program might serve to reawaken school spirit. After the founder's death, therefore, the university took tentative steps in that direction. In the spring of 1958, President Brown proposed that a men's intercollegiate basketball team be established on a trial basis for two years. A basketball team, he predicted, would "raise the school spirit" and John Brown University basketball players would "become a Christian testimony among other young men participating in competition with them." Both the board of trustees and the faculty organization approved the plan.[49]

The idea had some critics. Professor Woodland likened college athletic contests to the "gladiatorial combats of decadent Rome" and insisted that team sports "deliberately foster a point of view, an atmosphere, in which Socialism and Communism flourish." She recommended gardening, a more practical form of exercise. The university community on the whole, however, supported the idea. Adopting a name created years earlier by the freshman intramural team, the new basketball team called itself the "Golden Eagles." Despite mediocre records in its first few years, the basketball team

15. John Brown University's first intercollegiate basketball team in 1959.

seemed to have the desired effect on school spirit. After winning a tournament in California, for example, the team was met in Siloam Springs by "a caravan of over fifty decorated cars, a band, and all the cheerleaders." Back on campus, the basketball players, students, and faculty participated in a pep rally and a steak dinner. In 1961, the faculty organization voted to continue the basketball program indefinitely and added a track and field team.[50]

In a more subtle way, John Brown University also departed from the policies of its founder in the area of vocational education. One reason why John Brown Sr. opposed intercollegiate athletics was that he feared it would endanger the vocational component of the college. One could not devote time and resources to vocational training and also develop a college sports program, he believed. "It's a choice between athletics and vocational, specialized training," he remarked in 1955. Indeed, Brown Sr. had always seen vocational training as the heart of John Brown University and what set it apart from other Christian universities. "Probably the most important phase of the work of the John Brown University," he said in 1951, "centers back in vocational education." However, even before the founder's death in 1957, the university's vocational program was undergoing change.[51]

Originally, the purpose of vocational education at John Brown University had been for teaching students manual labor and, as the 1935 university catalog put it, "reducing the cost of operating the institution." John Brown Sr.'s brief plan in the late 1920s to decrease the vocational requirements for some students had been abandoned by 1935. "We have tried a shorter working period but have found it unsatisfactory," the university stated. Even if one's future career lay in ministry or business, spending four hours a day working in the university's industries gave one "a proper appreciation of the work done by others" and a skill to fall back on in hard times, since John Brown Sr. believed that blue-collar jobs would outnumber white-collar jobs in America. And the work was clearly perceived in terms of manual labor. Another stated purpose of the vocational training was "to acquire manual dexterity." In other words, the "Hand" training in "Head, Heart, and Hand" was understood quite literally—to teach students how to work with their hands. By the early 1950s, the institution had evolved away from this earlier ideal. As we have seen, programs in radio and engineering meant that rather than saving money, vocational education actually cost the university money. And learning to lay bricks or milk cows did not seem like a good use of one's time if one planned to become a radio broadcaster.[52]

Thus, by the 1950s the daily vocational work requirement had been reduced from four to three hours a day for all students, and the notion of vocational education itself was changing. In a 1953 article for the *John Brown University Bulletin*, Rogene Weathers, dean of vocational education, described the program in somewhat broader terms. "Hand training," as Weathers described it, was a "total program" to prepare students in "socially and economically useful remunerative occupations." This definition, Weathers noted, included "occupations commonly considered to be 'professional' as well as those commonly considered to be 'vocational.'" In other words, vocational training was now conceived broadly as career preparation, not simply training in manual labor. So vocational training could include any "supervised experiences directly related to occupational preparation," regardless of whether they contributed to the enterprises of the university. The "Hand" was now understood figuratively rather than literally.[53]

A broader conception of vocational training meant that concrete changes in the program would soon follow. Other factors also contributed to a revision of the university's vocational character. First, the university's emphasis on vocational programs had always been an obstacle to full accreditation. A university in which students spent three to four hours a day in manual labor would continue to find it difficult to be recognized as an academic institution. In 1954, a visitor from the North Central Association voiced his concern that the university overemphasized vocational aspects, especially in light of the fact that higher education, he said, was moving away from narrow specialization in job training. Moreover, he was concerned that John Brown University students were "working too hard" and thus not spending the time in study necessary to receive a true higher education. Throughout the late 1950s, the desire for accreditation would continue to promote a de-emphasis on vocational education as traditionally practiced at the university.[54]

Another problem was that by the late 1950s changes in the university had apparently made the vocational program unpopular among students. The *Threefold Advocate* observed in 1957, "each year many articles are written in criticism of the vocational program. . . . Many students have taken the attitude that vocation is either a three hour 'goof-off' period, or else it is a period of a non-paying forced labor program." An engineering student remarked, "it is not uncommon to hear the phrase, 'vocation is farcical and worthless, and should be removed.'" By 1957, the vocational element of the university had become perceived by many as an anachronism. One of the first steps taken by John Brown Jr. after the founder's death, therefore, was an extensive reconsideration and revision of the vocational program. In October, he announced to the faculty plans for reforming the vocational programming. "We should raise our sights in vocational training higher than mere floor sweeping and washing dishes," he asserted. New terminology might be needed, such as a "unit of experience," to replace outdated terms such as a "vocational hour."[55]

Significant changes came rapidly over the next four years. First, the hours per week mandated for vocational work were reduced from fifteen to ten, meaning that students now devoted only two hours a day to working at the university. Second, the nature of the student's vocational work itself was reformulated. Vocational hours were now recast as vocational training credits that could be satisfied in a variety of ways, as determined by the student's superintendent, including in some cases "outside experiences." Thus, the emphasis was now placed on "specific achievements" in the student's major, "rather than simply 'putting in time'" on a particular job. For example, a Bible major could now receive vocational credits for working as an assistant pastor at local churches, rather than by working in the college dairy barn. Prospective teachers would earn vocational credits by serving as assistants to faculty members instead of by learning carpentry.[56]

Early in 1961, the third and most significant step was taken. Throughout the history of John Brown University, all students had been required to take courses in the vocational division regardless of their particular major. Now the Educational Policies Committee recommended to the faculty that the vocational subject requirement for graduation be abolished. Such a measure brought up some crucial questions for the university, the committee recognized. A vocational subject requirement had always been part of John Brown University; would abolishing it represent a "disregard for the original objectives" of the institution? However, it was pointed out, "employment conditions today differ markedly from those which existed during the 1930s, when Dr. Brown had so much to say about 'the soup lines being full of graduates with high degrees, but with education which existed merely of theory.'" In today's world, what John Brown University was seeking to provide was not training in an "alternate occupation" but rather career preparation in the student's particular area of interest. The vocational requirement was abolished, therefore, "with the understanding that all divisions affected by this change in regulation will make it an occasion to strengthen their major programs with respect to occupational preparation."[57]

In other words, vocational preparation was to continue at John Brown University, but it was shifted from the vocational college to the respective departments. The transition from a work-study college to a Christian liberal arts university that emphasized career preparation was complete. Whereas in earlier years the purpose of the vocational program had been, for example, to train prospective teachers to work with their hands and to value manual labor, now it was to prepare specific majors for jobs in their fields. Emblematic of the changes, the university's dairy cows were sold in August.[58]

To a lesser degree, some changes occurred in the religious character of the university in the years following the founder's death. One important change that John Brown Jr. instituted was to decrease the religious insularity of the university. While the University Christian Fellowship still functioned as a local church for on-campus students, other students and faculty were encouraged to join local churches in the area, and John Brown Jr. himself set an example by joining the local Methodist church. It was believed that this step would improve relations between John Brown University and the local community. Concerning the student body, the religious makeup of the university seemed as heavily Christian as ever. In the fall of 1959, Dorothy Woodland estimated that 95 percent of incoming students were professed Christians.[59] Nevertheless, the school year in 1960 still began with a series of evangelistic services "for the specific purpose of presenting the Gospel to our students and urging them to commit their lives to Christ." In 1961, however, the emphasis during the opening week was shifted away from evangelizing nonbelievers toward discipling Christians, as evidenced by the adoption of the title, "Spiritual Emphasis Week." Said the administration, "It is the intention of John Brown University to make Spiritual Emphasis Week an annual event to serve in place of the evangelistic series formerly presented by the founder." The university was adjusting to the needs of a predominantly Christian student body, and to life without an evangelist founder.[60]

Despite these slight alterations, the university's religious identity continued largely unchanged after the founder's death. John Brown University had always relied on the personal influence of its founder rather than a written statement to safeguard its Christian orthodoxy. As John Brown Jr. remarked, "my father *was* the doctrinal statement." With the founder's dominating presence removed, John Brown Jr. believed that it was necessary to place the university's Christian identity on a more permanent foundation. In the spring 1958 meeting of the board of trustees, therefore, a committee was appointed to draft a doctrinal statement to present to the board for approval. A number of possible statements were drafted and discussed. Eventually seven "Articles of Faith," borrowed from the National Association of Christian Schools and covering the major points of orthodox Christian beliefs, were approved and included in the catalog for the 1959–60 academic year.[61]

John Brown University also continued its participation in the moderate evangelical wing of conservative Protestantism. The most obvious indication of John Brown University's religious identity during these years was Billy Graham's visit to the campus. Today the venerable evangelist hardly seems like a controversial figure, but in the 1950s Billy Graham was the lightning rod of the controversy between separatist fundamentalists and moderate evangelicals. As the evangelical magazine *Christianity Today* remarked of Graham, "the great irony of his career is that his most vehement opponents are fellow Bible believers." As noted earlier, Graham first achieved prominence as an evangelist with Youth for Christ in the mid-1940s, and his Los Angeles crusade in 1949 put him in the national spotlight.[62]

At this point in Graham's career, he still managed to span the growing divide between fundamentalists and evangelicals. But this became more difficult in the 1950s, as evidenced by Graham's deteriorating relationship with Bob Jones University. Graham actually attended Bob Jones University for a year before transferring to Wheaton College, and many members of his evangelistic team, including song leader Cliff Barrows, were Bob Jones University graduates. At the time of the Los Angeles crusade, Graham and his

16. Billy Graham's visit to John Brown University in 1959 illustrated the institution's affiliation with the more moderate "evangelical" wing of conservative Protestantism.

former university remained on good terms. Bob Jones University awarded Graham an honorary doctorate, and Bob Jones Jr. preached at one of Graham's rallies in California. In the early 1950s, however, as Bob Jones University became more militantly separatist, its attitude toward Graham changed considerably. What led to the final break was Graham's 1957 crusade in New York City in which he accepted the support of the National Council of Churches. Bob Jones Jr. publicly declared that "Billy is going to wreck evangelism and leave even orthodox churches, if they cooperate, spineless and emasculated."[63]

In 1957, John Brown Jr. received a letter from Bob Jones Sr. explaining his position on Billy Graham. Graham "has violated the Scripture," Jones insisted, by accepting the sponsorship of modernists. "It is one thing to preach to modernists," Jones argued, "but it is another thing to be sponsored by such modernists." Accepting sponsorship was tantamount to labeling someone a Christian, Jones believed, so that Graham was sinning by giving Christian recognition to modernists who denied the truths of the gospel. As a result, Jones claimed, "Billy Graham is having possibly the smallest percentage of conversions of any evangelist who has lived for fifty years." Because of Graham's actions, Jones concluded, "evangelism is in the greatest peril it has ever been."[64]

Inviting Billy Graham to John Brown University in the late 1950s, therefore, was a clear statement about where the institution stood in the fundamentalist/evangelical landscape. In September 1959, Graham visited the John Brown University campus and spoke at the semester-opening service in the Cathedral of the Ozarks. The overflow crowd, the *John Brown University Bulletin* reported, "received the evangelist enthusiastically." A few months later, John Brown Jr. received a poignant letter from the aging founder of Bob Jones University. Graham's visit to the John Brown University campus was clearly on his mind. After describing his long friendship with John Brown Sr. and the "good sense" that John Jr.'s father had, Jones reiterated his opposition to Billy Graham: "The type of evangelism he is carrying on is destructive, and it is not the type of evangelism your father stood for all his life." Jones urged, "John, you folks in Arkansas and California and we folks here at Bob Jones University ought to hold these bases." John Brown University, however, had long since ceased "holding the bases" in the way that Bob Jones Sr. advocated. Graham's visit to John Brown University served as a vivid closing symbolic expression of the college's migration from the old-time fundamentalism to mainstream evangelicalism.[65]

In the years following the death of John Brown Sr., John Brown University not only carried on the founder's evangelical, nonseparatist vision; it also accomplished his unfulfilled goal of national accreditation. In 1958, NCA officials made yet another visit to John Brown University. Once again, the report, boiled down to essentials, was, "Better, but not good enough." (At a faculty meeting, one exasperated professor asked if there was no agency other than North Central that the university could apply to.) After noting the university's strength in teaching, campus facilities, faculty/student interaction, and job placement, the officials explained what areas still needed to be improved upon for accreditation to be finally achieved.[66]

One weakness continued to be money. "One of the basic problems of the institution," NCA concluded, "is the matter of getting its financial business on a sound basis in order to provide adequate and stable income for support of the budget for current operations as well as capital improvements." Improvements came quickly. The Murray Sells bequest finally was settled in the courts in favor of John Brown University. Another friend of the institution, J. A. Chapman, donated a large trust to the institution. These developments significantly boosted the university's endowment. Smaller donations increased as well. Alumni giving jumped from $8,000 in 1957 to nearly $60,000 by 1960. At the same time, the university took steps to become less dependent on outside revenue. While still open to students without means, the university continued to move in the direction of a conventional tuition-based institution. Tuition was raised another $100 in 1959. This may have been unwelcome news to students, but it placed the university's finances on a more stable basis. Overall, the percentage of institutional income received from student fees climbed from about 10 percent in the early years to one-third in 1961. The university claimed that "financial aid now is being used to keep worthy students in college, rather than as an incentive to enroll."[67]

Concerning facilities, by the end of the 1950s John Brown University's infrastructure was adequate for an accredited university. In 1957, the cathedral group was finally completed. The final section of the cathedral, the auditorium, was completed in 1957, two months after the founder's death. The science building was finished a year later. The library had been completed in 1956, but in 1958 NCA officials noted another weakness: students were not actually using it. Library holdings were increased, and faculty members were instructed to assign projects that required library usage. By 1961, the university was able to claim a significant increase in use of the library.[68]

Money and buildings notwithstanding, the biggest hurdle to be cleared remained academic quality. Here, too, John Brown

17. The science building in 1958, part of the newly completed cathedral group.

University made significant progress in the late 1950s. Although NCA officials commended the faculty for the quality of its teaching, faculty credentials continued to be lacking. In 1958, only 17 percent of the faculty had earned doctorate degrees, which placed the university in the lowest quartile of NCA institutions. Once again, improvement followed quickly. The university began subsidizing the cost of graduate study for professors, and by 1961 24 percent of the professors held earned doctorates. Similar progress was reported for professors earning master's degrees. In addition, faculty salaries, still low, improved modestly. Faculty raises were implemented in 1958 and in 1961, so that by 1961 the university could claim that professors' salaries approached the mean for southeastern colleges, though they remained well below the national average for NCA-accredited institutions. Faculty standards remained relatively weak but were at least becoming acceptable by NCA standards.[69]

Another weakness of John Brown University as an academic institution continued to be student performance. John Brown had envisioned his university as a place that would be selective physically, morally, and intellectually, but historically that had not always been the case. NCA officials noted in 1958 that "virtually all who apply for admission are accepted." The result was a rather mediocre student body, academically, as university officials themselves acknowledged. Rogene Weathers observed in 1957, "the norms of John Brown University students in certain tests rank below the norms of other college and university students in the country." Perhaps one reason for this was that studying still did not seem to rank high among the priorities of John Brown University students. Noting what it called a "mediocre amount of studying" being done on campus, the *Threefold Advocate* remarked, "the general impression gained of the amount of serious study done on campus is almost certain to make you wonder what we are doing in school." Whatever the reason, the academic level among students remained fairly low, and this fact contributed to the continued high rate of student attrition. The university simply accepted a number of students who could not make the grade academically.[70]

Strengthening student academics was made difficult because of the university's sluggish enrollment. In 1959, fall enrollment failed to reach 300 students. Nevertheless, the university not only raised tuition the following year, it also introduced more stringent academic standards for admission through the use of entrance exams. Student enrollment survived the more selective criteria. Enrollment held steady for 1960, and in 1961, 326 students representing thirty states and ten countries attended the university. Thus, the student body improved both in quality and quantity. "Although the median ability of incoming freshmen is below average," the university noted, "screening of applicants is sufficient to assure a student body capable of doing college work." Furthermore, an honors program was begun in 1961 to challenge the university's superior students. John Brown University was still no Harvard, but it was at least approaching the standards required for NCA accreditation.[71]

With significant improvements to the finances, faculty, and student body, John Brown University was ready in 1961 to once again apply for NCA accreditation. Rumors swirled around the campus (again) that accreditation was imminent. One "very concerned" student exclaimed, "all you seem to hear are rumors and more rumors concerning the future and present accreditation of our John Brown University." Confronted with questions from the student body, John Brown Jr. was more cautious than his father had been. He informed students, "for any institution to presume to say 'we shall be accredited at such and such a time' would be presumptuous, indeed." He hoped, however, to proclaim news of accreditation by the spring of 1962. In June, therefore, the university formally applied for membership in NCA and submitted a lengthy self-study detailing the improvements to the institution made since 1958.[72]

At last, NCA officials who visited the campus in the fall of 1961 were satisfied with what they saw. In March 1962, North Central officially conferred accreditation status on the university. At the subsequent faculty meeting, Rogene Weathers and Dorothy Woodland were singled out for their work on accreditation over the years, and the faculty gave President Brown a standing ovation for his years of efforts toward that goal. The last unfulfilled dream of the founder for his university, national accreditation, was finally accomplished.[73]

In announcing the news, the university claimed that it had achieved accreditation "without our having to surrender even one of the basic features of the original institution." In retrospect, that assessment seems generally correct. The essential features of John E. Brown College were still recognizable in John Brown University in 1962. The university still seemed marked by a fervent piety in the broad evangelical tradition, as its founder had envisioned. John Brown Sr. would have braved criticism from fellow fundamentalists to welcome an ecumenical religious figure to John E. Brown College just as Billy Graham was welcomed to John Brown University. Academically, the university was probably closer in 1962 than it was in 1919 to John Brown Sr.'s stated goal of attracting the best students. And while no longer a school for young people who could not afford college, the university remained distinctive for its generous policy of financial aid to qualified students. Vocationally, the university had changed more than in any other area. Yet even here, one could argue, the original vision had been maintained and adapted to a new era. Prospective business leaders no longer laid bricks, but they did gain work experience in their chosen major. Moreover, by the 1960s, America was rapidly becoming an information-based society, not the industrial society that John Brown Sr. observed in the 1920s and 1930s. In an economy where flexibility, creativity, and critical thinking are the most marketable commodities, John Brown University's improving academic situation could be seen as another way of strengthening the university's purpose of preparing students to make a living.[74]

More important, John Brown University had not only survived the absence of John Brown Sr. but also thrived. In fact, the university's greatest progress to date as an academic institution probably occurred in the five years following the founder's death. John Brown University had moved out of the lengthened shadow of its founder. It had achieved permanence.

PART THREE

Pursuing Excellence, 1963–2000

Institutions that achieve excellence must adapt to changing surroundings while maintaining their core values. For John Brown University, this challenge was complicated by the fact that it had to adapt to two constituencies—American society in general and the evangelical subculture in particular—that were evolving in different ways in the late twentieth century. In response to changing social conditions, significant changes occurred at the university. Vocational education, for example, largely disappeared, while the home economics program became a casualty of the feminist revolution of the 1960s. Other aspects of the university's historic identity—such as the academic component—were strengthened, while the institution's commitment to interdenominational evangelicalism briefly wavered but ultimately survived. There was never full agreement about any of these developments, and some at the university feared that strengthening the "Head" might endanger the "Heart." Thus, while John Brown University managed to maintain some continuity with its past amid the changes of the late twentieth century, that continuity was never simple, nor was it always apparent to its constituents.

CHAPTER SEVEN

Decades of Turmoil and Transition

The decade of the 1960s was one of the most tumultuous in American history, especially on the nation's college campuses. The election of John F. Kennedy to the presidency in 1960, coinciding with the rise of the civil rights movement in the South, ushered in a spirit of reforming optimism among many of the nation's college students. Yet the assassinations of Kennedy and Martin Luther King Jr., urban riots, and an unpopular foreign war brought the decade to a turbulent and violent conclusion. More than any other event, the Vietnam War shattered the fabric of American society and helped to create the youth revolt of the 1960s. What began in the Kennedy administration as a minor involvement to prevent South Vietnam from falling to communist insurgents supported by North Vietnam became a full-scale war in all but name under Lyndon Johnson and Richard Nixon. By the end of the decade, over half a million American soldiers were deployed in Vietnam. As the number of body bags increased and graphic war footage became a common feature on the nightly news, many Americans began to question the nation's continued involvement in a remote corner of the world.[1]

Sparked by the Vietnam War, what had been a relatively minor radical student movement in the early 1960s blossomed into a major cultural event. War protests soon broadened to condemn much of modern American middle-class culture. Campus radicals castigated their universities as agents of the "establishment" that dehumanized students and helped propagate an immoral war in Vietnam. The tumult reached its peak in the late 1960s and early 1970s. In 1969, students at Columbia University in New York City seized the offices of the president and other administrators and occupied them for days until removed by local police. A year later, campus unrest seized the nation's attention when National Guardsmen shot and killed four students at an antiwar demonstration at Kent State University.[2]

Young radicals comprised only a minority of college students in the 1960s, but they received inordinate attention as symbols of the growing cultural divide in America. To many observers, it seemed as though America's universities were incubators of political radicalism, cultural rebellion, and personal immorality. The term "generation gap," describing the seeming gulf between America's cultural leaders and their baby boom offspring, entered the nation's vocabulary.

John Brown University and the Youth Revolt

Amid the turmoil of the 1960s, evangelical Christian colleges remained remarkably insulated from the maelstrom. The demonstrations and protests that swept America's campuses all but bypassed the Christian college campuses. Historian William Ringenberg has posited three reasons why Christian colleges remained so calm in the 1960s. First, evangelical students tended to favor traditional, individualistic evangelism over grand sociopolitical reform agendas. Personal piety and "soul-winning" were deemed more important than changing the system. Second, the students tended to be politically conservative in the first place. Wheaton College, for example, conducted a student poll in the mid-1960s that showed a strong majority of student opinion in favor of conservative Republicans. Only 7 percent of the students favored Democrats at a time when Democrats dominated the national government. Wheaton students generally did not join Vietnam War protests because their views on the war did not differ significantly from the policies of the Johnson and Nixon administrations. And if they did, college administrators made sure such views remained unvoiced. Administrators at Wheaton discouraged any discussion of Vietnam that might have deviated from support of governmental policies. Finally, the small size and personal nature of Christian colleges mitigated against student rebellions, which were often sparked by the perceived impersonal, uncaring nature of large secular campuses.[3]

Like other Christian colleges, John Brown University was generally immune to 1960s radicalism. Indeed, just as John Brown Sr. had promoted his "jazzless" university in the 1920s in opposition to cultural trends, so John Brown University in the 1960s trumpeted its insulation from the youth revolt. In 1965, John Brown Jr. lamented the "tragedies which have occurred on many of the large campuses" and expressed relief and enthusiasm that John Brown University had remained unscathed. He promised: "There is a very bright future for the small college and particularly John Brown University so long as we maintain the motto of 'Christ Over All.'" In 1969, at the height of the campus upheavals, John Brown University trustees issued a statement commending the students and faculty for their loyalty to the university and their firm stand on "Christian Americanism" amid the rebellions of the day. A summary of the 1968 school year testified to the insular nature of the campus. In a year that witnessed the Tet Offensive in Vietnam and the assassination of Martin Luther King Jr., among other things, the highlights mentioned in the *Threefold Advocate* were Campus Crusade meetings and a Spring Break missions trip to Mexico.[4]

As the above events indicate, the factors that insulated evangelical Christian colleges from campus radicalism existed in abundance at John Brown University. First, the university maintained a strong tradition of patriotism and support for the military, as evidenced by the numerous subsidiary military schools in its history. Throughout the 1960s and early 1970s, the John Brown University catalog opened with the motto "Under Two Flags," meaning the Christian and American flags. The purpose of the university, the catalog explained, was "to make our youth worthy of the names 'Christian' and 'American,'" and the promotion of "Christian Americanism" comprised one of the main goals of the general education curriculum.[5]

Political conservatism dominated the John Brown University campus. The clearest manifestation of the university's political stance was the institution of the Christian American Heritage Seminar in the early 1960s at the height of the cold war. For one week each fall, prominent politicians and businessmen were brought in to speak on the dangers of communism and the benefits of American democracy and free enterprise. Although some students questioned the ideological uniformity of the speakers and complained about having political science "crammed down their throats," the seminars seemed generally well received. Films and special convocations were also used to warn students against communism. Business leaders such as Walter Knott of Knott's Berry Farm and newscaster Paul Harvey occasionally visited the campus to deliver speeches against socialism and antipatriotism, which, they warned, were rampant among America's youth.[6]

John Brown University students, however, needed little prodding toward conservatism. A student poll during the 1968 presidential campaign showed overwhelming support for the Republican Richard Nixon, and as many students favored the southern segregationist George Wallace for president as the Democratic candidate for president. As opposition to the Vietnam War intensified, John Brown University students showed themselves more likely to condemn the protesters than criticize the war. The editor of the *Threefold Advocate* labeled University of California war protests "treason" and urged John Brown University students to write their representatives deploring the student uprisings. A month later, the student senate began selling "We Back Our Boys in Vietnam" stickers in the dining room. When Richard Nixon expanded the war into Cambodia, the student senate sent him a "vote of confidence" for his actions. One *Threefold Advocate* editorial went so far as to argue that the peace symbol symbolizing the hippie movement was Satanic.[7]

As at Wheaton and other Christian colleges, what student dissent that may have existed at John Brown University was not likely to be publicly expressed, since the university kept tight control over its students.[8] For example, all candidates for editor of the student newspaper and yearbook, as well as officers for student senate, had to be approved by the faculty. In 1966, when the two candidates for *Threefold Advocate* editor advocated a more independent voice for the newspaper, both were rejected, and a new policy was adopted. Candidates for newspaper editor and student senate had to appear in person before the faculty to present their platforms before their names could be announced to the student body. The following year, the successful nominee earned faculty approval by proclaiming, "Student viewpoints which are contrary to administration viewpoints should not be published in the paper." Her successor the next year pledged "continued support of the traditions and basic ideals of the university." Clearly, the movement for free speech on college campuses did not penetrate John Brown University.[9]

Like other Christian colleges, John Brown University's fervently evangelical, pietistic nature also discouraged campus radicalism. Many parents and students were attracted to John Brown University because they perceived it as a safe place amid an increasingly immoral and anti-Christian university culture. One parent whose son had been "caught up in the hippy movements" at another college commended the university for "standing solidly on the fundamentals of Christian Americanism." A student transferred to John Brown University from a well-respected private college in Pennsylvania, where he had become fed up with the dancing, smoking, liberalism, and agnosticism that he had experienced at this formerly Christian institution. In contrast, John Brown University seemed quite firmly evangelical and pietistic throughout the 1960s. Students were overwhelmingly conservative in theology. A student survey revealed that, out of 248 student responses, 237 believed the Bible to be infallible, 245 believed in a literal Virgin Birth of Christ, and 247 believed in a literal Second Coming of Christ. Moreover, a strong spirit of Christian service continued to characterize the campus. The Christian Workers Fellowship begun by John Brown Sr. evolved in 1970 into CAUSE (Council to Assist in the Unity of Student Evangelism). This council served as a coordinating organ for a number of student outreach groups that functioned or were organized under its influence such as Big Brother and Big Sister, visitation at Woodland Manor nursing home, and Neighborhood Bible Clubs.[10]

John Brown University also maintained its connection to national revivalist networks in the 1960s. In the 1940s and 1950s, that involvement had been exemplified in the university's connection with Youth for Christ. By the 1960s, a new organization called Campus Crusade had supplanted Youth for Christ as the most recognizable youth evangelistic initiative. Campus Crusade was founded by Bill Bright in 1951 at the University of California at Los Angeles to evangelize college students. By the mid-1960s the organization had spread to more than three hundred campuses and forty nations. Bright's evangelistic tract "The Four Spiritual Laws" spread throughout the evangelical subculture. Campus Crusade epitomized what Richard Quebedeaux has called "establishment evangelicalism," the broad institutional network of organizations committed to orthodox Protestant theology and evangelistic outreach. In 1964, Campus Crusade began hosting training sessions in campus evangelism at John Brown University. Soon John Brown University students were sending evangelistic teams to the nearby University of Arkansas and joining Campus Crusade Spring Break mission trips to Florida. Bill Bright himself visited the Siloam Springs campus in 1965 to receive an honorary doctorate and to give the commencement address.[11]

Campus Crusade's popularity at John Brown University can be explained in part by the university's historic identification with mass evangelism and missions. However, involvement in campus evangelism was also a religious response to 1960s youth radicalism. Campus Crusade, one student observed, was John Brown University's answer to the "rebellion and rioting among college students." Targeting campus radicals' souls was a way for John Brown University and other Christian colleges to address the troubling social issues of the decade with the traditional methods of personal evangelism. In 1970, for example, John Brown University students and about four hundred other Campus Crusaders visited one of the largest student antiwar rallies of the era, not to protest the war but to witness to the protesters.[12]

Nothing epitomized John Brown University's evangelical response to the youth revolt better than the Sound Generation, a student musical group that toured the nation representing the university in the late 1960s and early 1970s. Begun in 1967 by two John Brown University students, the group combined 1960s fashions, contemporary music styles, snappy stage routines, patriotic songs, and traditional revivalism to achieve great popular success. In the process, the Sound Generation gave John Brown University national exposure never experienced before or since.

The Sound Generation evolved out of the Harmonaires, a six-member musical gospel team that traveled for the university in the mid 1960s. In the summer of 1967, John Coates and Bill Hartman, two students who had spent the summer traveling with the Harmonaires, decided to start a larger musical group. That fall, under the sponsorship of campus pastor Jerry Hopkins, they assembled twenty-six John Brown University singers and musicians into the "Certain Sounds." When they discovered that a musical group in California already carried the "Certain Sounds" label, Coates and Hartman changed the name of the group to the Sound Generation.[13]

The group began auspiciously by taking first place among four hundred musical groups at the Tulsa State Fair talent show. Although originally planned as a campus group, after the Tulsa State Fair performance invitations came in for the Sound Generation to sing in a variety of venues. The group's popularity continued to increase throughout the year. Like John Brown Sr. had done decades earlier, the Sound Generation built its reputation in southern California. In the summer of 1968, John Brown University's vice president of West Coast operations Bill George set a California itinerary for the group that included 130 performances over eleven weeks. The Sound Generation performed at Disneyland and was the featured musical attraction at Knott's Berry Farm.[14]

The popularity of the group owed much to the musical talents of Coates and Hartman, but also to the contemporary style and sound of the group. V-neck sweaters replaced coats and ties for the men, and the hemlines of women's dresses fell alarmingly above the knees. The music, described as "exciting, swinging, controversial, and different," borrowed styles from modern brass and jazz. To

18. The Sound Generation at Disneyland in 1968.

standard gospel music the group added secular and patriotic numbers. Musical accompaniment included electric guitars and drums, instruments considered scandalous by many evangelicals at the time. These elements gave the Sound Generation a "with it" feel in the late 1960s—one that appealed to the young generation.[15]

However, what gave the Sound Generation its unique identity was its opposition to the radicalism of the young generation. The "sound" in the group's name referred not so much to its music as to its moral and political outlook. While hippies and war protesters made the headlines, the Sound Generation sought to communicate the idea that, as its publicity brochure stated, "despite small minorities to the contrary, the young people in our nation today are still a 'Sound Generation.'" As in so many other areas at John Brown University, Christianity and patriotism were intertwined. John Coates proclaimed at one concert, "We disagree with the stand taken by many young people today for we believe with all of our hearts that the United States of America is still the greatest nation on the face of the earth. And we believe that it is God's blessing that has made it so!" The group's underlying purpose, therefore, was to "translate the time-honored messages of faith and patriotism into the language of the youth today."[16]

Mindful of its purpose, the Sound Generation was careful to communicate as clean an image as possible while on tour. Group members received detailed instructions on proper behavior both on and off stage. When performing in churches or other conservative venues, "body movements" were restricted to avoid offense. "Weird, eccentric, and loud styles" of clothing were prohibited. Dating between members was allowed, but no physical contact was permitted. When staying in private homes, group members were instructed in how to eat properly and clean up after themselves. Since evangelism was also a goal of the group, performers received specific instructions on soul-winning as well. The Sound Generation's youthful zeal and old-fashioned patriotism were an appealing combination. One professor claimed that all the kids had to do was sing "God Bless America" and the audience was reduced to tears. One appreciative listener wrote to the university, "It is so wonderful to hear a group of young folks like yours. The good ones are the ones we seldom hear about."[17]

The Sound Generation promoted God and patriotism, but they also promoted John Brown University. When Bill Hartman graduated in January 1968, he was hired by the university to continue leading the group, which became part of the university's public relations department. Members of the Sound Generation were given a tuition credit of seven hundred dollars and spending money during their trips. Although some professors grumbled about classes missed by group members and the expense involved, the Sound Generation continued to expand their sphere over the next few years. They performed with celebrities such as Bob Hope, Pat Boone, Ray Stevens, Jonathan Winters, and Minnie Pearl. They played in Las Vegas (under the watchful eye of Bill George) and performed at the Sugar Bowl, the Rose Bowl, and Tulane Stadium. In 1970 the group traveled to Washington, D.C., to perform for President Nixon and other dignitaries at the Washington Prayer Breakfast. The Arkansas State General Assembly commended the Sound Generation for bringing "good publicity and good favor to John Brown University and the State of Arkansas" by symbolizing to America "the highly spiritual and patriotic aspirations of the youth of this generation." The Sound Generation's popularity reached its peak in 1972 when the group toured with country music singer Roy Clark and performed in eight episodes of the nationally televised "Hee Haw" show.[18]

Although the group's performances scandalized some trustees and professors (one music professor called the group "whirling dervishes"), the Sound Generation flourished because the group combined the revivalistic response to social problems typical of twentieth-century evangelicals with the latent conservatism of grassroots Americans. In 1968, Richard Nixon won the presidency by campaigning for the votes of the so-called silent majority of Americans who supported conservative values and the Vietnam War and who were alarmed by the youth revolt. In tapping the same clientele, the Sound Generation earned national fame for itself and brought favorable publicity to the university.[19]

John Brown University's evangelical character and political conservatism, traits epitomized by the Sound Generation, thus insulated the university from the radical tendencies of the 1960s. But the isolation was not total. In the late 1960s and early 1970s, some faint echoes of the youth revolt did extend to the university and produced some lasting changes to the institution. Ironically, some student activism at John Brown University was motivated by the fact that the students were in some ways more conservative than the administration, not less. As early as 1963, some professors noted unrest among the students of a conservative nature, and the "feeling among some that the school had gone liberal." Insufficiently orthodox chapel speakers and honorary degree recipients were a frequent complaint. Administrators often saw the awarding of honorary degrees and invitations to convocation speakers as ways to secure much-needed financial donations and public recognition, a rationale to which students were not particularly sympathetic. In 1968, the administration got more than it bargained for when it bestowed an honorary doctorate on Wendell Phillips, a wealthy entrepreneur and freelance archaeologist. After a rather irreverent chapel address, Phillips granted an interview with the *Threefold Advocate* in which he bluntly expressed his doubts concerning the infallibility of the Bible, the Virgin Birth, and the Second Coming of Christ. Students were outraged, and the normally docile *Threefold Advocate* reverberated with criticisms of the administration's judgment in inviting Phillips to campus.[20]

Concerns about intercollegiate athletics at John Brown University were another area where the religious conservatism of the student body was sometimes expressed. Throughout the 1960s, the university added new sports such as golf, track and field, women's volleyball, and baseball. Trustees and administrators saw the athletic teams as a way to boost the university's public image, and thus they recruited athletes regardless of their religious beliefs. Students, however, expressed concerns about the athletic program's impact on the university's Christian testimony. In 1966, a candidate for the student senate advocated eliminating intercollegiate athletics. His candidacy was immediately rejected by the faculty. The issue did not disappear, however. In 1971, the student senate proposed to the board of trustees that recipients of athletic scholarships, unlike other John Brown University students, be required to give a written testimony of their Christian conversion. The board rejected the proposal. Such protests availed little, but they did reveal that unlike the broader culture, student culture at John Brown University was in some ways more conservative than the university as a whole.[21]

In other areas, however, student unrest at John Brown University was more consistent with that of the student culture in general. Nineteen-sixty-nine was an especially turbulent year among the student body. The Wendell Phillips controversy sparked student outbursts, and throughout the school year students continued to air grievances about excessive rules, authoritative structure, and a lack of free expression. It was, president Brown admitted, "one of our most challenging years." A number of students were dismissed for disciplinary problems, and others simply left school. The *Threefold Advocate* called the year a "time of trial" at John Brown University. In particular, students demanded greater personal freedom, more racial diversity on campus, and above all more input in decision-making. Remarked one student in the pages of the *Threefold Advocate*, "we need to be given a voice and listened to."[22]

University leaders reacted to students' complaints with a mixture of denial and accommodation. President Brown blamed much of the unrest on outside agitators and "professional troublemakers" who were traveling from campus to campus organizing student protests. In general, however, the administration attempted to respond to student concerns and adapt to the new social environment. In April 1969, an outside consultant visited John Brown University to advise the university on the situation. Noting that "small colleges often are organized in an authoritarian manner," the consultant recommended that the university grant students more freedom and some voice in university governance. As a result, the administration began holding open forums in the dormitories to listen to students, and President Brown granted an interview with the *Threefold Advocate* in which he expressed a willingness to listen to student concerns.[23]

At the same time, the faculty turned over approval of *Threefold Advocate* editors and student senate candidates to the student affairs committee, which helped produce freer expression in the student newspaper. In 1971, for example, a student penned a scathing criticism of the "Christian Americanism" rhetoric of John Brown University and the "Christian America pep talks" that students were subjected to. Later in that year the *Threefold Advocate* printed a forum on the Vietnam War in which opinions ranged from continued support to immediate withdrawal from what some students considered an immoral war. Such diversity of views had typically been squelched in previous years.[24]

Students also gained more of a role in governing the university. In response to student requests, representatives from the student senate were granted seats on all faculty and administrative committees, and the student senate president began attending the monthly faculty meeting as a nonvoting member. The university responded to another student complaint, classroom instruction, by beginning a course evaluation system. Finally, a student judiciary board was formed to deal with disciplinary problems, thereby moving student discipline from administrative to student control.[25]

Along with more student governance came some relaxation of the strict rules that had historically characterized John Brown University. In the 1960s, men's hair length became a symbolic cultural issue. Sporting long hair, long sideburns, or a beard was a way of identifying oneself with the youth movement. When unkempt hair began appearing on campus in the late 1960s, administrators at first responded in the traditional way by issuing an order that beards must be shaved off and sideburns trimmed to the top of the earlobe. Students who failed to do so were even denied entrance to the dining room ("No shavey, no gravy" became the slogan of the day). After the predictable student uproar, administrators tried a new approach. To the surprise of students, the hair issue was turned over to the student senate to devise an appropriate policy. The senate decreed that students could wear their hair in any way that they saw fit, as long as the situation did not get out of hand. From that point on, hair length was deregulated; long sideburns and even some afros dotted the John Brown University yearbook throughout the decade of the 1970s.[26]

Restrictions for John Brown University women were relaxed somewhat as well. A month after the male hair controversy, female students received permission to wear slacks to classes. The change was justified at first simply as a concession to the cold January weather, but eventually a student committee was formed to examine the campus dress code. The result by 1972 was a dress code merely stipulating that clothing should "conform to good taste." "We are not policemen and have no desire to be such," the administration announced.[27]

If nothing else, then, the cultural trends of the 1960s helped produce a university more representative of and sensitive to the concerns of its students. The old "baby-sitting role" of earlier days, as President Brown called it, was replaced by a more collaborative model of university governance. Emblematic of the new spirit, the major building project on campus during this time was the Mabee Student Center. Unlike earlier projects, administrators solicited student recommendations before designing the building, and upon completion in 1972, the building was dedicated to enhancing student life on campus.[28]

The 1960s also witnessed a new activism and sense of identity among African Americans. The civil rights movement of the early 1960s, inspired by Martin Luther King Jr., was followed by the emergence of more radical groups such as Malcolm X's Nation of Islam. By the end of the decade, college campuses reverberated with "Black Power" symbols and rhetoric. Inspired by the civil rights movement, other groups such as women and Native Americans began pushing for equal rights or redress of old grievances. As with the youth movement, while no major eruption occurred at John Brown University, the changes in the national culture did produce faint echoes on the Siloam Springs campus.[29]

As we have seen, John Brown University, like most evangelical institutions, had historically been overwhelmingly white. While no evidence exists that the university ever applied race-based admissions standards, its position in America's social and geographical landscape meant that nonwhite students would rarely seek out the school. A smattering of Asian, Central American, and South American students did attend the college in the 1950s and 1960s, but even that handful of foreign students declined in the 1960s. Excluding Canadians, between four and ten international students attended John Brown University each year between 1958 and 1961. In 1965 and 1966, the university enrolled no foreign

19. The Mabee Student Center, completed in 1972.

students aside from two Canadians. African American students were not even a consideration.[30]

By the end of the decade, some John Brown University students decried the lack of racial diversity on campus. In 1969, the *Threefold Advocate* published an editorial endorsing Black Studies programs that were springing up in American universities and recommended the showing of a "Black Heritage" film series on campus. Later that year, a black musician from Oral Roberts University gave a concert on campus and received a standing ovation. Rumors circulated that this musician might transfer to John Brown University the following year. That same week, the *Threefold Advocate* published a student survey asking the question, "Would you welcome Negro students if some were enrolled at JBU?" Eighty-seven percent of the students responded in the affirmative. The momentum seemed to be building for the inclusion of minority students.[31]

By 1971, no African American students had yet attended the university, but their absence was becoming increasingly noticed, especially by students. The student senate organized a Minority Concerns subcommittee with the goal of integrating blacks into John Brown University through aggressive recruitment of minority students. Student Senate President George Korn remarked, "It is our responsibility to go out of our way to recruit Blacks and other minority students. . . . It means actively seeking and recruiting young people of all races."[32]

Minority recruitment at John Brown University, however, faced formidable obstacles. For one thing, private school tuition, even at John Brown University, made it difficult for the university to attract minority students. Furthermore, John Brown University's ethos was not tailored to black concerns. As one student noted, "there is little besides our spiritual commitment in our 'Christian-Americanism' middle-class orientation that would initially attract the victim of discrimination." Finally, the northwest Arkansas region was not known for being favorable to racial integration. Lee Netherton, a former John Brown University basketball player, recalled that in the 1950s and 1960s it was considered unsafe for African Americans to stay overnight in Siloam Springs. Basketball teams with black players that visited John Brown University typically drove to Oklahoma after games rather than stay overnight in Siloam Springs. Thus, while the basketball coach, Bill Haynes, had tried to recruit black athletes for years, without a support network of black students at the university, such efforts had been to no avail. As President Brown noted, "when blacks find out they are coming into an area that has no Negro population, they simply go elsewhere."[33]

In response to student calls for more aggressive attempts at racial integration, the administration's official policy remained racial neutrality. "John Brown University plans to continue its open door policy with the hope that all qualified students will feel perfectly free to apply," announced Vice President of Development John Terry. "Admissions practices for all students are the same." Nevertheless, beginning in 1972 a handful of African American students began trickling into the university via the athletic and music programs. Mike Elliot, a black basketball recruit from Camden, Arkansas, attended the university, and some black students joined the Sound Generation. Elliot became a popular student and was voted "Mr. JBU" in both his junior and senior years. John Brown University never boasted a sizable African American population, but neither did its all-white character continue after the cultural changes of the 1960s.[34]

The new perspectives of the day also effected modest changes for women at John Brown University. As mentioned earlier, one of John Brown Sr.'s goals for his institution was to train women for homemaking. Other majors were open to women, but all women regardless of major were required to take courses in homemaking. By 1966, the expectations for female students were codified to include three general areas: sewing skills, nutrition and meal planning, and "home furnishings and equipment." A Homemaking Proficiency Exam was administered to all incoming female students. Those who failed to achieve an adequate score were required to take two basic homemaking courses. Whether intentional or not, the formalization of homemaking requirements ironically coincided with the birth of the feminist movement in America. In 1963, Betty Friedan's *The Feminine Mystique* was published. Friedan deplored the idea that women should only seek fulfillment as wives and mothers, asserting instead that women should pursue careers as equals to men. In 1966, inspired by Friedan's book, female activists created the National Organization of Women to lobby for laws mandating equal hiring practices and equal pay, and to mobilize public opinion in support of feminism. Many Americans disagreed with NOW's goals and tactics, especially in the evangelical camp.

But, as with the civil rights movement, feminists succeeded in raising awareness of the issues among the American public. Terms such as *sexism* and *male chauvinist* entered the national vocabulary.[35]

Not surprisingly, no feminist movement emerged at John Brown University. In fact, in 1969, a year after radical feminists crowned a sheep Miss America to protest beauty pageants, John Brown University students were still electing a "Miss JBU" for each month of the year. Yet the university's homemaking requirements did disappear—not because of feminist protests but because of government legislation. In July 1972, Title IX of the Higher Education Act took effect, banning educational programs that discriminated based on gender at any institution receiving federal aid. The following fall, John Brown University eliminated the homemaking requirement for female students. The home economics major remained an option for women at John Brown University, but eventually this too fell prey to long-term cultural trends. In 1985, after years of declining student interest, the home economics program was dropped. The home economics building ended up housing the admissions department. Only the cryptic engraving "For Our Mothers" over the building's entrance hinted at its original purpose.[36]

The Trials of the Seventies

As the youth revolt of the 1960s wound down by the early 1970s, what little campus turmoil that existed at John Brown University receded. Students at John Brown University, like students nationwide, lost interest in big causes like the Vietnam War and civil rights. The student senate boasted of such accomplishments in the 1970s as getting peanut butter bins installed in the dining room. While administrators welcomed the absence of student rebellion, by the mid-1970s the university atmosphere had grown too quiet. An enrollment slump hit John Brown University that led to deep questions about the institution's identity and ultimately to a different type of university by the end of the decade.

Some perspective on American higher education is helpful here. The 1960s were an expansive time for the nation's colleges and universities. The baby boom generation of the post–World

War II years reached late adolescence in the 1960s, swelling the ranks of those attending college. Furthermore, the institution of a national draft for the Vietnam War meant that millions of young American males faced the choice of fighting in distant jungles or enrolling in college. Many chose the latter. The rising tide of students benefited nearly all educational institutions, including John Brown University. From a total of 325 students in 1961, the university grew steadily throughout the decade to a peak of 768 students in 1969. Optimistic administrators made plans for the university to grow to 1,500 students in the next decade.[37]

But the trend at John Brown University reversed itself dramatically in the early 1970s. Enrollment dipped slightly in 1970 to 757 students, then plunged alarmingly for the next four years. Only 526 students appeared on campus to begin the 1974–75 academic year, less than three-quarters of the student population in 1969. Administrators searched for explanations for the enrollment slump. Nationally, colleges and universities faced stiffer competition from community colleges and trade schools. Also, the cancellation of the military draft reduced that incentive for young men to attend college. Private institutions were especially hard hit. The percentage of college-bound youth enrolling in private institutions declined in the 1970s due to sharply rising cost differentials. The ratio of private to public college tuition grew from 3.5:1 in 1956–57 to 5:1 in 1974–75. And while John Brown University remained well below the average for private institutions, its cost was growing beyond that of the average public university.[38]

However, John Brown University could not simply chalk up the enrollment slump to national trends. Nationwide, the college population increased by 2.5 percent in 1973. Moreover, out of thirty-four Christian colleges surveyed that year, twenty-one of them reported enrollment increases. So the decrease in enrollment was to some extent unique to John Brown University. One problem seemed to be student retention. In 1970–71, for example, 45 percent of the nongraduating student body from the previous year did not return for classes that fall. Many transferred to public universities, while a significant number transferred to other Christian colleges. Student retention became such a concern in the 1970s that some professors were asked to ease the rigor of their courses so as not to discourage marginal students. Another possible factor for the enrollment decline may have been the emergence of a new local competitor. Oral Roberts University was founded in nearby Tulsa in 1965 and experienced rapid enrollment growth in the early 1970s. While primarily a Pentecostal institution, Oral Roberts University attracted enough non-Pentecostal Christians from the region that its growth may have contributed to John Brown University's sluggish enrollment.[39]

Accompanying the slump in student numbers were concerns about the spiritual vitality of the institution. As Vice President of Research and Planning Rogene Weathers admitted to the trustees at the spring 1973 board meeting, "Numerous students and faculty members feel that 'JBU has been slipping' in terms of its Christian idealism as exemplified by the founder." Of course, gauging spiritual zeal is a subjective endeavor, but, nevertheless, evidence exists that Weathers's remarks were an accurate reflection of the campus ethos at the time. In 1970, for example, a religious revival similar to the one twenty years earlier made the rounds of evangelical college campuses. Beginning in February at Asbury College, the wave of spiritual intensity spread to other Christian colleges such as Wheaton, Taylor, Spring Arbor, Houghton, Oral Roberts, and Greenville. However, to the chagrin of some students the revival seemed to bypass John Brown University.[40]

Concerns also surfaced about the quality of students being recruited by the most publicly visible group of the university, the Sound Generation. As the original members of the Sound Generation graduated, perceptions grew among students that subsequent members were simply hired performers who lacked the spiritual vision that had inspired the group in the first place. Founded to demonstrate the spiritual soundness of the young generation, the group took on a more professional flavor in the early 1970s. In 1971, the group was made a function of the university's development department. The group's directions for 1975 stated, "The Sound Generation is John Brown University's primary public relations thrust. We are responsible for 'selling' a product, a philosophy."[41]

Exacerbating the sense of spiritual malaise was tension between the administration and the Bible faculty concerning the proper spiritual direction of the university. Since the fundamentalist-liberal controversies of the 1920s, animosity had lingered between evangelical Protestants, descendants of the fundamentalists, and "mainline" Protestant denominations such as the United Methodists, Presbyterian Church, U.S.A., and the Episcopal Church that tolerated liberalism. When the National Association of Evangelicals was formed in 1941, founders adopted a clause barring any church that was a member of the mainline National Council of Churches from joining the NAE. Mainline organizations often responded in kind, dismissing evangelical groups as separatists and fundamentalist fanatics.[42]

In the 1970s, this tension manifested itself at John Brown University. President Brown, a longtime member of the local United Methodist Church, enjoyed a close friendship with the church's minister, Merle Johnson. The Methodist pastor perceived John Brown University's Bible faculty—most of whom graduated from the conservative Dallas Theological Seminary—as fundamentalistic and encouraged the president to move the university in a more mainline direction. One symbol of John Brown University's nonmainline identity was the Christian Fellowship, the interdenominational campus church that all students were required to attend. Under the vibrant leadership of Kelly Bihl, a former president of Youth for Christ, the Christian Fellowship began attracting members from local churches such as the United Methodist Church. In 1974, however, Bihl was transferred to the university's West Coast operations, the Christian Fellowship was disbanded, and members of the John Brown University community were instructed to attend a local church of their choice. The policy helped improve relations with the Siloam Springs community but was also perceived by some as an attempt to lessen the institution's evangelical identity. In 1975, Merle Johnson's friend Elton Trueblood, a highly respected but decidedly nonevangelical Quaker, was hired to serve as a consultant to the university. Soon thereafter, the chair of the Bible department, Dallas Seminary graduate Gilbert Weaver, was replaced by Trueblood's friend, Robert Johnson. Although Robert Johnson and the other Bible professors enjoyed a friendly relationship, tensions between the Bible faculty and the administration lingered throughout the decade.[43]

Needless to say, developments of the 1970s sparked some soul-searching that produced changes to the institution. Concerning enrollment, an emergency committee to study the issue was formed in 1973. The engineering faculty temporarily went to three-quarter workloads due to a shortage of student majors. A number of long-time professors, including science faculty Dorothy Woodland and Irwin Wills and music professor Mabel Oiesen, retired in the mid-1970s and were not replaced. To meet the challenge of community colleges, John Brown University introduced a two-year associate's degree program in career-oriented fields such as broadcasting, building construction, and church music.[44]

One casualty of the era was the Sound Generation. For university administrators, concerns about the spiritual commitment of group members were augmented by hefty expense accounts. Although not directly tied to the drop in enrollment, the group's size and budget at a time when the university was struggling to make ends meet was a crucial factor in its demise. Recruiting, equipping, and transporting such a large musical group required significant expense, and the group's budget dwarfed that of the music department. Members of the music department thus complained not only about the Sound Generation's musical style but also about funding inequities. The resentment was probably not reduced when the Sound Generation "donated" some of its old equipment to the music department to be used by the Cathedral Choir. By the mid-1970s, some were wondering if the Sound Generation tail was not wagging the John Brown University dog. The group's expenses had seemed justified by the public recognition it generated for the school; yet the Sound Generation's greatest national exposure coincided with the university's decline in enrollment. The time was ripe, therefore, for reassessment. When Elton Trueblood visited John Brown University as a consultant in 1975, one of his recommendations was that the Sound Generation be disbanded. The university accepted Trueblood's advice, and after the 1975–76 school year the Sound Generation ceased to exist.[45]

An even more fundamental change to John Brown University in the 1970s concerned the school's vocational program. By the end of the decade, it too had disappeared. As explained earlier, by 1960 John Brown University students were required to devote ten hours per week to vocational assignments. However, the "vocational" nature of these activities varied considerably. With a directive that vocational activities should relate to the student's field of study, a problem emerged in finding appropriate tasks for all students. This difficulty led to significant flexibility in defining "vocational" activities. In 1963, for example, basketball players received vocational credits for basketball practice. As the student population of the university grew in the 1960s, it became increasingly difficult to find meaningful vocational assignments for all students. A student poll concerning the vocational program reported that 67 percent favored reducing the number of hours involved.[46]

To meet these challenges, John Brown University's vocational program was revised again in 1965. Responsibility for the vocational program was dispersed to the separate departments of the university to define and administer as they saw fit. Some departments exempted freshmen from vocational requirements and granted "equivalence credit" for prior experiences and summer jobs. While some vocationally oriented departments such as engineering attempted to maintain strict requirements, by the late 1960s the general effect of these changes was a significant decrease in vocational emphasis and requirements. A 1971 university self-study found that only half of John Brown University students were involved in weekly vocational assignments, and that those students averaged only 4.3 hours of vocational work per week. Furthermore, the study found that many of the newer faculty members were either unfamiliar with the purpose of the vocational training program or "unsympathetic to its goals."[47]

Such changes alarmed the university's trustees, many of whom had directly benefited from the job training that John Brown

University had provided them. In 1970, John Brown University alumnus and board of trustee member Robert Jackson asked a current student about her vocational assignment. She responded, "I have none. They don't do this anymore as a work requirement until the senior year." Alarmed by this revelation, Jackson penned a letter to fellow trustees and university administrators expressing his concern that the university's historic distinctive of vocational training was being lost. Christian liberal arts colleges were "a dime a dozen," Jackson wrote. "If we are to become strictly a 'Christian Liberal Arts College,' I question the justification of our existence." In particular, Jackson criticized Vice President of Research and Planning Rogene Weathers for suggesting (as had been discussed in university committees for years) that the term *vocational training* be changed to something like *preoccupational experience* or *career orientation*. Jackson retorted, "I wonder how Dr. John E. Brown, Sr., were he alive, would react to this proposal?" Jackson urged that trustees who had directly benefited from the vocational training program take more aggressive leadership of the university to ensure that the ideals of the founder were preserved.[48]

In the wake of Jackson's letter, the university formed a Study Committee on Vocational Education to analyze the problem and make recommendations. The committee dissolved itself a few months later due to a lack of faculty interest and an inability to agree on a plan of action. Some faculty members, however, shared Robert Jackson's concerns, most notably Charles Willis, chair of the building construction department. Willis had taught at John Brown University since the 1940s, had chaired the building construction department since 1955, and had written a number of instructional manuals for vocational schools. Following the failure of the Study Committee on Vocational Education, Willis formed a new committee charged with revitalizing the vocational program at John Brown University. Calling the university's vocational training program the "reason for its existence," Willis's committee exclaimed, "the statement that we have remained true to the fundamental ideals of the founder in all respects is pure politics in the vocational training area."[49]

In 1973, the Willis committee issued its plan to revitalize vocational education. First, the name of the program would be changed to "Vocational Experience" to give the program increased stature in the university. Second, the committee proposed a universitywide minimum requirement of eight semester hours of vocational experience courses for all departments. This would result in increased vocational requirements for about 30 percent of the student body, the committee predicted. Finally, the committee proposed that an Office of Vocational Education with a head administrator be established to provide centralized leadership for the vocational program.[50]

Despite Willis's efforts, the trend away from vocational education continued throughout the 1970s. Of the committee's proposals, the only one to be enacted was the standard minimum credit hours of vocational experience; but these were reduced from eight to three hours. Moreover, what constituted "vocational experience" was left to the discretion of individual departments. Off-campus internships and summer jobs came to be classified as "practicums" that satisfied vocational credits in most departments. By 1976, the vocational program was being consistently referred to as "career orientation," and a practicum within each major had replaced the ideal of universitywide vocational training. The university's vocational distinctiveness was now defined by its emphasis on practicums in many of the programs and a few high-visibility career-oriented degree programs such as engineering, broadcasting, and building construction.[51]

The extent of the change is revealed in the John Brown University catalogs. The 1970 catalog, reflecting the university's traditional emphasis, began with a section entitled "Vocational Training." Explaining the university's distinctiveness, it quoted the oft-cited words of the founder that the John Brown University student is "educating himself to his life's work" through learning "the dignity of honest toil." In the 1975 catalog, an explanation of vocational training is still included, but it rests within a larger section on "A Philosophy of Education." The 1979 catalog makes no mention of vocational training or any occupational emphases. In fact, the terms *vocation* or *career preparation* do not appear anywhere in the catalog. The "Hand" was still emphasized by certain departments, but John Brown University no longer proclaimed itself a university of vocational specialization.[52]

The 1970s witnessed equally significant changes to the "Head" as John Brown University joined other evangelical colleges in attempting to recover Christian liberal arts excellence. To understand this transformation, it will be helpful to briefly consider some broader developments in Christian higher education in the twentieth century. Christians had dominated higher education in America from the 1600s to the mid-1800s. The Puritans established Harvard College in 1636, and over the course of the next 150 years Protestant groups founded prominent colleges such as Yale, Princeton, Dartmouth, and Brown. These colleges typically existed to train ministers, but their curricula also encompassed other areas of study.[53]

In the nineteenth century, evangelicals founded a host of denominational colleges and led the way in instituting the public university system. Curricula at these institutions consisted mostly of theology, classical studies, history, ethics, and natural science. But whatever the course of study, most nineteenth-century colleges proceeded on the assumption that Christian thinking can and should be applied to all areas of study, not just biblical studies and theology. Because, it was believed, the study of the natural world confirmed the truth of the Christian religion, the arts and sciences were studied for what they could reveal about God's nature and attributes. This educational philosophy was exemplified in the "moral philosophy" course taught by most college presidents and required of seniors as the unifying "capstone" of the college education. Historian Michael Hamilton describes it: "One part ethics, one part psychology, and one part natural theology, the mixture was served up in a broth of evangelical Protestantism that sought to confirm Christian teachings and find theological meaning in all branches of study." Such an approach was not without weaknesses (such as the assumption, soon to be seriously challenged, that natural science always affirmed the truths of Christianity). Nevertheless, for our purposes the important point to draw from the nineteenth century is that evangelical educators sought to integrate Christian faith into each discipline and to promote Christian thinking in all areas of study.[54]

This Protestant higher education enterprise collapsed in the late nineteenth century under the pressure of naturalistic science and new models of higher education. As explained earlier, modern universities, often based on naturalistic assumptions, existed to promote the values of intellectual inquiry and technical innovation that would produce leaders for a modern, technologically based society. Such changes, observes historian Mark Noll, "signaled the collapse of the effort by conservative evangelicals to construct a Christian mind in America." John Brown University and many other fundamentalist colleges begun in the early twentieth century were established partly in response to this disestablishment of Christianity in America's leading educational institutions.[55]

However, the fundamentalist movement in which such colleges were nurtured, while it effectively defended Christian supernaturalism from the attacks of liberal Protestantism, proved unable to reinspire the creation of a Christian mind. In their concern to defend Christianity from naturalism, fundamentalists often emphasized the supernatural to the exclusion of natural causes. For example, the fundamentalist fascination with biblical prophecy led to an almost complete inattention to studying and understanding the politics, economics, and history of the natural world. Moreover, fundamentalist spirituality, based on supernaturalistic slogans such as "letting go and letting God," tended to denigrate the intellect in the pursuit of holiness. As theologian Martin Lloyd Jones remarked to a group of conservatives in 1941, "If you teach that sanctification consists of 'letting go' and letting the Holy Spirit do all the work, then don't blame me if you have no scholars!" In all, fundamentalism promoted a kind of supernaturalism that, as Noll concludes, "for all its virtues in defending the faith, failed to give proper attention to the world." Whereas other Christian traditions have sparked vibrant scholarship in the natural sciences and liberal arts, fundamentalism tended to reduce interest in such seemingly mundane matters.[56]

For colleges nurtured in fundamentalism, therefore, learning was approached differently from the Christian ways of the past. Michael Hamilton delineates two models of learning that emerged in these twentieth-century institutions. The first he calls "triumphalist":

> The basic assumption of the new Christian triumphalism was that the prevailing intellectual culture was hopelessly flawed by nature of its secular assumptions. Its naturalistic materialism, being fundamentally erroneous, would eventually lead to its self-destruction. Christianity, however, being true, would endure and triumph. In this way of relating religion and education, faith always trumps learning. In this model, religious ways of knowing are by definition always superior to secular ways of knowing; secular ways of knowing become, by definition, more or less irrelevant.

This approach to learning expressed itself most often in relation to issues of science and religion. For example, at Wheaton College in 1961, trustees added a clause to the institution's doctrinal statement requiring belief in Adam and Eve as real historical persons, not having evolved from previously existing forms of life. The change was motivated by the fear among some trustees that modern science did not take the Bible seriously and that some Wheaton professors regarded scientific discoveries as a source of truth independent from the Bible. Such a clause concerning Adam and Eve made a literal reading of the Bible "the limiting framework within which all other knowledge would be pursued."[57]

While a triumphalist approach to faith and learning existed at some evangelical colleges, a more common model was what Hamilton calls the "value-added" model. This model of learning assumed that secular knowledge and sacred knowledge did not conflict because they occupied different spheres. Education consisted primarily of imparting knowledge and skills that would prepare students for various careers. The academic disciplines were considered value-neutral; faith could bring to learning an ethical dimension, but Christianity did not affect the actual content or methods of the particular academic disciplines. In this model of learning, the Christian college teaches basically the same things as a secular institution, but elements such as chapel, Christian relationships, Bible studies, and a safe environment constitute the "value-added" component that makes a college Christian. The value-added model, Hamilton claims, was and perhaps remains the most common approach to faith and learning at evangelical Christian colleges.[58]

By the 1960s, however, some of these colleges had begun to recover the historic Protestant approach to learning in which Christianity inspired attention to the visible world and made a difference in how one studied that world. The catalyst for this recovery was, strangely enough, the writings of Abraham Kuyper, a Dutch theologian and statesman of the late nineteenth century. Kuyper advocated broad Christian cultural engagement and an approach to learning in which Christian truths were integrated into all academic disciplines. As Kuyper put it, "There is not a square inch on the whole plain of human existence over which Christ, who is Lord over all, does not proclaim, 'This is Mine!'" In Kuyper's educational system, chemistry, psychology, history, and sociology have as much place in the Christian curriculum as theology and philosophy. Moreover, as James Bratt observes, "the guiding methodology for all these undertakings would be the desire to integrate Christian faith with learning in a particular discipline."[59]

Of course, few American evangelicals bothered to read Dutch theologians. Kuyper indirectly impacted American evangelical colleges through the vehicle of Calvin College, a Dutch Reformed school founded in 1876 in Grand Rapids, Michigan. Kuyper's educational approach became prominent at Calvin College in the mid-twentieth century. When the Christian College Coalition was formed in 1976, Calvin College exerted substantial intellectual influence on other institutions. Through contact with Calvin College, Arthur Holmes, a philosophy professor at Wheaton College, absorbed the Kuyperian worldview and began writing books articulating how a Christian college should pursue the distinctive task of relating faith, learning, and living. Holmes became a tireless advocate on Christian college campuses for the Kuyperian model of learning, and his book *The Idea of a Christian College* circulated widely among Christian college faculty and administrators. By the end of the 1970s, the "integration" model of faith and learning had become virtual dogma among Christian College Coalition institutions, inspiring efforts toward broad academic excellence and a distinctive approach to studying the disciplines.[60]

As with other aspects of American evangelicalism, John Brown University reflected these trends in Christian higher education. For example, much evidence exists that both triumphalist and value-added models of learning pervaded the university in the 1960s and early 1970s. Concerning the triumphalist model, a 1970 *Threefold Advocate* editorial claimed that John Brown University taught students that biblical knowledge trumped other forms of knowledge: "When any so-called authority in any area conflicts with a clear statement of God's inspired Word, then that writer is to be avoided." A John Brown University professor described a Christian college as a place where "people are trained to meet the world on its own ground and conquer it." The engineering department went so far as to invite as its banquet speaker for 1968 Henry Morris, the founder of scientific creationism and the epitome of a triumphalist approach to faith and learning.[61]

More commonly, however, John Brown University personnel expressed the value-added approach to learning. A 1973 faculty discussion on "The Role of the Christian College" yielded mainly value-added descriptions of the university's task. One professor described John Brown University as "an institution that puts the Lord first and offers adequate academic education with a plus." Another defined the Christian college as one in which professors "work with students with compassion and pray with them." A faculty exchange in the early 1970s exemplified the "separate spheres" notion of academic disciplines that the value-added approach implied. When asked by a Bible professor whether he integrated Christianity with his material, a science professor replied, "I don't teach Bible in my course; do you teach my subject in your Bible course?"[62]

The value-added model of learning at John Brown University

was best articulated by John Brown Jr. himself. In his annual report for 1967, President Brown described the university as one that "proclaims vigorously the fundamentals of the faith" within a "very positive Christian atmosphere." When asked in 1969 what distinguished John Brown University from other schools, Brown replied that "John Brown University stands in a very small group of positive Christian liberal arts colleges." He went on to explain what he meant by the term *positive* in words that embodied the value-added approach: "It insists that students take Bible courses, it insists that students have a certain high standard of moral behavior, it insists on church attendance on Sunday. In these things it is set apart from average Christian colleges which simply provide an academic program and the rest of the time as far as church attendance, as far as social activities, as far as out-of-class activities, provide very little incentive or program." In other words, John Brown University's "positive Christian" element consisted of the various activities that were added to the academic program. Brown's remarks reveal the university to be squarely in the mainstream evangelical tradition in the 1960s and early 1970s.[63]

In the mid-1970s, however, the recovery of the Kuyperian approach to learning promoted by the Christian College Coalition began to influence John Brown University. The effects could be seen in two ways. First, the university began to demonstrate a growing desire to improve academic quality in the liberal arts. Elton Trueblood's frequent visits to John Brown University in 1974 and 1975 were both symbolic of the change and important catalysts for improvement. Trueblood, a widely known scholar and professor of philosophy at Earlham College, had written *The Idea of a College* in 1959. In this book, Trueblood argued that colleges should emphasize the liberal arts and classical education, not career preparation. In his closing chapter, "A Vision of Excellence," Trueblood decried the trend toward egalitarianism in education that had compromised academic quality. Rather than trying to educate the masses, colleges should aim for academic excellence and seek to produce "intellectual aristocrats" who would be equipped to lead a democratic society, Trueblood believed. Inviting Trueblood, a liberal arts traditionalist, to John Brown University at the same time that the university's vocational program was shrinking represented a significant shift in direction.[64]

Trueblood first visited John Brown University in October 1974 to speak on "The Role of the Christian Intellectual." The next spring, as the university struggled with its future direction amid the crisis in enrollment, Trueblood made a series of consultation visits with faculty, administrators, and trustees. Not surprisingly, his prescriptions for John Brown University echoed his book. The university would survive as an institution, Trueblood concluded, but "John Brown University does need a change of mood." In order to thrive in the future the university would have to upgrade academic standards. A "great community of intellectuals" should be created. Faculty needed to write books, and students needed to be recruited who were capable of academic excellence. "High expectations toward high standards" should be expected of them. In short, Trueblood urged John Brown University to create the kind of vision of academic excellence articulated in *The Idea of a College*. Trueblood's visit reportedly made a significant impact. The next fall, President Brown boasted of a new attitude of optimism on campus and attributed the change to the work of Elton Trueblood. "The school has made a turn-around," he proclaimed.[65]

Trueblood's visits inspired John Brown University to seek academic excellence. Making that vision a reality, however, was another matter. Educational mediocrity had great inertia throughout the era. In 1963, John Brown University students placed in the 40th percentile nationwide on the Cooperative English Test. By the 1970s, after raising the minimum requirements for incoming students to 30 percent on college aptitude tests, John Brown University students remained at or just below the national American College Test norm of 20.3. John Brown University students remained around the national average throughout the 1970s. The students themselves continued to complain, as they had in earlier decades, of courses that resembled "high school type work" in requiring memorization of material rather than emphasizing thinking skills. A 1973 student poll revealed that only 54 percent of students agreed with the statement that "the intellectual atmosphere of this campus is on a college level."[66]

Professors continued to deride (as Trueblood had) the university's practice of awarding honorary degrees to persons of dubious academic distinction. In the 1970s, such recipients included country music star Roy Clark, football coach Tom Laundry, and even a Lawrence Welk Show singer. Efforts to improve the academic credentials of the professors themselves met with only moderate success. By the end of the 1970s, the percentage of faculty members with earned doctorates had increased from 20 to 60 percent. However, as accrediting agencies noted, an inordinately high number of professors were John Brown University alumni, and 40 percent of the doctorates held by John Brown University professors were from the nearby University of Arkansas, one of the nation's lower-rated public universities.[67]

Nevertheless, by 1977 students on campus detected, as the *Threefold Advocate* put it, an "increasing awareness of and motivation for academic excellence at John Brown University." The university was committed to recruiting students and faculty who were "purposefully committed to excellence in Christian higher education."[68]

In addition to taking academics more seriously, John Brown University also sought to move from a "value-added" philosophy of learning to the integration model that Abraham Kuyper, and later Arthur Holmes, had articulated. In 1975, Bible professor Jim Walters wrote a glowing review of Arthur Holmes's *The Idea of a Christian College* for the *Threefold Advocate*. Walters praised Holmes's definition of a Christian college as a community of scholars that sought to integrate faith and learning in all of the disciplines. A few years later, Vice President of Academic Affairs Richard Ruble mandated that John Brown University professors commit themselves to a thorough integration of faith and learning that went beyond a simple devotional time at the beginning of class. He recommended faculty development seminars to guide professors in this new endeavor and even suggested that those who failed to integrate faith and learning might not be retained as professors. In 1979, Arthur Holmes personally visited John Brown University to conduct a faculty workshop on integrating faith and learning. He was enthusiastically received and significant discussion of his book ensued. According to one professor, Holmes's visit significantly impacted several faculty members' thinking about integration.[69]

The impact of the integration model of Christian education at John Brown University can be seen by comparing two statements of the university's identity. In 1974, Vice President of Development John Terry defined a Christian college in traditional fundamentalist-evangelical terms as one that (1) accepts the Christian faith as set forth in the Bible, and (2) seeks to propagate that truth to others. Six years later, after the visits of Trueblood and Holmes, Richard Ruble wrote an article entitled "What Is a Christian College?" that differed dramatically from Terry's viewpoint. The primary purpose of a Christian college, Ruble asserted, was not to provide Bible training, prepare people for Christian ministry, shield students from sinful enticements, or to prepare students for a vocation. Rather, he insisted, "a Christian college exists to integrate the Christian faith into all areas of learning and then to produce a pietistic, knowledgeable, well-rounded student." It is a place where "all knowledge is looked at from a biblical perspective." Ruble's article was, of course, simply a restatement of Holmes's thesis in *The Idea of a Christian College*.[70]

The John Brown University catalog for 1979 thus revealed a university seeking to advance a new intellectual identity. Where previous catalogs had begun with a statement of Christian Americanism or the slogan "Under Two Flags," the cover page now asserted, "Above all this is a Christian institution seeking to integrate faith with learning." Though probably not endorsed by all of the university's constituents, the integration model of learning, along with a desire for academic excellence, had made significant inroads at John Brown University. The institution, along with a number of other Christian colleges, was seeking to recover and revitalize a Christian intellectual tradition that had been lost during the fundamentalist era.[71]

CHAPTER EIGHT

A Third Brown Presidency

In 1979, John Brown Jr. stepped down as president of John Brown University to become chancellor. Rather than running the institution, he planned to focus his attention on what had already been a major part of his job—overseeing the university's fund-raising activities and endowment properties (most notably radio stations in Houston and Long Beach and an academy in southern California). In 1976, John Brown University had launched the "Fulfillment of a Dream" capital campaign to raise five million dollars to expand the women's dormitory and build a new library. John Brown Jr. now dedicated his efforts to completing this campaign and increasing the university's fifteen-million-dollar endowment. For only the second time in John Brown University's sixty-year history, the question of presidential succession arose.[1]

It was answered in the same way that it had been approximately thirty years earlier—with a new President Brown. In October 1979, in a ceremony featuring Arkansas Gov. Bill Clinton, John Brown III was installed as the new president of the university. The transfer of power to a third Brown generation was not as inevitable as it might have appeared. John Brown III spent much of his childhood resisting associations with the university that his grandfather founded, and he was not pressured to follow in the footsteps of his father. In a fourth-grade essay assignment on future careers, the younger Brown wrote that he did not know what he wanted to be, but he knew what he did *not* want to be—president of John Brown University. After graduating from Siloam Springs high school, John Brown III left home to attend Hendrix College. A year later, he transferred to John Brown University—not to return home, he claims, but to be closer to his future wife, Stephania. After completing his undergraduate degree in 1971, John Brown III earned a

20. John Brown III assumed the presidency of the university in 1979.

law degree at the University of Arkansas in preparation for a career away from the "family business." In 1974, however, John Brown III sensed a duty to contribute to John Brown University, and he was sure enough of himself to return to the university despite his prominent name. He began working in development and legal affairs. He was named vice president in 1976 and gradually assumed more responsibilities in leading the university. The transition to president in 1979, therefore, was not a difficult one. Brown III recalls, "I picked up my pen set and Dad picked up his pen set, and we switched offices. It was an odd day, but we had been working together and it was comfortable."[2]

Building Academic Quality

John Brown III sought to promote a more open and collegial style of leadership than his predecessors. He frequently wrote columns in the student newspaper explaining university actions and policies in light of financial considerations. He also instituted a series of "fireside chats" in the dormitories in which he would listen and respond to students' questions and concerns. When students protested Brown's decision to schedule classes the Friday after Thanksgiving, John Brown III changed the policy and frankly admitted his mistake in the *Threefold Advocate*. "O.K., I was wrong," he remarked. "It looked great on paper, but it was a wash-out in Peoria." The same style marked John Brown III's relationship with university trustees. When he proposed at a trustee's meeting that the university consider changing its name to the "Brown University of Arkansas," the spirited response from some of the trustees quickly persuaded him to abandon the idea. Such a self-deprecating style of leadership characterized John Brown III's presidency.[3]

However, the young president did not shy away from making significant changes even when they were unpopular. One of John Brown III's first major tests as president concerned the university's popular, successful, and controversial baseball team. Begun in 1966, the team developed into an NAIA powerhouse under the leadership of Wally Moon, an ex–Los Angeles Dodger. Throughout the 1960s and 1970s the baseball team won numerous conference titles and made two appearances in the NAIA World Series. For a time, baseball, like the Sound Generation, was a major public relations engine for the university. Outsiders who knew little else about John Brown University recognized it for its strong baseball team.[4]

Success on the diamond, however, could not mask problems

with the baseball program. Long-standing concerns about the spiritual commitment and behavior of baseball players seemed to increase in the late 1970s. Athletic Director Robert Burns claimed that many John Brown University athletes over the years "were reached for Christ" as a result of their involvement in the sports program. Others, however, were not. One professor recalls that several baseball players simply "were not a good 'fit' for the expectations of the university." A longtime John Brown University employee bluntly declared them to be "arrogant and lacking in common courtesy or respect for anyone other than themselves." Apparently, students at the time were also concerned. A student survey revealed that student satisfaction with the athletic program dropped from a high of 80 percent in 1979 to 49 percent in 1981. Many students attributed the low ratings to behavioral problems involving baseball players.[5]

Spiritual concerns were augmented by practical problems. One of the main purposes of the intercollegiate athletics program, explained Robert Burns, was "to serve as a 'rallying point' in the lives of JBU students, alumni, faculty, staff, and the community." However, as John Brown III noted, the baseball team did not fulfill this function well since its playoff games did not begin until mid-May, after other students had left campus for the summer. Furthermore, the university incurred significant expense in housing and feeding the baseball players on campus when classes were not in session. The student body would be better served, Brown believed, by a popular sport in the fall that could unite the campus community and make freshmen students feel excited about the school. Soccer, which had begun as a club sport in the late 1970s, seemed to fill that role. John Brown III recalls looking out the window of his office on a Saturday afternoon in the fall and seeing two hundred people cheering for the soccer team. It seemed to Brown that soccer could boost campus spirit more effectively than baseball did.[6]

Having decided to reduce baseball expenses in favor of soccer, Brown next chose to cut the program immediately rather than let the program "limp around with continuing concerns." On April 13, 1981, the president announced that the current baseball season would be the team's last. Not surprisingly, Brown's announcement drew criticism. Athletic Director Burns thought the decision was a mistake but supported it publicly. Local newspapers, which had enjoyed having a winning team in the community, published editorials critical of the decision.[7] Many students, however, apparently agreed with the president. Student approval of the athletic program leapt from 49 percent the year before the baseball team was cut to 87 percent the following year, and it remained high in ensuing years. It surely did not hurt that the soccer team proved even more successful than the baseball team had been. After only two years as a varsity sport, the Golden Eagles soccer team won the 1983 National Christian College Athletic Association championship.[8]

21. The John Brown University baseball team was successful throughout the 1960s and 1970s but was disbanded in 1981.

President Brown defended his decision to drop the baseball team as a matter of putting principle ahead of athletic success. At a Christian college, Brown said, winning is not everything. "Christian education is the substance. Baseball or other such activities, while having a worthy purpose, are still but a shadow." Indeed, John Brown III's presidency was marked above all by a desire to strengthen Christian education and make it the university's top priority. If the completion of the Mabee Student Center in 1972 epitomized that era's major trend of making the university more responsive to students, the completion in 1980 of the new library, known as the Arutunoff Learning Resource Center, epitomized the theme of John Brown III's presidency: building academic quality. Although trained as a lawyer, not an academician, the new president understood the academic task of a Christian college and began implementing measures to improve academic quality. As he grew into his role as an academic leader, the young president earned credibility among his peers. In 1986, Brown was elected to the board of directors of the Christian College Coalition.[9]

John Brown III adopted wholeheartedly the coalition's integration credo promoted by Arthur Holmes and others. The new president declared his main goal to be, as he informed the *Threefold Advocate*, to "increase the integration of faith and learning in quality education." After quoting Arthur Holmes's explanation of integration extensively, Brown concluded, "This standard is the ideal to which John Brown University aspires." John Brown III even commended Holmes's institution, Wheaton College, as a model for John Brown University. In 1981, Brown visited Wheaton College and declared himself to be "impressed and inspired by the Wheaton ideal." The institution exemplified a "great Christian college" in its clear commitment to "high academic quality." The following spring, John Brown University invited Wheaton College president Hudson Armerding to speak at its commencement services and bestowed on him an honorary doctorate.[10]

Although John Brown III praised Wheaton's approach to learning, it was left to the John Brown University faculty to implement the integration of faith and learning into the curriculum. Initially, this took the form of a new worldviews curriculum proposed by some professors in 1980. The worldviews program, and the controversy it provoked, illustrated both the extent to which integrationist views had impacted John Brown University and the significant resistance to the growing liberal arts emphasis that such views implied.

In the spring of 1980, physics professor Jim Holliday proposed a substantial revision of the university's general education program. Quoting from Arthur Holmes, who advanced a Christian worldview as the educational goal of a Christian college, Holliday proposed a "World Views Study Program," consisting of several team-taught interdisciplinary courses, that would replace the current general education curriculum. Such courses would increase the philosophy component in education and, as history professor William Burnside stated, "introduce integration earlier and in a more systematic fashion" into the curriculum. After considerable discussion, the faculty voted to adopt a required freshman worldviews course on a trial basis for the fall 1980 academic year.[11]

That fall, the first worldviews course was taught to freshmen, and an evaluation committee gave the course mixed reviews. The basic objectives of the course seemed to have been achieved, the committee concluded, but students were only "mildly enthusiastic" about the class. Some felt that the class size was too large and the content too "deep," while other students felt that professors pushed their own worldview rather than encouraging students to develop one of their own. Overall, the committee gave the course moderate approval. When proponents attempted to expand the worldviews program to a full four-year curriculum, however, objections to expansion revealed a faculty deeply divided over the merits of the program and the purpose of the institution.[12]

One prominent opponent of the worldviews program was Robert Johnson, chair of the Bible department. Johnson challenged the integrationist ideal promoted by Arthur Holmes and his advocates at John Brown University. Integration had always occurred at John Brown University, Johnson claimed. "It takes place when there is a committed Christian teacher in every classroom. The history of the school as well as a great host of alumni testify to the extent of this integration in past years." Professors could do a better job of integrating faith and learning "by deepening our own spiritual commitment" rather than devising a course to do it. In other words, for Johnson integration was something that naturally occurred whenever spiritually committed professors taught; it did not require a self-conscious attempt to view the subject matter itself from a Christian perspective. Johnson was articulating the value-added understanding of the Christian college as providing a standard education plus spiritual commitment and Christian fellowship between professor and student. Clearly, not everyone at John Brown University had been converted to Holmes's integrationist educational philosophy.[13]

A different sort of attack on the worldviews program was launched from the university's vocational education proponents. Their concern was not so much integration but the increasingly liberal arts orientation of the university that the worldviews curriculum seemed to reflect. Predictably, longtime building construction professor Charles Willis most adamantly expressed this concern. Willis's written response to the worldviews program began: "If you repeat a statement often enough people will come to believe it. 'John Brown University is a liberal arts college.' This statement continues to be used in spite of the fact that we are not now or never have been such an institution. We are compared to other Christian colleges but very few have program offerings similar to ours. Practically every consultant or expert who comes on campus is of the liberal arts persuasion and encourages us to fall into line." Liberal arts requirements were constantly increasing, Willis complained, making it more and more difficult for the university's professional programs to build a solid curriculum. "The trend seems to be," Willis observed, "toward a major in general studies with a minor in music or engineering, etc." The worldviews program, Willis believed, further eroded the university's professional programs by piling on even more general education requirements. Fellow building construction professor Kent Davis concurred, the worldviews proposals "showed a lack of sensitivity toward professional programs."[14]

Such variety of opinion concerning the worldviews program resulted in a series of rancorous faculty meetings convened in the spring of 1981 to determine the fate of the program. Supporters of the worldviews program proposed expanding it to four required courses, one for each year of a student's life at John Brown University.

Charles Willis, with considerable backing from other professors, proposed eliminating two of the worldviews courses. Bible professor Andy Bowling proposed eliminating the program altogether. Eventually, a faculty vote was taken on the original proposal to implement four worldviews courses. The proposal failed by a vote of 28 to 21. In an effort to salvage something of the program, William Burnside proposed that the freshman worldviews course be continued in the fall of 1981. A nearly evenly divided faculty approved this proposal by a 23 to 20 vote. The following fall, however, the worldviews program was weakened even further when the faculty voted to make the worldviews course optional rather than required.[15]

The worldviews program thus continued in a weakened form, but its days were numbered. What eventually doomed the program were practical concerns that augmented the philosophical ones. One practical difficulty concerned students transferring to or from John Brown University. What transfer courses would be accepted as fulfilling a worldviews requirement? What credit would students who left John Brown University be given for a worldviews course that other colleges typically did not offer? Furthermore, the team-taught aspect of the course caused difficulty with faculty teaching loads. Finding professors who were willing and available to help teach the class was a continual problem. Finally, in the fall of 1984, the worldviews course was dropped, a victim of declining student enrollment and insufficient faculty support.[16]

The worldviews controversy illustrated the conflicted identity of an institution moving from emphasis on vocational education to Christian liberal arts. Some professors saw no need to change the curriculum to emphasize the integration of faith and learning. Others saw the worldviews program as further evidence that the university was abandoning its vocational heritage. In the wake of the program's failure, President Brown reaffirmed the institution's commitment both to "a foundational program in the liberal arts and religious studies" and to "an integrative, stimulating core curriculum." In the future, however, integrating faith and learning would be promoted not through a worldviews curriculum but by individual professors in their courses. For example, the university instituted a policy in which professors undergoing their fourth year review were required to write a paper explaining their understanding of the "integration of faith and learning" and how they implemented it in their teaching.[17]

More important than any specific program to promote integration was an overall commitment by the young president to emulate Wheaton College in its pursuit of academic excellence. While such a goal had of course been stated in the past, John Brown III showed himself willing to devote significant financial resources to achieving it. For example, in order to recruit quality professors, the university aspired to climb into the top 25 percent of Christian College Coalition institutions for faculty salaries and benefits. A series of significant across-the-board pay increases in the early 1980s enabled the university to achieve this goal. By 1986, full professors' salaries at John Brown University ranked in the top 12 percent of CCC institutions, and assistant professors ranked in the top 10 percent. John Brown III also sought to build a community of scholarship by encouraging professors to write books. He pledged a special effort to raise funds for endowed chairs—faculty positions funded by external contributions that would have reduced teaching loads to allow professors more time for research and writing.[18]

As with previous attempts to improve faculty credentials, John Brown III's efforts achieved only partial success. Faculty salaries, which improved significantly in the early 1980s, actually lost ground in the latter half of the decade. By 1989, full professors' salaries at John Brown University ranked only in the top 40 percent for CCC institutions. Graduate degrees for faculty changed little from 1980 to 1990: The percentage of professors with earned doctorates remained at approximately 60 percent, while the number of John Brown University alumni on the faculty actually increased from 16 to 22 percent. Faculty scholarship seemed to improve somewhat, but other than the work of biology professor Gaston Griggs, faculty research was typically in teaching-related areas such as textbooks and papers for pedagogy conferences. The "five to ten" endowed chairs envisioned by John Brown III never materialized.[19]

One area that did witness significant progress in the 1980s was faculty independence. An accreditation team visit in 1981 noted as a weakness the passivity of the faculty, most likely a vestige of days when individual professors could be dismissed unilaterally by John Brown Sr. or John Brown Jr. In response, a faculty association consisting of full-time faculty members was created to facilitate communication between professors and the administration. While not a governing body, the association would serve as a forum for individual professors to voice concerns that would then be communicated to the administration. John Brown III gave full support to the faculty association as a way to give the faculty an independent voice in decisions made by the university. Furthermore, the president encouraged academic freedom and the expression of diverse opinions among the faculty. The decade of the 1980s, therefore, witnessed moderate gains in the quality and independence of the John Brown University faculty.[20]

Of course, improving the quality of the teachers affected only one side of the educational coin. The learners were equally important to the academic enterprise. Upon assuming office, John Brown III stated as one of his goals to upgrade the academic quality of the student body. Such attempts in the past had often floundered against the countervailing need to keep enrollment at a healthy level. Despite rhetoric concerning student quality in earlier decades at John Brown University, it was not until the 1980s that the university experienced a significant increase in the academic quality of the student body. One way that this was achieved was by raising minimum entrance standards. In 1980, John Brown III announced a departure of sorts from previous policies in stating that the "primary consideration" in the selection of John Brown University students during his presidency would be academic preparation, as evidenced by American College Test scores or high school academic achievement. Eventually, minimum entrance requirements were raised from a 2.0 to a 2.5 high school grade point average, and students had to score in at least the twenty-fifth percentile on the ACT for college bound students. As a result, the average ACT percentile for John Brown University freshmen rose from 55 percent in 1985 to 64 percent in 1986. The minimum was raised further to the thirtieth percentile in 1989.[21]

At the same time, the university began using scholarship money to recruit academically gifted students. In 1987, ten presidential scholarships providing full tuition remission were awarded to students who scored in the 95th percentile in the ACT and achieved at least a 3.9 high school GPA. Twenty-five divisional scholarships providing partial tuition remission were awarded to students who scored above the 90th percentile in the ACT and achieved at least a 3.5 high school GPA. The following year, in addition to maintaining the presidential and division scholarships, the university awarded an automatic five hundred dollar scholarship to any student scoring above the 80th percentile on the ACT.[22]

The changes to the academic program at John Brown University were best symbolized by the inauguration of a university honors program in 1988. The idea of a separate program within a college for gifted students had emerged back in the 1920s as a reaction to expansion of American higher education to the masses. As historian Frederick Rudolph noted, the honors idea rejected "the popular notion that the average man was superior to the most able man, a notion that had had a powerful history in the United States." Given John Brown University's egalitarian nature, it is no wonder that an honors program had failed to take root earlier. In the 1960s, when a university honors program was first proposed, the idea aroused considerable opposition and was not successfully implemented. Fears of academic elitism prevented such a program from taking root. In 1987, however, English professor Shirley Thomas began a university honors program, ostensibly to help attract and retain gifted students. Vice President of Academic Affairs A. J. Anglin defended the program to critics as a way to benefit students and professors across the campus by improving intellectual stimulation in classes, not as an attempt at elitism. Under Thomas's leadership, the John Brown University honors program developed into one of the leading programs among Christian colleges.[23]

Together, higher minimum standards, academic scholarships, and an honors program significantly improved the intellectual quality of John Brown University students. The average freshman ACT score, which had been 18.5 in 1985, climbed to 22.0 in 1991. This figure placed John Brown University in the "liberal arts—selective" category for national college and university rankings. Seventy years after John Brown Sr. had vowed to attract "above average" students to his college, that goal finally seemed to be a reality.[24]

Maintaining Historic Distinctives

While improving academic quality, John Brown University did not simply seek to become another Wheaton College. In 1990, the *Threefold Advocate* sparked a flurry of student letters when it printed a story stating that the university was seeking to attract "Wheaton-type" students. The newspaper's faculty adviser Fred Lollar responded with an editorial clarifying the story and explaining how John Brown University was different from—and in his opinion superior to—Wheaton College. Lollar mentioned two traits in particular that distinguished John Brown University from Wheaton and other prestigious Christian liberal arts colleges. John Brown University students, he asserted, receive "good hands-on experience" in their majors, and they "pay less for a quality education than students do at Wheaton." Despite changes in other areas, these two historic distinctives—practical experience and affordability—continued to characterize John Brown University into the 1990s.[25]

With a vocational program no longer in place, John Brown University still sought to maintain "strong career fields," as John Brown III called them, to give it a competitive edge over other colleges. Most liberal arts colleges by the 1980s typically offered career-oriented degrees, so John Brown University actually differed from other colleges only in the number of its career-oriented majors, not in its basic philosophy of combining "Head" and "Hand." Moreover, the university's increasing liberal arts emphasis was itself articulated as contributing to career-oriented education. In 1989, a university committee on general education revised the curriculum to include seven more hours of liberal arts courses. Justifying the changes, committee member Doyle Butts explained, "This component will make graduates more attractive to employers who are now looking for students with a more diversified education that liberal arts institutions offer." In such remarks, one can see a merging of the university's vocational heritage with the "cultural education" established by the founder. Once viewed by some as antithetical to practical education, liberal arts courses were now promoted as a means to providing better career opportunities for graduates.[26]

Affordability also remained a distinguishing characteristic of the university during John Brown III's tenure, but only if one compared John Brown University to the right institutions. In general, just as the university's career emphasis came to be promoted in relation to other Christian liberal arts colleges, not vocational colleges, so its affordability came to be defined in relation to other private colleges, not to public universities. Such a change was simply a result of the changing economic realities of higher education. Throughout the 1960s and 1970s, the rising costs of private education far outpaced that of public education. The trend continued into the 1980s. As soaring inflation rates drove up the cost of education, increased government funding for public institutions allowed them to keep costs down, thus making it increasingly difficult for private institutions to compete for a dwindling supply of students in the post–baby boom generation. At the same time, changes to federal tax policy reduced the incentives for donations to charitable organizations. John Brown III summarized the difficult situation that private colleges faced in the 1980s: "We must compete for fewer students with even more precious dollars. On the other hand, we are met with a public policy which artificially suppresses the real costs of public higher education, even while it reduces the traditional incentives for private sector philanthropy." Given such realities, competing economically with public universities was increasingly unrealistic.[27]

However, when compared to other private Christian colleges, John Brown University's financial situation looked fairly strong due to its relatively large endowment. The key to the university's financial health was the Chapman Trust, established in 1966. James A. Chapman, an Oklahoma oil and ranch millionaire, met John

Brown Sr. in the 1940s during one of Brown's speaking tours of Oklahoma. The son of rural Oklahomans who himself never finished high school, Chapman's humble beginnings resembled those of John Brown, and he shared the evangelist's desire to help young people gain an education. For years Chapman made anonymous donations to John Brown University. When he died in 1966, a five-million-dollar trust fund for the university was established from Chapman's considerable assets. For a private institution the size of John Brown University, such a fund was a considerable boost. John Brown Jr. called Chapman's gift "the event which takes place that starts the institution toward greatness." He likened the Chapman Trust for John Brown University to tax support for a public university. By 1979, the Chapman Trust was generating over $700,000 in annual income for the university. The Chapman Trust significantly augmented John Brown University's diversified endowment consisting of traditional stocks and securities, radio stations, hotel properties, a military academy, and other enterprises. By 1982, the university's total endowment had reached approximately twenty-five million dollars.[28]

All of this meant that John Brown University's financial position compared quite favorably to that of other Christian colleges. A 1982 study by *Christianity Today* magazine found that in terms of endowment income per student, John Brown University's $31,130 per student far outpaced other Christian College Coalition institutions. Wheaton College was a distant second at $12,020 per student. Thus, John Brown University students continued to benefit from substantial financial aid. In the 1982–83 school year, for example, students were charged $4,400 for room, board, and tuition, while the university spent approximately $8,000 to educate each student. In other words, students were paying about half price for their John Brown University education.[29]

Despite the seemingly rosy financial picture, however, the decade of the 1980s made John Brown University's historic commitment to affordable education more problematic. For one thing, the university's programs in expensive majors such as engineering and broadcasting continued to push costs higher than those of other institutions. While the university ranked toward the bottom of eighty CCC colleges in terms of cost to the student, its annual expenditures on education per student ranked in the top twenty of those institutions. Another challenge was that the endowment dollars had to cover a growing number of students due to increasing enrollment in the late 1980s. After the enrollment slump of the 1970s, the number of students attending John Brown University gradually climbed well into the eight hundreds in the mid-1980s, despite grim predictions of a nationwide decline in college enrollees. In 1987, the university announced a goal of "1001 Students by 1991." This was rather ambitious, given that enrollment had declined to 817 students in 1987. Nonetheless, marketing and recruitment efforts were stepped up, and in the fall of 1991 the university managed to enroll 1,044 students.[30]

The good news on the enrollment front meant, however, that the university's endowment dollars were spread over a larger student body, and cash flow became tight. John Brown III, steadfastly committed to both student financial aid and a balanced budget, did not hesitate to cut university programs that failed to justify their costs. In early 1990, for example, a $250,000 budget shortfall led to a host of program cuts. One casualty was JoySong, a promotional/ministry musical group founded in 1977 to succeed the Sound Generation. Despite the group's success in the 1980s, the budget shortfall led the university to cut funding for the group, effectively killing it off. Other casualties of the "Valentine's Day Massacre," as it came to be called, included the university's cross-country team, tennis team, and cheerleading scholarships. Faculty salaries and financial aid, however, remained at the then-current levels.[31]

Such cash flow problems led the university to alter its pricing and marketing strategy. At an October 1990 executive team meeting, university administrators agreed to raise tuition and to make a concerted effort to attract more full-paying students from beyond the south-central geographical region. Even though John Brown University had at the time the third highest tuition level among private Arkansas colleges, the university followed a 9.2 percent tuition increase in 1989–90 with a 9.1 increase in 1990–91, bringing total student fees up to $8,550, or about twice as much as students had paid a decade earlier. John Brown III acknowledged that John Brown University was no longer inexpensive in its particular geographical region, even in relation to other private colleges. Instead, the university's affordability was now defined in relation to Wheaton and other nationally known Christian colleges. Said Brown, "We are comparable to a number of different schools. In fact, we are a bargain compared to some." Facts seemed to bear him out; despite the cost increases, the university remained in the lowest quartile of Christian College Coalition institutions. The reference point for affordability, however, had clearly changed. Due to its relatively large endowment, John Brown University remained less expensive than most other private Christian colleges across the nation. But it no longer described itself as a place for promising young people who could not otherwise afford a college education. It was certainly not the first option for penniless rural Americans, as its founder had once described it.[32]

As the university sought to attract more full-paying students, one rather unexpected source emerged from Central America. As early as 1970, when students began advocating more aggressive recruiting of minorities, John Brown University had attempted to become more racially and ethnically diverse. In 1973, a consultant, Dr. John E. King, visited the campus and issued a number of recommendations, one of them being that John Brown University develop a climate in which students from wide-ranging ethnic backgrounds would feel welcome on campus. Particularly, King had in mind Native Americans in nearby Oklahoma who could benefit from John Brown University's generous financial aid program. Two years later, the university hired Dennis Snell, who was half Cherokee, as an admissions counselor to recruit Native American students from Oklahoma. Although the hiring of Snell brought little in the way of tangible results, the university remained committed to increasing the racial diversity of its student body. Institutional goals for the years 1981–86 included increasing the percentage of minority students to 5 percent by 1985. The university ultimately achieved this goal—and picked up a substantial number of full-paying students—by attracting not African Americans or Native Americans but Central Americans.[33]

In July 1985, Wal-Mart founder Sam Walton announced that he was donating $3.6 million to three Arkansas colleges—College of the Ozarks, Harding University, and John Brown University—to fund scholarships for students from Central America. Walton's announcement consummated a growing partnership between the retail giant and John Brown University that produced many dividends for the university. By turning a modest collection of Arkansas five-and-dime stores into the world's largest retail chain, Sam Walton came to embody the American values of free enterprise capitalism and rugged individualism. John Brown University had promoted such values for decades, most notably through its Christian American Heritage seminars. In 1981, Wal-Mart Executive Vice President Don Soderquist spoke at John Brown University's "American Heritage Week" and presented a check for $30,000 to help renovate the Cathedral of the Ozarks. He later joined the university board of trustees. In 1988, the university named its newly completed multimillion dollar recreational facility the Walton Lifetime Health Complex in honor of Sam Walton's considerable donations to that project.[34]

Walton's most enduring legacy for John Brown University, however, was the Central American scholarship fund that he created. The Walton scholarship fund meshed nicely with John Brown University's patriotic and anticommunist emphases. Walton hoped to counteract communist influence in Central America by bringing students to study in U.S. colleges, where they would learn the values of democracy and free enterprise and spread those values in their own countries upon their return. As a result of the Walton fund, fifteen new international students arrived at John Brown University for the 1985–86 academic year.[35]

The Walton students joined thirty-five other international students on campus (including children of American missionaries). To handle this growth, the university created a new position called director of international programs. A year later President Brown personally traveled to Central America to recruit eighteen Central American students to be sponsored by the Walton fund. By 1987, forty-eight Walton students were attending John Brown University, and instead of attempting to boost the international student population, university trustees actually passed a motion to limit the international student population to 15 percent of the student body.[36]

Aside from the increase in Central American students, John Brown University continued to struggle to create racial diversity in regards to African American students. Despite efforts to "attract all races," according to Dean of Student Life Lee Demarais, the number of black Americans enrolled at John Brown University in 1988 was less than 1 percent of the student body. Nevertheless, the infusion of Central American students helped to broaden and diversify the campus community. In 1990, the university's Central American students began broadcasting a Spanish language news program for the Latino population of northwest Arkansas. The university created an Intercultural Studies major and instituted an annual Cultural Awareness Week to help students understand issues of cultural differences. With roughly 10 percent of its student body originating from foreign countries, John Brown University in the 1990s displayed a surprising degree of ethnic diversity for a small Christian college in northwest Arkansas.[37]

The Walton Scholarship Program thus fulfilled a number of functions for John Brown University. It provided a steady stream of the full-paying students that the university sought, and it enhanced the diversity of the campus. It also provided a new outlet for the university's evangelistic emphasis by bringing a largely nonevangelical population to the campus. Gilberto Campos of Panama, for example, was not a Christian when he came to John Brown University as a Walton student in 1987. Through the influence of Christian students and professors, Campos converted to Christianity during his freshman year. "I knew God had something for me," he remarked, "because if I would have known this was a Christian college, I wouldn't have come." Campos's experience revealed that amid the many changes during John Brown III's tenure as president, John Brown University retained its strong evangelical ethos.[38]

Key figures in American evangelicalism continued to visit the Siloam Springs campus as they had in earlier decades. Well-known pastor and radio preacher J. Vernon McGee visited the university frequently during these decades. Kenneth Kantzer, managing editor of the leading evangelical magazine *Christianity Today*, spoke at commencement in 1981 and joined John Brown University's board of trustees in 1983. Charles Colson, author of the best-selling book *Born Again* and one of the most influential evangelical leaders in America, gave the university's commencement address in 1988.[39]

As in most Christian colleges, some concerns were expressed about possible spiritual decline among the student body. Some students regularly violated the university's prohibition of alcohol consumption. Bible professor Jim Walters warned that although student responses to a Campus Crusade survey of religious activity seemed favorable, students' behavior did not always match their responses. Less than half of the students were attending church regularly, he claimed, and only 20 percent of the students were involved in CAUSE ministries. One student decried a "prevailing spirit of apathy" across the campus.[40]

On the whole, however, John Brown University students seemed to maintain the religious devotion of earlier generations, especially when one compared them to other campuses. Ninety-nine percent of John Brown University students labeled themselves "reborn Christians," compared to 30 percent nationally. Forty-five percent of the students came from a Baptist or independent Bible church background. A 1980 survey of recent alumni asked what led them to choose John Brown University. Of nine possible reasons, the college's Christian character was overwhelmingly the most important factor, cited by 93 percent of the respondents. The two least significant factors cited were academic reputation and occupational emphasis, suggesting that to students, at least, the Heart aspect of the university was far more important than the Head or the Hand. Furthermore, while chapel services remained mandatory, little evidence exists of student complaints about required chapels.

Rather, the complaints made about chapel typically concerned a dearth of biblical content or a lack of emphasis on evangelism. A transfer student from the University of Oklahoma expressed amusement at the suggestion that John Brown University was spiritually tepid. "Take it from me," he exclaimed, "to a heathen this campus reeks of spirituality."[41]

John Brown University's religious character did not remain completely static, however. The chapel program, for example, adapted itself to changing evangelical musical tastes. In the mid-1960s, Christian teenagers inspired by the Beatles and Bob Dylan began forming garage bands that married Christian lyrics to rock 'n' roll music. These "Jesus rock" pioneers such as Larry Norman and Chuck Girard led an underground circuit of musicians who played in parks, coffeehouses, and other venues outside the evangelical mainstream. While most churches disdained the new style, the Calvary Chapel in southern California, a church that ministered to hippies, welcomed the innovations. In 1973, Calvary Chapel founded Maranatha! Music to spread the new music to other churches. Eventually the new style shed the stigma of its rock 'n' roll origins and achieved widespread acceptance in evangelicalism under a new name, "praise and worship" music.[42]

Like other developments in American evangelicalism, the changes in worship style eventually impacted John Brown University. While John Brown Sr. had spiced up chapel services in the 1950s with Youth for Christ evangelistic choruses, worship in chapel remained largely traditional in the 1960s and early 1970s. Jim Walters, who arrived on campus in 1968, recalled, "When I came, Dr. Oiesen was the chair of the music department. She made comments like, 'When you hear the music, does it make you want to worship, or does it make you want to tap your foot?'" By the mid-1970s, many students were answering, "Both." New musical styles appeared in chapel, and Christian rock guru Larry Norman gave a concert on campus in 1977. Guitars became common in chapel worship, and a praise chorus book joined the traditional hymnal in the cathedral pews. By the late 1980s, hymn books disappeared altogether as contemporary worship pervaded chapel. In the 1990s,

Thursday chapel evolved into "Community Worship" sessions led by a student praise band. To Walters, it seemed that in a few decades the university had gone from the belief that anything contemporary was inappropriate to the view that anything traditional had no value. Predictably, the praise songs that won out in American evangelicalism triumphed at John Brown University as well.[43]

John Brown University chapels developed a greater openness to other theological traditions as well as new musical styles. In 1989, for example, John Michael Talbot, a Roman Catholic monk and professional musician, gave a concert in chapel. Students' reactions varied widely. One student called it "the most appalling and sacrilegious concert of my entire life," while others expressed enthusiastic approval. Apparently it was Talbot's tunic, sandals, and worship style that sparked the controversy, not so much his theology. Talbot and his group danced on the platform and encouraged the audience to raise their hands during worship. A month later, another Catholic, Brennan Manning, spoke in chapel and was well received by the student body. A visit by Talbot three years later (minus the dance team) went largely unopposed. A reporter observed, "many students found it a peaceful, soothing intrusion into their hectic lives." By the 1990s, dozens of John Brown University professors and students were attending Grace Episcopal Church, the local Episcopal congregation. While still fervently evangelical, the university community as a whole demonstrated more tolerance of other Christian traditions. The tendency toward sectarianism typical of fundamentalism seemed to have largely disappeared.[44]

Further relaxations in campus rules also revealed a university less dominated by its fundamentalist heritage. Some policies remained largely unchanged. In addition to required chapels twice a week, the university maintained firm prohibitions against alcohol and tobacco.[45] In other areas, however, John Brown University followed and in some cases surpassed other Christian colleges in granting students more freedom. The campus dress code, for example, was further modified to emphasize general principles of modesty rather than particular items such as skirt lengths and blue jeans. The goal, Lee Demarais explained, was to make the dress code "conform to what we really want around here." Even dancing, which had been unthinkable in earlier eras, merited reconsideration. In 1984, the university began allowing square dances and folk dances on campus. Two years later, university policy was modified to allow off-campus dancing at "non-alcoholic dance clubs." Enterprising students took advantage of the new loophole to organize an off-campus dance for John Brown University students, prompting university officials to hastily clarify the policy. President Brown declared, "We have NOT sanctioned JBU students organizing and promoting an off-campus dance." Dance tensions notwithstanding, the university had clearly come a long way from the highly restrictive policies of earlier eras. John Brown III observed correctly in 1991, "Students at John Brown University are granted an extraordinary amount of personal freedom compared to many other Christian colleges."[46]

While such changes could be perceived as evidence of secularization, from a broader historical perspective the relaxation of rules more accurately reflects simply a dwindling of the fundamentalist legacy at John Brown University. Strict rules governing Christian living arose not from the Protestant Reformation but from nineteenth-century evangelicalism and early-twentieth-century fundamentalism. As sociologist James Davison Hunter notes, belief in the moral impropriety of such behaviors as drinking, dancing, and card playing "was characteristic of only a portion of ascetic Protestantism for a relatively brief period—roughly 1870–1960." Reformation Protestantism, on the other hand, tended to emphasize Martin Luther's notion of "the freedom of the Christian" and a life of grace rather than a litany of proscribed behaviors. Therefore, as John Schmalzbauer and C. Gray Wheeler argue concerning Christian colleges, "Contemporary changes in rules have actually represented a recovery rather than an abandonment of Protestant orthodoxy among evangelicals." Like the renewed emphasis on the Christian mind, the relaxation of rules reflects John Brown University's attempt to move from its fundamentalist past into the broader tradition of historic Protestantism.[47]

Many members of the John Brown University community attributed the university's continued strong religious atmosphere to the leadership of the president. While John Brown Jr. was a skilled businessman who brought financial stability to the institution, John Brown III helped bring spiritual vitality to the university that some felt was lacking in the 1970s. Remarked one alumnus, "Many alumni thought John Brown III restored the spiritual element to the school that existed during his grandfather's time." Science professor Lee Netherton recalled "spiritual modeling" as one of John Brown III's most memorable traits as president. Jim Walters speculates that John Brown University in the 1970s was coming to resemble a mainline denominational college until John Brown III strengthened the university's ties to conservative evangelicalism in the 1980s.[48]

Whatever the case, John Brown III clearly played a crucial role in the university's spiritual and academic vitality. It was a momentous occasion, therefore, in September 1992 when John Brown III, at the age of forty-three, announced in chapel that he would be resigning at the end of the 1992–93 school year. Brown had never planned on remaining the school's president for his lifetime, he said, and by 1992 a number of major initiatives had been achieved. New buildings such as the Walton Lifetime Health Complex and the Mabee Learning Resource Center had been completed, and existing buildings such as J. Alvin Dormitory and the Cathedral of the Ozarks had been substantially renovated. Enrollment surpassed one thousand students, and student retention reached a record high. "It's better to go out when you've had a winning season," Brown remarked. Besides, he said, after seventy years it was time for John Brown University to have someone other than a Brown as president.[49]

Plans to select the first non-Brown president commenced immediately. On September 9, 1993, the executive committee of the board of trustees met to design the search process. The trustees hired David McKenna, president of Asbury Theological Seminary and a respected evangelical leader, to serve as consultant for the search and allocated $43,000 for the task. In October, McKenna prepared a survey that was distributed to John Brown University faculty, administration, students, and alumni asking about institutional priorities and preferred presidential characteristics. A Campus Search Committee was formed to approve a list of ten to twelve candidates, from which the Trustee Selection Committee would select three candidates to invite to the campus. The process would culminate in April 1993 with the announcement of a new president. With such careful preparation, university leaders were confident of success. John Brown III exclaimed, "I am firmly optimistic that God will direct an outstanding leader to our campus to take over as president."[50]

The search process yielded three finalists, one of whom was Dr. George Ford, senior vice president of advancement at Roberts Wesleyan College in Rochester, New York. Ford's credentials were impressive. An experienced administrator and fund-raiser at a Christian college, he had completed a Ph.D. in educational administration the previous year at the State University at New York in Buffalo. Ford visited John Brown University in March, and when the other two finalists withdrew their names from consideration, the board of trustees unanimously elected Ford to assume the presidency effective July 1, 1993. Vice Chairman Nick Petelski expressed the board's enthusiasm for working with Dr. Ford in future years, and Ford spoke for all parties when he exclaimed, "the future is bright." An exciting new era seemed imminent. Instead, what ensued was one of the most difficult years in the history of John Brown University.[51]

CHAPTER NINE

New Leadership, New Directions

Amid the expressions of optimism, some misgivings concerning the incoming president arose even during the search process itself, which one administrator later described as "extremely scripted and rigid." Many John Brown University employees felt that they had little input into a process that was dominated by consultant David McKenna and the trustees. Lee Netherton, who served on the Campus Search Committee, recalled that despite faculty and staff representation, the consultant "for the most part ran the show." Some professors were concerned that George Ford's references came from his administrative peers rather than from faculty or others below him at Roberts Wesleyan University. Even Ford's campus visit in March had provided little opportunity for members of the university to get to know him. After the visit, professors speaking through the faculty association complained of being insulated from the candidate and requested that they be more involved in future presidential searches.[1]

Despite possible problems with the search process, members of the university were ready to welcome the new leader. For his part, George Ford said all of the right things as the university's first non-Brown president. At a dinner with senior staff and spouses in April, Ford pledged that he would spend his first six to nine months in office listening to them as much as possible to gain all the input he could. The cabinet would function as a team, he told them, and any changes to the structure would be done "in concert with you rather than in isolation from you." That summer, the John Brown University Bulletin described the new president as a down-to-earth, approachable "team-builder" who sought to work with the faculty and who typically ate in the student dining room.[2]

When the academic year began, however, problems rapidly

22. George Ford, fourth president of John Brown University.

developed between the new president and members of the university. President Ford proposed significant changes to the institution almost immediately. Speaking to a freshman class in September, Ford announced that he planned to grow the university to fifteen hundred students. This may require, he acknowledged, lowering the school's academic standards, a change contrary to the trend of the John Brown III era. For the faculty, what was disturbing about this news was not so much the plan to grow but a complete lack of input into such a decision. From their perspective, students had been informed of the new goal before they were. "We are out of the communication chain," professors complained. Tensions were exacerbated when Ford sought to institute a more formal dress code for the faculty and have members of the community address each other by their official titles. What Ford saw as an attempt to foster a greater sense of professionalism in a small Arkansas college was perceived by others as unnecessary meddling in a close-knit, informal university culture.[3]

Amid such tensions, even trivial matters assumed outsized significance. When Ford designated three thousand dollars to be spent combating dandelions on the campus lawn, the faculty complained of concurrent cuts to the library budget. In October, students at an open forum asked Ford about expensive renovations and repairs that were being made to the president's home. Ford's response indicated the strain that was developing: "Do you really want to get into the details of this? There's sort of an accusation behind questions like this. Like we have been spend-thrifts or we have not been good stewards of the money." Whether necessary or not, the spending of such funds contributed to rapidly deteriorating relations between the new president and the university.[4]

Ford's relationship with the board of trustees got off to an equally rocky start. At the fall 1993 board meeting, disagreements about the proper relationship between president and trustees surfaced between Ford and the board members, who expected to assume a more supervisory role over the university following John Brown III's retirement. By the end of Ford's first semester as president, serious misgivings were already arising among those above and those below the president in the university structure. However, little communication occurred between members of the university and the board of trustees, since administrators feared that communicating with board members without Ford's permission would result in dismissal. An atmosphere of uncertainty prevailed. As one cabinet member later remarked, "We all had our resumes ready."[5]

During the winter of 1993–94, tensions between President Ford and the faculty came to a head. In a December meeting of the faculty association (a meeting of professors only), Bible professor Jim Walters read a letter outlining concerns that many professors had with president Ford's leadership style. The discussion among the faculty revealed "a high level of mutual apprehension and distrust" between President Ford and members of the faculty. The tension increased in January when Ford unilaterally announced a plan to reorganize the university into four colleges. Soon thereafter, the faculty voted to reissue a Faculty Climate Survey that had last been circulated in 1989.[6]

With matters at an impasse, two professors, Walters and mathematics professor Cal Piston, wrote separate letters to Board of Trustees Chair Don Soderquist informing him of the problems and requesting the board's help in resolving matters. These letters prompted a series of closed-door meetings in which Ford, trustees Soderquist and Mark Simmons, and administrators and faculty members sought to state and resolve the issues of contention.[7]

In early February, George Ford met with the faculty association and apologized for initiating too many new changes. He vowed to listen more and be less defensive in the future. Events, however, had seemingly reached a point of no return, as the results of the Faculty Climate Survey revealed later in the month. Responses to survey questions revealed a faculty feeling significantly less informed about university affairs, less trustful of leadership at the university, and less optimistic about the university's future than they had five years earlier. Nearly half of the fifty-two respondents responded affirmatively to the statement, "If offered an equivalent job at another University, I would move." Exclaimed one professor, "It is extremely difficult to keep a positive attitude about the future direction of John Brown University!"[8]

Later that spring, as university officials continued meeting to discuss the crisis, President Ford and his wife left Siloam Springs. On April 12, Ford faxed the board his resignation effective immediately. A special chapel service took place on Friday, April 15, to announce the news to students. Bill George, a longtime board member and retired vice president of the John Brown schools in California, agreed to serve as interim president until a new leader could be selected. George Ford's brief presidency was officially over.[9]

In retrospect, one would be tempted to interpret the Ford debacle as a simple case of a sophisticated urbanite from the North trying and failing to civilize a small-town Arkansas institution. In some ways, the events fit that pattern. Ford himself noted a "perception that I am a New Yorker," and his penchant for designer suits contrasted with the more modest tastes of most faculty members. Ford's wife apparently had difficulty making the transition to Siloam Springs and had doubts about the compatibility between the Fords and Arkansas. Not surprisingly, amid rising tensions Ford's discomfort with the university culture did not seem to dissipate. Throughout the 1993–94 academic year his personal belongings remained boxed up in a corner of his office.[10]

Yet the cultural incompatibility explanation falls short of the reality. John Brown University throughout its history maintained only an indirect relationship to its small-town Arkansas surroundings. A majority of its students, faculty, and administrators had always come from elsewhere. Virtually all of the major figures in the events of 1993–94, including Jim Walters, Don Soderquist, Bill George, and cabinet members Don Crandall, Pat Gustavson, and Jim Barnes, were nonnative Arkansans. Many of them, like Ford, hailed from the urban North or East. Participants in the events of that year claimed that the basic source of Ford's difficulties was not cultural disconnect but rather that he "did not take time to establish trust or to understand the John Brown University community." Doing so was especially important as the first non-Brown president of the university. Ford's successor Lee Balzer noted, "It is difficult for a new leader to achieve early success after a successful leader, and certainly after a series of successful family-led administrations, as was the case at John Brown University." A post-Brown presidency was not necessarily doomed from the start, but such a crucial period of organizational transition did require a high level of patience, communication skills, and cultural sensitivity.[11]

After nearly a year of turmoil, no one relished the idea of beginning a presidential search process again. Fortunately, that did not prove necessary. Lee Balzer, president of Tabor College in Kansas, had been one of the three finalists for the John Brown University presidency in the spring of 1993. At the time, however, Balzer cited firm commitments he had made to Tabor and withdrew his name from consideration. When John Brown University trustees contacted Balzer again after Ford's resignation, he felt that the timing

23. Lee Balzer assumed the university presidency in 1994.

was right to accept the presidency. Thus, in August 1994 Lee Balzer became the fifth president of John Brown University.[12]

Balzer's first few months began a rapid healing process at the university. With a Ph.D. in biology from Ohio State University and administrative experience at Seattle Pacific University and Tabor College, Balzer clearly had solid academic credentials. Yet Balzer's upbringing in rural Oklahoma gave him an understanding of the regional culture that many felt Ford had lacked. In words oddly reminiscent of the previous year, Balzer pledged to involve the university community in decision making and to practice participatory leadership. Balzer proved true to his word. Gustavson recalled, "He was very intentional about taking time to understand the culture and history of John Brown University as an organization before he began to suggest changes." Balzer was also careful to subject the presidency to the policies and desires of the board of trustees. At the new president's request, the board of trustees began holding a closed-door executive session during every board meeting with no president or cabinet members present. At the fall meeting of the board of trustees, Balzer and the board created a long-range planning committee, comprised of trustees, alumni, administrators, professors, and students, to set the future goals and priorities of the university. The following spring, the board of trustees, along with Balzer, reaffirmed the university's mission statement and authorized the use of two university mottoes, "Head, Heart, Hand" and "Christ Over All."[13]

Relations between the president and the faculty also improved under Balzer. The Faculty Climate Survey for 1995 showed drastic improvements in faculty responses compared to the previous year. Professors felt more secure in their jobs, expressed greater optimism about the future of the university, and believed that the president gave positive leadership in academic affairs. In all, by the end of Balzer's first year as president it seemed that the trauma of the previous year was already a dim memory. Some even believed that the adversity of the Ford year brought the John Brown University community closer together and helped pave the way for Lee Balzer's success.[14]

Even during George Ford's presidency, tensions within the university seemed to have little effect on the overall strength of the institution. The growth in size and academic quality that had characterized the John Brown III era continued despite the turmoil in administrative circles. Student enrollment in the spring of 1994 reached a record level, and the 1994–95 academic year began with a record enrollment of 1,083 students, due in part to Ford's insistence on stepping up marketing and recruiting efforts. That same year, John Brown University was ranked as one of the top ten liberal arts colleges in the South by *U.S. News and World Report* and was named to the Templeton Honor Roll for Character-Building Colleges for the sixth year in a row.[15]

With a decade of solid growth behind it, John Brown University in the 1990s began seeking ways to expand its mission and activities outside of Siloam Springs and beyond undergraduate education. In the fall of 1991, officials at Crichton College, a small, church-related, financially strapped school in Memphis, Tennessee, approached John Brown University about the possibility of a relationship between the institutions. After extensive investigation, John Brown University agreed to affiliate with Crichton College on a three-year trial basis. John Brown University loaned the college half a million dollars and assumed responsibility for recruiting students and administering the school for the 1992–93 academic year. John Brown University's vice president for marketing, Larry Brooks, assumed the presidency of Crichton. The agreement also called for future exchanges between faculty, students, and staff on the two campuses. A possible merger between the institutions seemed to be in the foreseeable future. With few John Brown University students coming from the southeast, affiliation with Crichton College seemed like an effective way to expand John Brown University's influence and visibility in this region of the country.[16]

Despite early optimism, the relationship with Crichton College proved temporary. Even with financial and administrative assistance from John Brown University, Crichton retained an operating deficit of one million dollars. Moreover, Crichton's accrediting organization, the Southern Association of Colleges and Schools, disapproved of affiliation between the two institutions from different educational regions. As a result, John Brown University followed the Southern Association's recommendation and severed its relation with Crichton College in 1994. Nevertheless, John Brown University's assistance at a critical time enabled Crichton to stay afloat and eventually achieve stability. By the end of 1998, Crichton had achieved an operating surplus and repaid the $500,000 loan to John Brown University. John Brown University's ability to rescue a struggling college attested to its own institutional and financial strength by the 1990s.[17]

John Brown University's expansion into nontraditional education proved more permanent—and financially rewarding—than its geographical expansion into Memphis. In 1991, the university began researching the idea of offering a two-year off-campus educational program that would enable working adults to complete a bachelor's degree in organization management. As president, George Ford threw his influence behind the idea, and in 1993 the advance program began holding night classes in Springdale, Arkansas, for twenty-two adult students. With Ford's departure, some worried about the fate of the advance program, but the board of trustees affirmed its commitment to the degree completion program and approved plans to expand it. The following year, the advance program grew to 105 students and added sites in Fayetteville and Bentonville. By the end of the 1990s, the advance program enrolled 349 students in sites ranging from northwest Arkansas to Little Rock. In addition to expanding John Brown University's educational mission to nontraditional students, the advance program generated extra funds to enhance the traditional undergraduate program.[18]

While not strictly a vocational program, the advance program's emphasis on a practical degree to enhance working adults' career opportunities did hearken back to the "Hand" ideal of John Brown University's earlier years. So too did the graduate programs and centers that emerged on campus in the late 1990s. In the fall of 1995, the teacher education division of the university began a master's degree program in counselor education for twenty-seven students. John Brown University's modest endeavor in graduate education received a boost from the creation of externally funded centers. In 1997, the university announced the creation of the Center for Marriage and Family Studies. The Windgate Foundation pledged four million dollars to the program if the university could raise another four million, which it accomplished a few years later. The Center for Marriage and Family Studies implemented a graduate degree program to train future marriage and family therapists. It also offered relationship counseling for John Brown University undergraduates and an array of services designed to strengthen families in the region and around the nation. The new center's national visibility was enhanced when it hired as its director Dr. Gary Oliver, a well-known author, counselor, and speaker from Denver, Colorado.[19]

John Brown University's center for family studies was soon joined by a second one for business ethics. In August 1998, the university announced the creation of the Donald G. Soderquist Center for Business Leadership and Ethics. Named after Wal-Mart's chief operating officer and the chairman of the board of trustees at John Brown University, the center sought to promote the application of ethical principles to the business world—something that Don Soderquist had embodied throughout his career. The Soderquist Center organized conferences, seminars, guest lectureships, and residence programs designed to inform and motivate business executives in the area of leadership and ethics. It also supported the development of master's degree programs in leadership and ethics and business administration.[20]

Thus, by the year 2000 John Brown University enrolled 132 students earning graduate degrees in the areas of school counseling, family counseling, and business ethics. Together with the advance program, the centers and graduate programs represented a more direct approach to practical education than occurred in many undergraduate departments since the disappearance of vocational requirements in the 1970s. These programs could be seen as a reemphasis on the "Hand" in particular areas to replace the vocational ideal that had characterized the university until the 1970s.[21]

Of course, funding the centers, as well as maintaining a vibrant undergraduate program, required money. Nothing demonstrated the university's growing stature in the 1990s better than its unprecedented success in raising funds to support its expansion. In 1998, John Brown University launched "JBU Campaign 2000," a fund-raising drive far more extensive than anything the university had attempted before. In addition to raising money to support the two centers, the university sought funds to build a campus community center and a new science building, and to increase the endowment and the student scholarship fund. The estimated needs totaled more than thirty million dollars, a seemingly unrealistic amount given the fact that John Brown University's previous capital fund-raising campaign twenty years earlier had achieved a modest five million dollars.[22]

However, like other evangelical institutions John Brown University's fund-raising methods had become much more sophisticated since the 1970s, and American evangelicals themselves had grown wealthier over the years. Vice President for University Advancement Al Cureton aggressively cultivated relationships with large donors and encouraged stepped-up giving by alumni and supporters. As a result, John Brown University not only met but far exceeded its campaign goals. In January 2000, President Balzer announced that the campaign had generated more than thirty-nine million dollars in gifts and pledges.[23]

The unprecedented amount illustrated not only the increasing affluence of American evangelicalism but also John Brown University's growing stature and significance within that subculture. President Balzer and other university officials occupied leadership positions within the Council for Christian Colleges and Universities.[24] The university continued to be ranked by *U.S. News and World Report* in the top tier of southern liberal arts colleges, selected by the Templeton Foundation to its Honor Roll for Character-Building Colleges, and named as one of America's "100 Best College Buys." Meanwhile, overall enrollment continued to climb. While undergraduate enrollment remained steady at around one thousand students, the rapidly growing advance program and graduate programs pushed total enrollment past fifteen hundred by 1999. At no time in its eighty-year history had John Brown University enjoyed as much enrollment, financial support, and external recognition as it did by the end of the twentieth century.[25]

Two years after the completion of "JBU Campaign 2000," John Brown University officially dedicated the $13.5 million Pat and Willard Walker Campus Community Center. Meanwhile, just a short distance away from the new Walker Center, California Residence Hall, once the heart of the college, sat empty and decaying. New dormitory rooms in Walker had made it possible to abandon California, which no longer met current building safety codes. The cost of renovating the building was estimated to be higher than that of destroying it and building something new, yet demolishing the structure would risk offending alumni who cherished memories of their years in the building. Plans were made to construct a business and conference center on the California site, but a major grant to fund the project did not materialize. With its future status uncertain, the California building slowly decayed.[26]

The contrast between the Walker Center, complete with skylights and a Starbucks cafe, and its deteriorating neighbor vividly illustrated the social odyssey of American evangelicals in the twentieth century. When fundamentalists left the mainline churches in the early twentieth century, one historian has noted, they left behind "paid-for buildings, established fund-raising networks, and access to most of America's wealthy businessmen and large foundations." In other words, conservative Protestants became poor for the sake of the gospel as they understood it.[27]

John Brown University's early years exemplified this phenomenon. Deprived of funds from major denominations or large foundations, John Brown Sr. worked tirelessly to scrape together enough donations to keep the school afloat. The dirt roads and rustic wooden buildings of the campus hardly resembled those of a stately, well-endowed denominational college. Fundamentalist students also reflected the relative poverty of the subculture. In the 1930s, 80 percent of students at Wheaton College worked their way through school, compared to the national average of 50 percent.[28] At John Brown University, of course, all of them did. The completion of California Residence Hall in 1927 largely through student labor represented a significant achievement for this generation. The tile roof and large veranda made for an attractive exterior, but the building itself was designed to be as simple, functional, and inexpensive as possible. The fanfare that accompanied the completion of this relatively modest building reflected the humble social status of American evangelicals' fundamentalist ancestors.

But something happened to evangelicalism in the second half of the twentieth century. Numerically, the movement exploded.

24. The Walker Student Center, completed in 2002.

While most scholars of American religion expected conservative Protestantism to wither and die in the modern world, in fact the very opposite occurred. Today evangelicalism has far surpassed mainline Protestantism in population, and over one-quarter of Americans consider themselves evangelical. Evangelicals also became wealthier. Nearly all of the large new church buildings constructed in recent years have been built by evangelicals. Luxury cars and sport utility vehicles dot the parking lots of middle-class suburban evangelical megachurches. Evangelical parachurch ministries have reaped the harvest of the movement's new wealth. Christian colleges, evangelistic and missions organizations, communications media agencies, and the like together comprise a combined annual budget that one scholar has estimated to be around twenty-two billion dollars. Given the social changes that have occurred in modern American evangelicalism, John Brown University's recent fund-raising success seems less astounding. Clearly, the contrast between the Walker Center and the California building reflects broader trends within American religion.[29]

All of this raises the age-old question of whether there is a spiritual cost that accompanies economic success. In 1789, John Wesley warned his upwardly mobile Methodist flock:

> Wherever true Christianity spreads, it must cause diligence and frugality, which, in the natural course of things, must beget riches. And riches naturally beget pride, love of the world, and every temper that is destructive of Christianity. So, if there be no way to prevent this, Christianity is inconsistent with itself and, of consequence, cannot continue long among any people, since, wherever it generally prevails, it saps its own foundation.

Wesley's remarks had their counterpart in the early years of John Brown University. Fundamentalist preacher G. Campbell Morgan warned John Brown Sr. in 1921:

> I regret that the time will come when you will be compelled to leave these limited, rustic, inadequate quarters. There is always, in a school like this, working under handicaps and disadvantages, a spirit of vision and sacrifice that you will lose when you move into larger and more permanent quarters. Buildings do not make a school. Sometimes they wreck them.

By the end of the century, John Brown University had large, permanent quarters in abundance. But have the buildings distracted the school from its original vision?[30]

In some ways, the university's newest building itself answers that question, for the Walker Center is neither simply a student center nor an educational building. The building houses classrooms and the Department of Biblical Studies, exemplifying the university's central commitment to academics. It also serves the university's spiritual and social functions by housing a student commons area as well as the offices for student development, campus ministries, and the CAUSE student ministries. Finally, the university's commitment to practical training and ministry is reaffirmed by the presence of the Center for Marriage and Family Studies on the second floor directly above the student commons. For eighty years, John Brown University has sought to combine head, heart, and hand in higher education. Its newest and largest building etches into brick and mortar that threefold philosophy of education—a fitting testament to the continuing vitality of the founder's education vision.

Epilogue

As this epilogue is being written, demolition crews are at work tearing down California Residence Hall in preparation for a new business and conference center. Students have assembled lawn chairs nearby to watch the spectacle. While some alumni may bemoan the destruction of this venerable building, for most this is just another indication of John Brown University's progress. Indeed, virtually all indicators are that the quality of the university is improving every year. The fall 2002 student body was the largest and brightest ever, if standardized test scores are any indication. The faculty are better educated and produce higher quality scholarship than ever before. Facilities continue to improve with each new and renovated building. The completion of the Bell Science Hall in December 2002 means that the old science building can be renovated to house digital media and art programs that are bursting at the seams.

Among Christian institutions, John Brown University has lots of company in its upward trajectory. The Council for Christian Colleges and Universities is thriving. New colleges are being added to the ranks, and enrollment at such institutions has skyrocketed in the past decade. Leading Christian colleges such as Wheaton College and Calvin College regularly appear in the *U.S. News and World Report* rankings among the top schools in their regions. Evangelical scholarship has blossomed under the hefty financial backing of the Pew Charitable Trust and the Lilly Endowment. A few hours down the road from John Brown University in Texas, Baylor University has launched a ten-year campaign to become a nationally regarded Protestant research university—the evangelical Notre Dame, its advocates hope. To do so, the school is spending enormous sums of Southern Baptist money to lure nationally renowned scholars from the ivory towers of the north to Waco.

Clearly, these are heady days for American evangelicals in higher education, both in Siloam Springs and beyond. Yet one suspects among some a certain sense of uneasiness with all of the seeming signs of progress. Does all of this represent a return to earlier days when Protestants were the intellectual and cultural leaders of their society and dominated American higher education? Or is this simply a recapitulation of those dreary examples of once-Christian colleges from Harvard on down going secular, lured away by visions of large endowments and prestigious faculty—a process described in excruciating detail in James Burtchaell's *The Dying of the Light: The Disengagement of American Colleges and Universities from Their Christian Churches?* Offspring of fundamentalists who became social outcasts for their faith, today's evangelicals retain enough of a separatist edge to be suspicious of worldly success. And if not trained by their parents to be wary of success, their premillennialist beliefs, reinforced by the popular *Left Behind* bestsellers, condition evangelicals to expect decline and catastrophe in the future, not triumph and success.

Historians prefer to focus on particular events and avoid metanarrative, but in this case the question of where evangelical higher education is headed cannot be avoided, for much is riding on the outcome. George Marsden, for one, evinces optimism about the future. In *The Outrageous Idea of Christian Scholarship*, he concludes by questioning the seeming inevitability of secularization in higher education. Marsden believes one crucial difference separates our era from earlier ones in American history. Because we live in a post-enlightenment age in which it is no longer assumed that science and rationality have all of the answers, Christian colleges do not have to abandon religious commitments in order to be considered intellectually respectable. Marsden concludes, "For academic communities there should no longer be the assumption that the move to embrace the more enlightened and more secular standards of the culture of the research university is a course to improvement." In a culture liberated from the dominance of secular scientific notions of rationality, Christian colleges are now free to build vibrant intellectual communities that do not conform to the oppressive secular norms of the research university.[1]

But given their position within the popular (and historically anti-intellectual) evangelical subculture, will Christian colleges do so? Other scholars are less sanguine about the future. Calvin College English professor Ed Ericson Jr., in a review of *The Dying of the Light*, finds little room for optimism that today's Christian colleges will avoid the pitfalls of their Protestant forbears. He notes a recent advertisement listing the top ten reasons why students at Christian colleges like their schools. The reasons run the gamut from caring residence-hall staff to availability of weekend activities to variety of intramural sports. "There is not a word about Christian minds," Ericson laments. "There is not a word about anything explicitly Christian." Like Burtchaell, Ericson sees little to prevent today's Christian colleges from treading the worn path "from light to lite to night."[2]

Those of us involved in Christian higher education would of course like to side with Marsden. We work for and hope that evangelical colleges are moving toward a reclamation of the historic Protestantism of Luther, Calvin, and the Puritans with their concern for intellectual excellence in all areas of knowledge. However, the study of history leads one to maintain a sense of modesty about our understanding of the direction that history is moving and the role of individual human actors to affect the larger drama. The poet William Henley boasted, "I am the master of my fate," while F. Scott Fitzgerald closed his classic novel *The Great Gatsby* with the words, "So we beat on, boats against the current, born back ceaselessly into the past." For Christians, the truth lies somewhere in between. Like the hobbits in J. R. R. Tolkien's fantasy world of Middle Earth, we do the best we can and pray for wisdom, all the while aware that greater, deeper powers shape the larger destiny.

Will the revival of Christian higher learning at colleges such as John Brown University succeed, or will they become yet another example of secular drift? Institutions such as John Brown University are betting that one can nurture the head *and* the heart; that intellect and piety, so often uneasy bedfellows in American history, can not only coexist but actually embrace. Time will tell.

NOTES

Part One: Starting from Scratch, 1879–1934

Chapter One: The "Laughing Evangelist"

1. J. Ellis Williams, "Memories of '27 and '28," *Christian Fellowship*, December 20, 1934, 8. Most of the primary sources on which this book is based are John Brown University publications housed in the university archives. *Christian Fellowship*, for example, was the university's weekly publication from 1934 to 1936. Other university publications cited below include the *Southwestern* (published from 1919 to 1922) and the *American Wayshower* (published 1922 to 1933). These publications often do not contain volume numbers or page numbers; thus, many of the citations given below will simply refer to the date of publication. Unless otherwise indicated, these publications were written by John Brown himself.

2. Earl Williams, "John Brown University: Its Founder and Founding, 1919–1957" (Ed.D. diss., University of Arkansas, 1971), 31–32; Ralph Kennedy and Thomas Rothrock, *John Brown of Arkansas* (Siloam Springs, Ark.: John Brown University Press, 1966), 1–2.

3. Williams, "John Brown University," 33–35; Kennedy and Rothrock, *John Brown of Arkansas*, 4.

4. Williams, "John Brown University," 35–36; T. P. Morgan, "The Long Boy from the Lime Kilns," *Country Gentleman*, December 1919, 10. *Country Gentleman* was an early-twentieth-century popular magazine that featured an article on John Brown. *American Wayshower*, December 1933, 6.

5. John Brown, *Sowing and Reaping* (Osage, Iowa: Wolverton and Co., 1902), 27.

6. Williams, "John Brown University," 37; Kennedy and Rothrock, *John Brown of Arkansas*, 7.

7. Quoted in Kennedy and Rothrock, *John Brown of Arkansas*, 2–3.

8. Kennedy and Rothrock, *John Brown of Arkansas*, 3; *American Wayshower*, November 1928, 3. Much recent work has been done on the idealization of nineteenth-century Victorian womanhood. See, for example, Nancy F. Cott, *The Bonds of Womanhood: "Women's Sphere" in New England, 1780–1835* (New Haven: Yale University Press, 1997).

9. *American Wayshower*, August 1926, 3; May 1926, 7. *Southwestern*, October 1920, 6.

10. *American Wayshower*, December 1928, 6; *Boston Sunday Post*, January 22, 1928, available in the John Brown University archives.

11. Williams, "John Brown University," 38; Morgan, "The Long Boy from the Lime Kilns," 10; Carl Moneyhon, *Arkansas and the New South, 1874–1929* (Fayetteville: University of Arkansas Press, 1997), 95–98.

12. Brown, *Sowing and Reaping*, 27; Kennedy and Rothrock, *John Brown of Arkansas*, 8–9.

13. Kennedy and Rothrock, *John Brown of Arkansas*, 9.

14. Ibid., 11.

15. For a discussion of the significance to American Protestants of the evangelical conversion narrative, see Virginia Brereton, *From Sin to Salvation: Stories of Women's Conversions, 1800 to the Present* (Bloomington: Indiana University Press, 1991).

16. See Diane Winston, *Red-Hot and Righteous: The Urban Religion of the Salvation Army* (Cambridge: Harvard University Press, 1999).

17. *American Wayshower*, December 1928, 6; Williams, "John Brown University," 44–46.

18. Kennedy and Rothrock, *John Brown of Arkansas*, 14. See also David F. Trask, *The War with Spain in 1898* (Lincoln: University of Nebraska Press, 1997).

19. Ibid., 15.

20. *American Wayshower*, December 1928, 6; Kennedy and Rothrock, *John Brown of Arkansas*, 15.

21. "Revivalism," in *Dictionary of Christianity in America*, ed. Douglas Reid (Downers Grove, Ill.: Intervarsity Press, 1991), 1012. The most complete book on the history of American revivalism is William McLoughlin's *Modern Revivalism: Charles Grandison Finney to Billy Graham* (New York: Ronald Press, 1959). See also Nathan Hatch, *The Democratization of American Christianity* (New Haven: Yale University Press, 1991); Harry Stout, *The Divine Dramatist: George Whitefield and the Rise of Modern Evangelicalism* (Grand Rapids: Eerdmans Publishing, 1991); and Charles Hambrick Stowe, *Charles Finney and the Spirit of American Evangelicalism* (Grand Rapids: Eerdmans Publishing, 1996).

22. The best recent work on D. L. Moody is Lyle Dorsett's *A Passion for Souls: The Life of D. L. Moody* (Chicago: Moody Press, 1997).

23. Jones quoted in McLoughlin, *Modern Revivalism*, 288.

24. McLoughlin, *Modern Revivalism*, 407–8, 415; Sunday quoted in Sidney Ahlstrom, *A Religious History of the American People* (New Haven: Yale University Press, 1972), 748. See also Lyle Dorsett, *Billy Sunday and the Redemption of Urban America* (Grand Rapids: Eerdmans Publishing, 1991).

25. McLoughlin, *Modern Revivalism*, 448–49.

26. Quoted in Brown, *Sowing and Reaping*, 3, 30.

27. Kennedy and Rothrock, *John Brown of Arkansas*, 21–22.

28. Ibid., 17, 26; Williams, "John Brown University," 62.

29. Williams, "John Brown University," 58–59.

30. *American Wayshower*, December 1928, 6; Kennedy and Rothrock, *John Brown of Arkansas*, 25.

31. Williams, "John Brown University," 63.

32. *Santa Ana Daily News*, 1911; *Los Angeles Times*, July 22, 1912; Kennedy and Rothrock, *John Brown of Arkansas*, 31. The John Brown University archives houses a collection of newspaper articles on John Brown's evangelistic career, from which much of

the information in these pages is drawn. On the history of early-twentieth-century California, see Roger Lotchin, *Fortress California, 1910–1961: From Warfare to Welfare* (New York: Oxford University Press, 1992).

33. *Southwestern*, August 1922, 4; Williams, "John Brown University," 67; *El Paso Morning Times*, March 17, 1918.

34. *Pasadena Daily News*, May 17, 1915; Williams, "John Brown University," 69–70.

35. *El Paso Morning Times*, March 17, 1918; Ms. Sunday quoted in McLoughlin, *Modern Revivalism*, 391.

36. *Harrisonburg Times*, no date; McLoughlin, *Modern Revivalism*, 403.

37. *Los Angeles Tribune*, July 31, 1911; *Knoxville News-Sentinel*, March 14, 1927; *Norfolk Public Ledger*, no date. The bonfire account is in John Brown, *Slime Pits* (Siloam Springs, Ark.: International Federation Publishing Co., 1922), 153.

38. John Brown, *A Great Woman* (Siloam Springs, Ark.: International Federation Publishing Co., 1924), 31; *Watsonville Register*, 1913.

39. *Los Angeles Tribune*, July 28, 1913; *Mason City Globe Gazette*, no date; *Pasadena Daily News*, November 10, 1913; Morgan, "The Long Boy from the Lime Kilns," 10.

40. *Boston Sunday Post*, January 22, 1928; *American Wayshower*, February 1928, 3.

41. Letter to Juanita Brown, October 10, 1926; Letter to Juanita Brown, no date. All of John Brown's personal correspondence cited in this chapter and the following chapters is available in the John Brown University archives.

42. Among the historical works on the origins of Protestant liberalism, probably the best is William Hutchison's *The Modernist Impulse in American Protestantism* (New York: Oxford University Press, 1976). See also Kenneth Cauthen, *The Impact of American Religious Liberalism* (New York: University Press of America, 1983); Martin Marty, *Modern American Religion: The Irony of It All, 1893–1919* (Waco, Tex.: Word Publishing, 1986); and Ferenc Szasz, *The Divided Mind of Protestant America,*

1880–1930 (Tuscaloosa: University of Alabama Press, 1982).

43. The historical literature on American fundamentalism is large and growing, but the best single work remains George M. Marsden's *Fundamentalism and American Culture, 1875–1925: The Shaping of Twentieth Century Evangelicalism* (New York: Oxford University Press, 1980). Other helpful works include Ernest Sandeen, *The Roots of Fundamentalism: British and American Millenarianism, 1800–1930* (Chicago: University of Chicago Press, 1970), and C. Allyn Russell, *Voices of American Fundamentalism: Seven Biographical Studies* (Philadelphia: Westminster John Knox Press, 1976). Fundamentalist views on gender and 1920s cultural trends are explored in Betty DeBerg, *Ungodly Women: Gender and the First Wave of American Fundamentalism* (Minneapolis: Fortress Press, 1990).

44. John Brown, *The Foundation of God* (Siloam Springs, Ark.: International Federation Publishing Co., 1920), 8, 19.

45. Brown, *Sowing and Reaping,* 14; *American Wayshower,* August 1933.

46. Williams, "John Brown University," 53–55. See also Gene Getz, *MBI: The Story of Moody Bible Institute* (Chicago: Moody Press, 1986), and Roger Martin, *R. A. Torrey: Apostle of Certainty* (Grand Rapids: Baker Book House, 1982).

47. Kennedy and Rothrock, *John Brown of Arkansas,* 31–32. On the history of fundamentalist Bible conferences, see Sandeen, *The Roots of Fundamentalism.* The history of the most prominent Bible conference, Winona Lake, is explained in Mark Sidwell, "The History of Winona Lake Bible Conference" (Ph.D. diss., Bob Jones University, 1988.)

Chapter Two: Creating a New Kind of College

1. *American Evangelist,* September 1919, 8; *American Evangelist,* October 1919, 8. This publication, housed in the John Brown University archives, was issued monthly by John Brown during his evangelistic career and evolved into the *Southwestern* soon after the founding of the college.

2. Williams, "John Brown University," 72, 74.

3. Kennedy and Rothrock, *John Brown of Arkansas*, 40.

4. Ibid., 41.

5. Mark Noll, quoted in Joel Carpenter and Kenneth Shipps, eds., *Making Higher Education Christian: The History and Mission of Evangelical Colleges in America* (Grand Rapids: Eerdmans Publishing Co., 1987), 101. For other historical works on the history of American higher education, see Frederick Rudolph, *The American College and University: A History* (New York: Vintage Books, 1962), and William Ringenberg, *The Christian College: A History of Protestant Higher Education in America* (Grand Rapids: Eerdmans Publishing Co., 1984).

6. Carpenter and Shipps, *Making Higher Education Christian*, 100–101. On the transition from traditional to modern universities, see George M. Marsden, *The Soul of the American University* (New York: Oxford University Press, 1994), and George Marsden and Bradley Longfield, eds., *The Secularization of the Academy* (New York: Oxford Press, 1992).

7. Ringenberg, *The Christian College*, 134.

8. John Brown, *Is Our Modern System of Education Doomed?* (Siloam Springs, Ark.: John E. Brown College Press, 1933), 116–17.

9. Brown, *The Foundation of God*, 148; *Ozark American*, October 1922, 11. The *Ozark American* was a monthly general news magazine published by John Brown for a time in the 1920s and housed now in the university archives. It was intended to complement rather than replace the college publications. On the relationship between theological modernism and American universities, see Marsden, *The Soul of the American University*, 167–78.

10. *American Wayshower*, June 1929, 6; John Brown, *America's Startling Need* (Siloam Springs, Ark.: John E. Brown College Press, 1926), 9.

11. Brown, *America's Startling Need*, 4, 12–13.

12. Ibid., 16.

13. Brown, *A Great Woman*, 33; Brown, *America's Startling Need*, 19. Ironically, female students typically outnumbered male

students in fundamentalist colleges; but they usually were trained for full-time Christian work such as foreign missions rather than secular careers (see Margaret Bendroth, *Fundamentalism and Gender, 1875 to the Present* [New Haven: Yale University Press, 1996]). On male fundamentalists' ambivalence toward women, see Betty DeBerg, *Ungodly Women: Gender and the First Wave of American Fundamentalism* (Minneapolis: Fortress Press, 1990).

14. *Southwestern*, June 1921, 5; *Ozark American*, March 1923, 8.

15. *American Evangelist*, October 1919, 10–11.

16. Ibid., 10; Brown, *America's Startling Need*, 8.

17. *Ozark American*, November 1924, 8.

18. Brown, *America's Startling Need*, 23.

19. Ibid., 31; *American Wayshower*, May 1926, 6.

20. Ringenberg, *The Christian College*, 71, 77; Wayland is quoted in Ringenberg, *The Christian College*, 65.

21. Rudolph, *The American College and University*, 255–63. Public universities in the South also displayed a trend away from classical education and toward more practical education in the early twentieth century. Michael Dennis observes, "New South educators believed that economic regeneration required professional education and training in the practical sciences. Advocates of classical training, they subjected the classical tradition of the antebellum southern colleges to withering criticism (*Lessons in Progress: State Universities and Progressivism in the New South, 1880–1920* [Urbana: University of Illinois Press, 2001], 3).

22. Ringenberg, *The Christian College*, 78, 76. See also Rudolph, *The American College and University*, 96–109.

23. Quoted in Williams, "John Brown University," 25–28.

24. See Virginia Brereton, "The Bible Schools and Conservative Evangelical Higher Education, 1880–1940," in Carpenter and Shipps, *Making Higher Education Christian*, 110–36. On the role of Bible institutes in fundamentalism, see Sandeen, *The Roots of Fundamentalism*; Virginia Brereton, *Training God's Army: The American Bible School, 1880–1940* (Bloomington: Indiana University Press, 1990); and Marsden,

Fundamentalism and American Culture, 62.

25. Brereton, "The Bible Schools," 115.

26. *American Evangelist*, October 1919, 11; Brereton, "The Bible Schools," 124–26.

27. Brown, *America's Startling Need*, 15.

28. *American Evangelist*, October 1919, 11.

29. Ibid., August 1919, 9.

30. Ibid., October 1919, 9; August 1919, 10. Kennedy and Rothrock, *John Brown of Arkansas*, 41.

31. *American Evangelist*, September 1919, 9; Williams, "John Brown University," 82.

32. *Southwestern*, April 1920, 11; May 1920, 2.

33. Ibid., June, July, December 1920.

34. See Sandeen, *The Roots of Fundamentalism*, 242–43.

35. *Southwestern*, June, July 1921.

36. Ibid., June 1921, 2.

37. Ibid., 1.

38. Morgan, "The Long Boy from the Lime Kilns," 10–15; John Brown to Robert Leflar, March 18, 20, 22, April 11, 1924; *Ozark American*, March 1925; *Ozark American*, December 1924. Brown's correspondence, as well as articles in the popular press about John Brown, are available in the university archives.

39. Williams, "John Brown University," 83, 86, 87.

40. *Southwestern*, February, 1921, 1.

41. *American Wayshower*, September 1925; *Southwestern*, August 1922; Williams, "John Brown University," 96–97, 115.

42. *Ozark American*, May, December 1924.

43. Ibid., April 1924.

Chapter Three: From John E. Brown College to John Brown University

1. *Ozark American*, November, 1924, 1.

2. Ibid., 1; Williams, "John Brown University," 103.

3. John Brown, "An Explanation" (1924). This public letter, apparently printed in the local newspaper, is contained in the correspondence of John Brown available in the John Brown

University archives. It is difficult to verify the extent to which Brown's comments accurately depicted the state of Siloam Springs in the 1920s.

4. *Ozark American*, October, November 1924; Williams, "John Brown University," 104. Jazz music was a powerful symbol to conservatives of the alarming new trends of the 1920s. See, for example, Frederick Lewis Allen, *Only Yesterday: An Informal History of the 1920s* (New York: Harper and Row, 1931).

5. John Brown to Robert Leflar, April 11, 1924; John Brown to John Engles, December 31, 1923.

6. Robert Leflar to John Brown, February 13, 1924; Williams, "John Brown University," 101.

7. *Ozark American*, November 1924, 1.

8. McLoughlin, *Modern Revivalism*, 447–48.

9. *American Wayshower*, August 1926, 7.

10. *Ozark American*, February 1925. On the denominational conflicts of the 1920s, see Ferenc Szasz, *The Divided Mind of Protestant America, 1880–1930* (Tuscaloosa: University of Alabama Press, 1982); Bradley Longfield, *The Presbyterian Controversy* (New York: Oxford University Press, 1993); and Marsden, *Fundamentalism and American Culture*.

11. *Ozark American*, July 1925; *American Wayshower*, February 1926; Williams, "John Brown University," 107–8.

12. *American Wayshower*, September 1925.

13. Ibid., April 1926.

14. Ibid., April, October 1926.

15. Kennedy and Rothrock, *John Brown of Arkansas*, 50; *American Wayshower*, July 1926.

16. *American Wayshower*, September, December, 1926.

17. Ibid., March 1927.

18. Ibid., March 1928.

19. Ibid., March, 1927.

20. Hatch, *The Democratization of American Christianity* (New Haven: Yale University Press, 1991). See also Finke and Stark, *The Churching of America, 1776–1900: Winners and Losers in Our Religious Economy* (New Brunswick: Rutgers University Press, 1992).

21. John Brown, "An Attack on Our Schools: Why?" (1927). This pamphlet is found in the John Brown University archives. *Christian Fellowship*, May 1934; *American Wayshower*, August 1928. The *Christian Fellowship* succeeded the *American Wayshower* as the college's periodical in 1934.

22. *American Wayshower*, April, October, May 1927.

23. Ibid., July 1927, April 1928.

24. Ibid., July 1928; John Brown, "By Way of Explanation," *Sulphur Springs American*, August 18, 1928 (found in the John Brown University archives). *American Wayshower*, August 1928.

25. *American Wayshower*, July 1927; Clyde Kilby, "Some Memories of John Elward Brown and the John Brown Schools Long Ago" (unpublished manuscript available in the university archives, 1984), 14.

26. *American Wayshower*, January 1929, January 1931.

27. Ibid., March 1932; John Brown to Richard Hodges, October 1, 1932.

28. *American Wayshower*, August 1933.

29. *Boston Evening American*, January 4, 1928; *American Wayshower*, February 1928. The Boston article can be found in the university archives.

30. *American Wayshower*, February 1931, December 1932.

31. See Harry Stout, *The Divine Dramatist: George Whitefield and the Rise of Modern Evangelicalism* (Grand Rapids: Eerdmans Publishing, 1991), and Lyle Dorsett, *A Passion for Souls: The Life of D. L. Moody* (Chicago: Moody Press, 1997). On the use of radio among fundamentalists in the 1920s, see Gene Getz, *MBI: The Story of Moody Bible Institute* (Chicago: Moody Press, 1969), 163–74.

32. *American Wayshower*, January, February, September 1933; Williams, "John Brown University," 119.

33. Anonymous, "The Life Story of John Brown: Evangelist and Educator" (unpublished biography available in the university archives, n.d.), 33–34; *American Wayshower*, September 1933.

34. *American Wayshower*, April 1930.

35. Ibid., August 1930, July 1931.

36. Ibid., September 1932.

37. Ibid.

38. Ibid., March 1933.

39. Williams, "John Brown University," 115, 126.

40. Ibid., 120–26; *American Wayshower*, April 1933.

41. *American Wayshower*, November 1933.

42. Ibid., September 1932, November 1933.

43. *Interstate American*, June 14, 1934. This news periodical produced by John Brown was essentially a successor to *Ozark American*. *Christian Fellowship*, July 5, 1934.

44. *Christian Fellowship*, July 12, 1934.

Part Two: Achieving Permanence, 1935–1962

1. Bruce Shelley, "Counter-Culture Christianity," *Christian History* 14:1 (1995): 34.

Chapter Four: College Life in the Early Years

1. *Ozark American*, March 1923; *American Wayshower*, January 1927.

2. *American Wayshower*, June, April 1928; April 1929.

3. Ibid., September 1925, 1931; J. Ellis Williams, "Memories of '27 and '28, Part Four," *Christian Fellowship*, October 11, 1934, 8.

4. *American Wayshower*, November 1928, March, 1929. John Brown University's national and international character continued throughout the twentieth century, despite a stereotype as a rural Arkansas institution. John Brown once took offense when a local pastor, upon introducing the university choir to his church, "gave the impression to the congregation that they were representing a hill-billy school back in the Ozark Hills." Brown pointed out that the choir at the time comprised students from fourteen different states and three foreign countries (*John Brown University Bulletin*, August 1954).

5. Clyde Kilby to Committee, 1928 (in John Brown University archives); Williams memoir; *American Wayshower*, March, February 1927. This trend continued at John Brown

University. In 1961, a survey of alumni occupations was conducted. Of the 356 returns, ninety-five graduates were in education and music, sixty-six were in engineering-related professions, forty-nine were in business, forty-four were full-time housewives, twenty-nine were in full-time Christian ministry, and only seven graduates were in farming (Subcommittee on Vocation Education, "A Report on Post-Graduate Study and Occupations of John Brown University Graduates," May 1961, p. 10, John Brown University archives).

6. On racism in high school textbooks, see Edward Larson, *Summer for the Gods: The Scopes Trial and America's Continuing Debate over Science and Religion* (Cambridge: Harvard University Press, 1997), 23–24; On William Bell Riley, see William V. Trollinger, *God's Empire: William Bell Riley and Midwestern Fundamentalism* (Madison: University of Wisconsin Press, 1990), 62–82. See also George Marsden, *Fundamentalism and American Culture*, 210.

7. The Ku Klux Klan episode is related in Kennedy and Rothrock, *John Brown of Arkansas*, 83; Clyde Kilby mentions Brown's African American revival services in "Some Memories of John Elward Brown and the John Brown Schools Long Ago" (unpublished manuscript, John Brown University archives, 1984), 1; John Brown, *Common Sense or Chaos* (Siloam Springs, Ark.: John Brown University Press [1940]), 1; Brown, *Slime Pits*, 35, 122. While continuing to condemn racial intermarriage, John Brown seemed to moderate his view of other races later in life. Nonwhite races, he claimed in 1953, had their own particular qualities that "would not be strengthened or made greater by intermingling and intermarrying with the white race. There would be desperate loss all the way around!" (*One World: Is It of God or Satan?* [Siloam Springs, Ark.: John Brown University Press, 1953], 78).

8. John Brown, *Is Our Modern System of Education Doomed?* (Siloam Springs, Ark.: John E. Brown College Press, 1933), 141; *American Wayshower*, December 1928; *Ozark American*, April 1925. One Asian student graduated in 1948, and a 1951 *John*

Brown University Bulletin printed a testimonial from a Puerto Rican alumnus (*John Brown University Bulletin*, June 1948, July 1951). A student from Brazil attended in 1940, but it is unclear whether he was a native Brazilian or a son of missionaries (*Threefold Advocate*, October 1940). Interestingly, no evidence exists that John E. Brown College ever employed a race-based admissions policy. This is most likely because no African American student ever bothered to apply, given the overwhelmingly white character of northwest Arkansas during this era.

9. Harry Huey, "The Diary of Jim Branson at John Brown University," John Brown University promotional pamphlet, 1936, in John Brown University archives.

10. *Ozark American*, December 1924; *Ozark American*, February 1925; *American Wayshower*, March 1927.

11. *Christian Fellowship*, July 1934; Huey, "The Diary of Jim Branson."

12. *American Wayshower*, June 1932; *Hillbilly*, July 6, 1929; *Spizzerinktor*, January 27, 1933. The *Hillbilly* and the *Spizzerinktor* were student publications that predated the emergence of the *Threefold Advocate* in 1937.

13. John Brown to Richard Hodges, November 18, 1933; John Brown to Richard Hodges, April 30, 1934 (letters found in John Brown University archives).

14. *Southwestern*, October 1919; *American Wayshower*, September 1931; Huey, "The Diary of Jim Branson"; *Ozark American*, October 1922; Stewart Springfield to John Brown University students, October 10, 1939; *American Wayshower*, March 1933.

15. Huey, "The Diary of Jim Branson"; *American Wayshower*, March 1933.

16. *American Wayshower*, March 1929, December 1929, June 1933; J. Ellis Williams to John Brown University Archives, 1972; *John Brown University Bulletin*, January 1939. This periodical replaced the *Christian Fellowship* as the university's monthly informational publication in 1937.

17. *Ozark American*, December 1924; *American Wayshower*,

September 1929; John Brown, *Sharks, Gulls, and Little Fishes* (Siloam Springs, Ark.: John Brown University Press, 1935), 111; *Southwestern*, October 1921.

18. *Spizzerinktor*, November 4, 1933.

19. Williams, "Part Five," *Christian Fellowship*, October 18, 1934, 8; *Hillbilly*, April 3, 1928; Huey, "The Diary of Jim Branson."

20. Williams, "Part Eight," *Christian Fellowship*, December 13, 1934, 8; Huey, "The Diary of Jim Branson"; *Spizzerinktor*, March 17, 1934; *American Wayshower*, September 1929.

21. *American Wayshower*, September 1931.

22. Huey, "The Diary of Jim Branson"; *American Wayshower*, September 1926, March 1932.

23. *American Wayshower*, June 1929.

24. Ibid., May 1933; *Christian Fellowship*, September 1934; Williams, "John Brown University," 129.

25. *Spizzerinktor*, March 17, 1934; Fessenden quoted in the *John Brown University Bulletin*, October 1989; J. Ellis Williams memoir, "Part Eight," *Christian Fellowship*, November 22, 1934, 8; John Brown to J. Ellis Williams, September 24, 1934; the poem was published in the *Christian Fellowship*, September 1934.

26. William Ringenberg, *The Christian College: A History of Protestant Higher Education in America* (Grand Rapids: Wm. B. Eerdmans Publishing Co.), 183.

27. *American Wayshower*, June 22, June 29, 1933.

28. Quoted in Kennedy and Rothrock, *John Brown of Arkansas*, 19.

Chapter Five: Foundations for Growth

1. Joel Carpenter, *Revive Us Again: The Reawakening of American Fundamentalism* (New York: Oxford Press, 1997), 126, 130–31.

2. Williams, "John Brown University," 135–37; Kennedy and Rothrock, *John Brown of Arkansas*, 64–65; *John Brown University Bulletin*, January 1939. For another example of the importance of radio networks to fundamentalist empire-building, see Gene Getz, *MBI: The Story of Moody Bible Institute* (Chicago:

Moody Press, 1969), 163–74. The creation of the engineering division is explained in Williams, "John Brown University," 189.

3. *John Brown University Bulletin*, August 1956; Williams, "John Brown University," 140–42; Kennedy and Rothrock, *John Brown of Arkansas*, 70.

4. *John Brown University Bulletin*, October 1938, January 1939, Panage quoted May–June 1974, 4.

5. Dorothy Woodland's recollections are found in John Brown III and Edward Nichols, eds., *By These Stones: Biographies and Writings of Former Faculty at John Brown University* (Siloam Springs, Ark.: John Brown University Press, 1984), 53; *Threefold Advocate*, December 17, 1937; Clyde Kilby, "Some Memories of John Elward Brown and the John Brown Schools Long Ago" (unpublished manuscript, John Brown University archives, 1984), 4, 8; transcript of John Brown University Archives interview with Ralph Kennedy, February 21, 1997, 17.

6. Kennedy interview, 5; *Threefold Advocate*, December 10, 1937; December 27, 1940.

7. Academic College Faculty Meeting Minutes, John Brown University Archives, August 3, 1938; *Threefold Advocate*, October 31, 1946.

8. Williams, "John Brown University," 147; Academic Staff Meeting Minutes, John Brown University Archives, May 6, 1941; *Threefold Advocate*, December 11, 1948.

9. Williams, "John Brown University," 110; Kilby, "Some Memories of John Elward Brown," 7.

10. Williams, "John Brown University," 159; *John Brown University Bulletin*, September 1947, February 1952; Faculty Organization Meeting Minutes, October 6, 1947.

11. Williams, "John Brown University," 138. Counting students is difficult for this period because the numbers given often included the high school students. Thus, Ralph Kennedy recalled that when he came to John Brown University in 1939, the "advertised figure" for the school was 450, but this included high school students. The actual number of college students was closer to 250 (Kennedy interview, 6–7).

12. Williams, "John Brown University," 138–39, 145; Kennedy interview, 10.

13. Williams, "John Brown University," 155; Faculty Organization Meeting Minutes, October 22, 1945; *Threefold Advocate*, October 4, 1946; John Brown to Juanita Brown, June 9, 1947; John Brown University Self-Study (1961), 3.

14. *John Brown University Bulletin*, September 1947, October 1949. John Brown to staff, July 19, 1947.

15. *John Brown University Bulletin*, February 1939, September 1947.

16. Ibid., March 1937.

17. Williams, "John Brown University," 151; John Brown to staff, December 24, 1939; John Brown University Self-Study (1961), 24; John Brown to Executive Committee, November 4, 1941.

18. John Brown to Executive Committee, October 14, 1941; John Brown to bondholders, September 11, 1941; John Brown to Executive Committee, November 4, 1941.

19. Williams, "John Brown University," 151–52.

20. John Brown to Bondholders, September 11, 1941; John Brown to Executive Committee, November 4, 1941.

21. Kennedy interview, 18.

22. John Brown to Juanita Brown, August 23, 1944.

23. Ibid.

24. *Ozark American*, September 1922; John Brown to Juanita Brown, August 17, 23, 1944.

25. Telephone interview with John Brown Jr., July 14, 2000; *John Brown University Bulletin*, June 1947.

26. Kennedy and Rothrock, *John Brown of Arkansas*, 115–17.

27. Faculty Organization Meeting Minutes, July 2, 1946, July 23, 1946, November 5, 1948. All minutes are available in the John Brown University archives.

28. *Threefold Advocate* (February 19, 1949, October 22, 1949, November 4, 1949).

29. *John Brown University Bulletin*, June 1947, July 1949.

30. *Time*, April 19, 1948, 69; *Newsweek*, September 5, 1949, 2; Kennedy and Rothrock, *John Brown of Arkansas*, 124.

31. *John Brown University Bulletin*, February 1947, September 1947, January 1949, July 1949.

32. Carpenter, *Revive Us Again*, 33–34. Carpenter's book is the best on mid-twentieth-century fundamentalism. See also George M. Marsden, *Reforming Fundamentalism: Fuller Seminary and the New Evangelicalism* (Grand Rapids: Eerdmans Publishing, 1987), and David Beale, *In Pursuit of Purity: American Fundamentalism since 1850* (Greenville, S.C.: Bob Jones University Press, 1987). On liberal Protestant control of radio access, see William Hutchison, ed., *Between the Times: The Travail of the Protestant Establishment, 1900–1960* (Cambridge: Cambridge University Press, 1991).

33. Carpenter, *Revive Us Again*, 34, 335. Edmund Morgan's *The Puritan Dilemma* (New York: Addison-Wesley Publishing, 1999) is a brief, clear study of American Puritanism.

34. Quoted in Mark Dalhouse, *An Island in the Lake of Fire: Bob Jones University, Fundamentalism, and the Separatist Movement* (Athens: University of Georgia Press, 1996), 55.

35. Quoted in Dalhouse, *An Island in the Lake of Fire*, 61. See also Carpenter, *Revive Us Again*, 141–60.

36. Dalhouse, *An Island in the Lake of Fire*, 61; Carpenter, *Revive Us Again*, 194. On the creation of Fuller Seminary, see Marsden, *Reforming Fundamentalism*, 53–68.

37. *John Brown University Bulletin*, October 1938; *Threefold Advocate*, September 25, 1942.

38. Carpenter, *Revive Us Again*, 116; John Brown, *Death in the Pot* (Siloam Springs, Ark.: John Brown University Press, 1954), 97. On the history of American Protestant opposition to alcohol, see Norman Clark, *Deliver Us From Evil: An Interpretation of American Prohibition* (New York: Norton Publishing, 1985). See also Marsden, *Fundamentalism and American Culture*, 66–68.

39. *Threefold Advocate*, November 21, 1941; Martha

Londagin, "Benton County Wet/Dry Election of 1947" (research paper available in the John Brown University archives, 1998), 5–11, 22.

40. Earl Smith, "Our Foundations in the Faith," in Brown and Nichols, *By These Stones*, 27–29. By way of contrast, see Paul Boyer's study of conservative Protestant prophecy belief, *When Time Shall Be No More: Prophecy Belief in Modern American Culture* (Cambridge: Harvard University Press, 1994).

41. Schimpf's experience is recalled in Brown and Nichols, *By These Stones*, 65; *Threefold Advocate*, March 28, 1947.

42. Carpenter, *Revive Us Again*, 164–65.

43. Ibid., 162, 165.

44. Kennedy and Rothrock, *John Brown of Arkansas*, 114; *Threefold Advocate*, February 12, 1949.

45. *John Brown University Bulletin*, June 1947, 1949.

Chapter Six: Emerging from the Founder's Shadow

1. John Brown Jr. to Frank Sewell, September 22, 1948; *Threefold Advocate*, April 16, 1948. John Brown Jr.'s correspondence is available in the John Brown University archives.

2. John Brown, *Death in the Pot* (Siloam Springs, Ark.: John Brown University Press, 1954). On the decline of moral invectives in evangelical evangelism, see Joel Carpenter, *Revive Us Again*, 223–24. On Billy Graham's evangelistic career, see William Martin, *A Prophet with Honor: The Billy Graham Story* (New York: William Morrow and Co., 1994).

3. *John Brown University Bulletin*, October 1953; Kennedy and Rothrock, *John Brown of Arkansas*, 126.

4. *John Brown University Bulletin*, October 1953, December 1953, April 1955; John Brown to staff, July 15, 1953; Kennedy interview, 126.

5. *Threefold Advocate*, February 24, 1951; February 25, 1950.

6. Ibid., February 4, December 16, 1950; Faculty Organization Minutes, March 22, 1955.

7. Faculty Organization Minutes, December 1, 1954.

8. *John Brown University Bulletin*, August, November 1951; telephone interview with John Brown Jr., July 24, 2000.

9. Brown and Nichols, *By These Stones*, 66; Stuart Schimpf, "Personal Reflections on John Brown," John Brown University archives, no date, 3; *John Brown University Bulletin*, April 1953.

10. *Threefold Advocate*, February 18, 1950.

11. *John Brown University Bulletin*, November 1951; Faculty Organization Minutes, December 16, 1955.

12. Mark Dalhouse, *An Island in the Lake of Fire*, 7, 21.

13. Ibid., 35, 39, 44, 136.

14. Bob Jones Sr. to John Brown Jr., April 18, 1960 (available in the John Brown University archives); *Threefold Advocate*, May 23, 1941; Brown and Nichols, *By These Stones*, 66.

15. Dalhouse, *An Island in the Lake of Fire*, 64–65, 205–6; Carpenter, *Revive Us Again*, 204–6.

16. Bob Jones Jr.'s criticism of Moody Bible Institute and Youth for Christ is quoted in Dalhouse, *An Island in the Lake of Fire*, 85–86; criticism of evangelicalism is quoted in Carpenter, *Revive Us Again*, 241.

17. Carpenter, *Revive Us Again*, 51.

18. Dalhouse, *An Island in the Lake of Fire*, 21, 65–78. On post–Civil War southern society, see C. Vann Woodward, *The Strange Career of Jim Crow* (New York: Oxford University Press, 2001).

19. Recounted in Brown and Nichols, *By These Stones*, 65.

20. Quoted in Dalhouse, *An Island in the Lake of Fire*, 84.

21. *John Brown University Bulletin*, February 1952.

22. Ibid., December 1951, November 1953.

23. Kennedy and Rothrock, *John Brown of Arkansas*, 120–22; *John Brown University Bulletin*, October 1952.

24. John Brown Sr. to staff, August 15, 1952; October 22, 1953.

25. Kennedy and Rothrock, *John Brown of Arkansas*, 127–29; *John Brown University Bulletin*, April 1951; Williams, "John Brown University," 169.

26. *John Brown University Bulletin*, August 1956. At this

point in its history, John Brown University had a full summer school program, which meant that students could pay $1,200 to attend year-round and graduate in three years.

27. John Brown Sr. to staff, August 16, 1951; April 4, 1952.

28. Williams, "John Brown University," 150; *John Brown University Bulletin*, April 1949; John Brown University Self-Study (1961), 26.

29. *John Brown University Bulletin*, March 1951; John Brown Sr. to staff, August 16, 1951; John Brown Sr. to staff, n.d.

30. *John Brown University Bulletin*, December 1953; Williams, "John Brown University," 165–69.

31. John Brown Sr. to staff, December 30, 1954.

32. Faculty Organization Minutes, May 11, 1951, January 16, 1953; Educational Policies Committee Minutes, May 26, 1956; *John Brown University Bulletin*, February 1952, September 1953; John Brown University Self-Study (1961), 58.

33. Faculty Organization Minutes, April 22, October 13, 1953; January 10, 1954. John Brown University Self-Study (1961), 7. Faculty Organization Minutes, December 16, 1955.

34. Bob Jones III quoted in Dalhouse, *An Island in the Lake of Fire*, 120; Roger Cox, "The Christian Teacher in the Christian College," in Brown and Nichols, *By These Stones*, 20–21.

35. John Brown III, "Dr. Panage, Walking Prof. Since '39," in Brown and Nichols, *By These Stones*, 33–35.

36. Quoted in Brown and Nichols, *By These Stones*, 39; Faculty Organization Minutes, September 8, 1955, February 24, 1942.

37. Brown and Nichols, *By These Stones*, 53; *Threefold Advocate*, April 9, 1947.

38. Dorothy Woodland, "The Climate of Learning," John Brown University archives, c. 1957, 1; Faculty Organization Minutes, October 24, 1956.

39. Woodland, "Christianity, Nuclear Energy, and a Horse's Teeth," chapel address, John Brown University archives, February 1950. In Brown and Nichols, *By These Stones*, 58–59.

40. Faculty Organization Minutes, October 3, 1952; *John Brown University Bulletin*, February 1954.

41. *John Brown University Bulletin*, February 1950, October 1950, February 1954, November 1955.

42. *John Brown University Bulletin*, August 1951, June 1953 (advertisement), June 1954. Faculty Organization Minutes, February 14, 1947.

43. *John Brown University Bulletin*, February 1954.

44. Pastor quoted in *John Brown University Bulletin*, August 1956. *Threefold Advocate*, December 4, 1953.

45. *John Brown University Bulletin*, June, July, 1954.

46. Kennedy and Rothrock, *John Brown of Arkansas*, 133–34; John Brown Sr. to John Brown Jr., March 14, 1956.

47. Kennedy and Rothrock, *John Brown of Arkansas*, 134–36; Williams, "John Brown University," 196; John Brown Sr. to Juanita Brown, August 23, 1944.

48. John Brown Jr. to Mrs. Johns, March 1957.

49. *Threefold Advocate*, September 19, 1954; telephone interview with John Brown Jr., June 14, 2000; Board of Trustees Minutes, April 11 and 12, 1958; Faculty Organization Minutes, May 6, 1958.

50. Woodland speech, John Brown University archives, no date; *Threefold Advocate*, November 19, 1937; March 15, 1962. John Brown University Self-Study (1961), 69.

51. *John Brown University Bulletin*, August 1951, February 1955.

52. *John Brown University Catalog*, 1935–36, 15.

53. Rogene Weathers, "Vocational Education in a Threefold Program," in *John Brown University Bulletin*, September 1953.

54. Faculty Organization Minutes, November 8, 1954.

55. *Threefold Advocate*, October 25, 1957; *John Brown University Bulletin*, January 1960; Faculty Organization Minutes, October 30, 1957.

56. "Observations and Status Report" (in Faculty Organization Minutes, November 19, 1958); *John Brown University Catalog*, 1958–59, 15–16.

57. Education Policies Committee "Memorandum to Faculty," in Education Policies Committee Minutes, March 28, 1961.

58. Announcement, in John Brown University archives, August 24, 1961.

59. Though the university remained interdenominational, one trend did seem to be developing. Whereas in earlier years Baptists, Presbyterians, and Methodists attended the university in roughly equal numbers (the latter being the denomination of the founder), by the late-1950s the university began reflecting more Baptist influence. One faculty member advised the university to "watch closely that we are not swamped by Baptists" (Faculty Organization Minutes, October 6, 1959); John Brown University Self-Study (1961), 11.

60. John Brown University Self-Study (1961), 46; Virginia Cox, "John Brown University: A Unique I-II-III" (unpublished paper, John Brown University archives, n.d.), 13; Faculty Organization Minutes, September 29, 1959; *John Brown University Bulletin*, September 1960, September–October 1961.

61. Telephone interview with John Brown Jr., June 14, 2000; Board of Trustees Minutes, May 31, 1958; Faculty Organization Minutes, May 18, 1959. At this point in the university's history, individual faculty members were not required to formally subscribe to the Articles of Faith. Faculty members were expected to display "at least a sympathetic understanding in these matters" (John Brown University Self-Study [1961], 15). A more informal system of evaluation characteristic of the founder's era remained in place for the time being.

62. Quoted in Dalhouse, *An Island in the Lake of Fire*, 78.

63. Ibid., 80–82.

64. Bob Jones Sr. to John Brown Jr., March 6, 1957.

65. *John Brown University Bulletin*, October 1959; Bob Jones Sr. to John Brown Jr., April 18, 1960.

66. North Central Association, "Report of an Examination of John Brown University" (in John Brown University archives, December 1958; hereafter cited as NCA Report); Faculty

Organization Minutes, September 11, 1958.

67. NCA Report, 6; *John Brown University Bulletin*, November 1960; John Brown Self-Study (1961), 25–26.

68. Williams, "John Brown University," 173; NCA Report, 25; John Brown University Self-Study (1961), 22.

69. NCA Report, 8; John Brown University Self-Study (1961), 15–16, 58.

70. NCA Report, 4; Faculty Organization Minutes, September 16, 1957; *Threefold Advocate*, February 14, 1958.

71. *John Brown University Bulletin*, November 1960; September 1961. Faculty Organization Minutes, September 9, January–September 1960. John Brown University Self-Study (1961), 44. *John Brown University Catalog*, 1961–62, 18.

72. *Threefold Advocate*, February 17, 1961; *John Brown University Bulletin*, March–April, July–August 1961.

73. *John Brown University Bulletin*, March–April 1962; Faculty Organization Minutes, April 3, 1962.

74. *John Brown University Bulletin*, March–April 1962.

Part Three: Pursuing Excellence, 1963–2000

Chapter Seven: Decades of Turmoil and Transition

1. See Tom Wells, *The War Within: America's Battle Over Vietnam* (Berkeley: University of California Press, 1994).

2. On campus radicalism, see William O'Neill, *Coming Apart: An Informal History of America in the 1960s* (New York: Times Books, 1974); Charles Kaiser, *1968 in America: Music, Politics, Chaos, Counterculture, and the Shaping of a Generation* (New York: Grove Press, 1988), 154–66, and Gitlin, *The Sixties: Years of Hope, Days of Rage* (New York: Bantam Books, 1987).

3. Ringenberg, *The Christian College*, 186; Michael S. Hamilton and James A. Mathisen, "Faith and Learning at Wheaton College," in *Models for Christian Higher Education*, ed. Richard Hughes and William B. Adrian (Grand Rapids: Eerdmans Publishing, 1997), 278; Ringenberg, *The Christian College*, 203.

4. Annual Report to the Board of Trustees, 1964–65

(hereafter cited as Annual Report); Board of Trustees Minutes, April 26, 1969; John Brown University Self-Study (1991), 6; *Threefold Advocate*, May 24, 1968. All minutes and annual reports used in this chapter are available in the university archives.

5. *John Brown University Catalog*, 1964–65, 3; Faculty Organization Minutes, December 1967.

6. Faculty Organization Minutes, December 15, 1964; March 2, 1965. *Threefold Advocate*, December 13, 1963; February 14, 1965, October 10, 1967; Faculty Organization Minutes. Josh Hofer, "Patriotism and Politics in America and at John Brown University" (undergraduate research paper, fall 2000), 5 (available in the university archives).

7. John Brown University professor A. P. Vohs headed the Wallace for President campaign in Benton County (*Threefold Advocate*, January 28, 1966); *Threefold Advocate*, February 18, 1966, May 10, 1968, September 30, 1968, April 26, 1969, September 2, 1970.

8. In the mid-1960s, a group of male students in J. Alvin dormitory burned their student handbooks to protest what they saw as their condescending nature. Interestingly, while students were reprimanded, no severe punishments were meted out, and no mention of the incident ever appeared in either the *Threefold Advocate* or the *John Brown University Bulletin*. In the minds of the administration, it was as if the incident never occurred (interview with Arnie Mayer, June 15, 2001).

9. Faculty Organization Minutes, April 19, May 10, 1966; March 7, 1967; March 5, 1968.

10. Annual Report, 1967–68; *Threefold Advocate*, March 31, 1966; October 5, 1971; September 16, 1972; July 19, 1982.

11. Richard Quebedeaux, *The Young Evangelicals* (New York: Harper & Row, 1974), 30; *Threefold Advocate*, December 7, 1967; October 30, 1964; January 28, 1966.

12. *Threefold Advocate*, December 7, 1967; November 11, 1970.

13. Luke Afeman, "The Sound Generation" (undergraduate research paper, fall 2000), 2 (available in the university archives).

14. *Threefold Advocate,* October 10, 1967; November–December 1967; July–August 1968.

15. *Threefold Advocate,* October 10, 1967.

16. Ibid., September 1968, July–August 1968, November–December 1967.

17. "Performance Tips" (instruction packet available in the university archives); Afeman, "The Sound Generation," 4; *Threefold Advocate,* November–December 1967.

18. Afeman, "The Sound Generation," 12–13; *Threefold Advocate,* February 21, 1970, March–April 1971, March–April 1972.

19. Interview with Shirley Thomas, August 6, 2001; interview with Lee Netherton, August 20, 2002. On the "Silent Majority," see Herbert Parmet, *Richard Nixon and His America* (William S. Konecky Publishing, 1990). See also Ferenc Szasz, *The Grassroots Mind in America: The American Sense of Absolutes* (New York: New Viewpoints, 1977).

20. Faculty Organization Minutes, May 14, 1963; *Threefold Advocate,* September 30, October 17, 1968.

21. Interview with Ed Klotz, June 18, 2001; Board of Trustees Minutes, April 21, 1971.

22. Annual Report, 1969; *Threefold Advocate,* March 15, 1969; February 21, 1970.

23. *Threefold Advocate,* March 22, May 23, 1969; Faculty Organization Minutes, April 15, 1969.

24. *Threefold Advocate,* March 11, 1969; January 27, 1971; April 14, 1971.

25. Ibid., September 12, October 10, December 18, 1969; September 2, 1970. John Brown University Self-Study (1971), 61–62.

26. *Threefold Advocate,* January 24, 1970. Travis Vaughn, "The Seventies: Promise of a Bright Future" (undergraduate research paper, fall 2000), 8–9 (available in the university archives).

27. *Threefold Advocate,* February 7, 1970; Board of Trustees Minutes, July 14, 1972.

28. *Threefold Advocate*, January 27, 1971; Annual Report, 1972–73.

29. See, among other works, O'Neill, *Coming Apart and Stephen Oates, Let the Trumpet Sound: A Life of Martin Luther King, Jr.* (New York: HarperCollins, 1982).

30. Annual Report, 1966–67.

31. *Threefold Advocate*, May 23, November 15, 1969.

32. Ibid., October 5, 1971, February 25, 1972.

33. Interview with Lee Netherton, August 21, 2001; *Threefold Advocate*, October 5, 1971, October 27, 1972; telephone interview with John Brown Jr., August 16, 2001.

34. *Threefold Advocate*, November 19, 1971, July–August 1973, February 3, 1975, November 17, 1975, April 12, 1976.

35. Faculty Organization Minutes, March 3, 1966; Education Policies Committee Minutes, May 1967; *John Brown University Catalog*, 1966–67, 49. On 1960s feminism, see William Chafe, *The American Woman: Her Changing Social, Economic, and Political Role*, *1920–1970* (New York: Oxford University Press, 1972).

36. *Threefold Advocate*, May 23, 1969; Faculty Organization Minutes, August 19, 1972; John Brown University Self-Study (1991), 28.

37. Annual Report, 1967–68. On the expansion of universities in the 1960s, see Gitlin, *The Sixties*, 20–21.

38. *John Brown University Bulletin*, February 1977; *Threefold Advocate*, January 29, 1980; Ringenberg, *The Christian College*, 210; Faculty Organization Minutes, October 3, 1972.

39. Board of Trustees Minutes, October 22, 1973; Faculty Organization Minutes, October 2, 1970; interview with Larry Seward, August 9, 2001; interview with Jim Walters, August 23, 2001; On Oral Roberts University, see Ringenberg, *The Christian College*, 191–92.

40. Board of Trustees Minutes, May 17, 1973; Threefold Advocate editorial (September 2, 1970). The 1970 campus revival is recounted in Ringenberg, *The Christian College*, 201–2.

41. Luke Afeman interview with John McCullough, November 3, 2000; Minutes of the John Brown University Cabinet, September 13, 1971; Sound Generation "Performance Tips," 1975.

42. On the NAE and separatism, see Carpenter, *Revive Us Again*, 152–54.

43. *Threefold Advocate*, October 28, 1974; Walters interview.

44. Board of Trustees Minutes, January 7, 1975, April 17, 1974; Faculty Organization Minutes, February 20, 1974; John Brown University Catalog (1975–77).

45. McCullough interview; Walters interview; Afeman, "The Sound Generation," 18–19.

46. Educational Policies Committee Minutes, October 6, 1964, October 4, 1963; Threefold Advocate (May 7, 1965).

47. John Brown University Progress Report, January 10, 1967; John Brown University Self-Study (1971), 82–84.

48. Letter from Robert Jackson to trustees and administrators, January 20, 1970 (available in university archives).

49. Study Committee on Vocational Education Report, October 5, 1970; Coordinating Committee on Vocational Education Report (February 12, 1973), 4–5.

50. Coordinating Committee on Vocational Education Report (February 12, 1973).

51. John Brown University Self-Study (1981), 73; Faculty Organization Minutes, May 6, 1975; *John Brown University Bulletin*, January 1976.

52. John Brown University Catalog (1970–71), 14; (1975–77), 6; (1979–81).

53. On colonial higher education, see Rudolph, *The American College and University*, 3–22, and George Marsden, *The Soul of the American University: From Protestant Establishment to Established Unbelief* (New York: Oxford Press, 1994), 29–47.

54. Hamilton and Mathisen, "Faith and Learning at Wheaton College," 269. See also Marsden, *The Soul of the American University*, 79–100. Also helpful is Bruce Kuklick,

Churchmen and Philosophers: From Jonathan Edwards to John Dewey (New Haven: Yale University Press, 1985).

55. Mark Noll, *The Scandal of the Evangelical Mind* (Grand Rapids: Eerdmans Publishing, 1995), 113. On the origins of fundamentalist Bible colleges, see Virginia Brereton, *Training God's Army: The American Bible School, 1880–1914* (Bloomington: Indiana University Press, 1990), 55–77.

56. Noll, *The Scandal of the Evangelical Mind*, 124, 132. See also Timothy Weber, *Living in the Shadow of the Second Coming: American Premillennialism, 1875–1982* (Chicago: University of Chicago Press, 1987), and Douglas Frank, *Less Than Conquerors: How Evangelicals Entered the Twentieth Century* (Grand Rapids: Eerdmans Publishing, 1986).

57. Hamilton and Mathisen, "Faith and Learning at Wheaton College," 269, 277.

58. Ibid., 270.

59. James Bratt and Ronald Wells, "Piety and Progress: A History of Calvin College," in Hughes and Adrian, *Models for Christian Higher Education*, 143, 158. See also James Bratt, *Dutch Calvinism in Modern America: A History of a Conservative Subculture* (Grand Rapids: Eerdmans Publishing, 1997).

60. Hamilton and Mathisen, "Faith and Learning at Wheaton College," 279–80.

61. *Threefold Advocate*, October 30, 1970. Faculty Organization Minutes, August 28, 1973; March 5, 1968.

62. This exchange is recounted in the Faculty Organization Minutes, January 16, 1985.

63. Annual Report, 1967; *Threefold Advocate*, October 10, 1969.

64. Elton Trueblood, *The Idea of a College* (New York: Harper & Row, 1959), 186–87.

65. Faculty Organization Minutes, February 25, 1975; Board of Trustee Minutes, February 28, 1975; April 24, 1975; October 31, 1975.

66. Faculty Organization Minutes, November 12, 1963; John

Brown University Self-Study (1971), 139; *Threefold Advocate*, February 24, 1971; March 30, 1973.

67. *John Brown University Bulletin*, May–June, 1974; Annual Report, 1979; John Brown University Self-Study (1971), 22; (1981), 19.

68. *Threefold Advocate*, October 17, 1977; November 21, 1979.

69. Ibid., December 8, 1975; February 6, 1978. Interview with Jim Pearson, September 10, 2001.

70. *John Brown University Bulletin*, October 1974; Ruble, "What Is a Christian College?" in "Faculty Writings," John Brown University brochure, 1980.

71. *John Brown University Catalog*, 1979–81.

Chapter Eight: A Third Brown Presidency

1. *John Brown University Bulletin*, July 1976; *Threefold Advocate*, September 18, 1976. See also Travis Vaughn, "The Seventies: Promise of a Bright Future" (undergraduate research paper, fall 2000), 2–3 (available in university archives).

2. *Threefold Advocate*, September 18, October 25, 1979; *Arkansas Democrat Gazette*, November 5, 2000.

3. *Threefold Advocate*, February 25, 1983; February 11, 1982. Interview with John Brown III, August 20, 2002.

4. A. J. Neufeld, "The Three John Browns and the Role Sports Played at Their School" (undergraduate research paper, fall 2000), 12–13 (available in the university archives).

5. *Threefold Advocate*, February 12, 1981; email interview with Lee Netherton, August 21, 2001; email interview with Jan Lancaster, August 24, 2001.

6. *Threefold Advocate*, February 12, 1981; April 16, 1981. Interview with John Brown III, August 16, 2001; Neufeld, "The Three John Browns," 15–16.

7. Of course, the decision was not popular with the baseball team either. A number of young trees were toppled on campus later that spring, apparently the object of the wrath of some

baseball players (interview with Jim Walters, August 23, 2001; Netherton interview).

8. *Threefold Advocate*, April 16, 1981; February 11, 1983; December 2, 1983. John Brown III interview.

9. John Brown III commentary in *Arkansas Herald-Democrat*, June 11, 1981; *Threefold Advocate*, February 28, 1986.

10. *Threefold Advocate*, September 18, 1979; October 14, 1980; April 15, 1982.

11. Faculty Organization Minutes, May 2, 1980; *Threefold Advocate*, September 30, 1980.

12. "Report to the Faculty on GS 113 World Views I," January 1981. All documents concerning the "World Views" course controversy are available in the university archives.

13. Johnson, "Some Observations Regarding the World Views Course," February 3, 1981.

14. Charles Willis, untitled document, February 17, 1981; Faculty Organization Minutes, February 19, 1981.

15. Faculty Organization Minutes, February 3, 17, 19, March 10, November 17, 1981.

16. *Threefold Advocate*, March 17, 1981; December 7, 1984.

17. John Brown III, "Faculty Address," August 26, 1983; Board of Trustees Minutes, October 21, 1988.

18. John Brown University Self-Study (1991), 121; Annual Report, 1985.

19. John Brown University Self-Study (1991), 118–21, 128–29; Board of Trustee Minutes, November 11, 1983. In 1990, a McGee Endowed Chair in Biblical Studies was instituted that provided funding for one-half of the faculty workload to be devoted to writing. In 1993, Dr. Ron Habermas was hired to fill this position.

20. John Brown University Self-Study 1991, 50–51; John Brown III, "Faculty Address," August 26, 1983.

21. Faculty Organization Minutes, August 27, 1980; *Threefold Advocate*, January 29, 1980; October 9, 1986. John Brown University Self-Study (1991), 66.

22. *Threefold Advocate*, September 25, 1987; October 7, 1988.

23. Rudolph, *The American College and University*, 457. Faculty Organization Minutes, February 4, November 3, 1964. *Threefold Advocate*, September 21, 1990; *Arkansas Democrat Gazette*, November 18, 2001.

24. John Brown University Self-Study (1991), G-6; Board of Trustees Minutes, October 25, 1991.

25. *Threefold Advocate*, October 26, 1990.

26. Ibid., April 29, 1989.

27. John Brown III, "Challenges to the Christian College," in "Faculty Writings," John Brown University brochure, 1980 (available in university archives).

28. *Threefold Advocate*, September 19, 1966; December 11, 1979; December 10, 1982. Annual Report, 1966–67.

29. *Threefold Advocate*, December 10, 1982.

30. Ibid., October 22, 1981; December 10, 1982; April 9, 1987; March 1, 1991. John Brown University Self-Study (1991), G-2. *John Brown University Bulletin*, October 1991, winter 1998.

31. *Threefold Advocate*, October 5, February 28, September 21, 1990.

32. Ibid., April 30, October 5, 19, November 9, 16, 1990.

33. Consultant's Report, July 5, 1973, available in university archives; *John Brown University Bulletin*, October 1975. John Brown Self-Study (1981), 139.

34. *Threefold Advocate*, November 19, 1981; January 25, 1988. On Sam Walton and Wal-Mart, see Sam Walton and John Huey, *Sam Walton: Made in America: My Story* (New York: Bantam Books, 1993).

35. *Threefold Advocate*, July 1985.

36. Ibid., August 1985; April 8, 1987; September 25, 1987. Board of Trustees Minutes, February 20, 1987.

37. *Threefold Advocate*, January 29, 1988; February 9, 1990; February 1, 1991; December 11, 1992.

38. Ibid., October 23, 1987.

39. Ibid., April 16, 1981; Board of Trustees Minutes, April 16, 1983.

40. *Threefold Advocate*, November 22, 1985; December 2, 1988; April 21, 1989.

41. John Brown University Self-Study (1981), 12; (1991), 31. Alumni Survey, in Faculty Organization Minutes, February 1980. *Threefold Advocate*, April 1, 1980; December 2, 1988; February 24, 1989.

42. Michael Hamilton, "The Triumph of the Praise Songs," *Christianity Today*, July 12, 1999, 28–35.

43. *Threefold Advocate*, October 17, 1977; Cherissa Dees, "Worship Tradition Transforms into Modern Praise," in *Threefold Advocate*, November 29, 2001.

44. *Threefold Advocate*, September 15, October 27, 1989; April 16, 1993. Ryan Marr, "A Historical Study of Grace Episcopal Church in Siloam Springs, Arkansas" (undergraduate research paper, fall 2001), 12–13.

45. Indeed, in testament to its vigorously prohibitionist past, the university in 1983 attempted to prevent Bailey's Pizza Emporium of West Siloam Springs, Oklahoma, from selling beer. The university had once owned the land and claimed that a "restrictive covenant" placed on the land by John Brown Sr. prohibited the sale of alcoholic beverages by subsequent owners of the property. The university lost the legal battle and Mr. Bailey continued to serve beer to his customers (*Threefold Advocate*, December 2, 1983; January 27, 1984).

46. Board of Trustee Minutes, October 23, 1986; *Threefold Advocate*, November 20, 1987; September 28, 1984; September 11, 1986; November 11, 1988; February 8, 1991.

47. John A. Schmalzbauer and C. Gray Wheeler, "Between Fundamentalism and Secularization: Secularizing and Sacralizing Currents in the Evangelical Debate on Campus Lifestyle Codes," *Sociology of Religion* 57, no. 3 (1996): 241–57.

48. Lancaster interview; *Threefold Advocate*, April 23, 1993. Interview with Jim Walters, October 5, 2001.

49. *Threefold Advocate*, October 2, 1992.

50. John Brown University Executive Committee Minutes, September 9, 1992; Board of Trustees Minutes, October 24, 1992; *Threefold Advocate*, October 16, 1992.

51. Board of Trustees Minutes, April 3, 1993; *Threefold Advocate*, April 9, 1993.

Chapter Nine: New Leadership, New Directions

1. Email interview with Pat Gustavson, January 18, 2002; email interview with Lee Netherton, January 22, 2002; email interview with Jim Walters, January 18, 2002; Faculty Association Minutes, March 24, 1993, April 28, 1993; Graham Jones, "Trust in the Vacuum: Communication of Leader and Led at John Brown University" (undergraduate research paper, fall 2000), 8–9. This paper and other documents related to the George Ford presidency are available in the university archives.

2. Notes on Senior Staff and Spouses Dinner Meeting, April 3, 1993 (available in the university archives); *John Brown University Bulletin*, summer 1993.

3. *Threefold Advocate*, October 8, 1993; Faculty Association Minutes, September 22, 1993, February 11, 1994; Jones, "Trust in the Vacuum," 11–12.

4. Faculty Association Minutes, September 22, 1993; *Threefold Advocate*, October 8, 1993.

5. Jones, "Trust in the Vacuum," 12–13; interview with Don Crandall, January 30, 2002.

6. Faculty Association Minutes, December 1, 1993; January 26, 1994.

7. Email interview with Cal Piston, January 18, 2002; Walters interview; Jones, "Trust in the Vacuum," 17–18.

8. Faculty Association Minutes, February 11, 1994; Faculty Climate Survey, spring 1994.

9. John Brown University Executive Committee Minutes, April 12, 1994; Board of Trustees Minutes, April 15, 1994; *Threefold Advocate*, April 22, 1994.

10. Faculty Association Minutes, February 11, 1994; Jones, "Trust in the Vacuum," 11–12; Crandall interview. In the fall of

1993, President Ford asked the Board of Trustees to pray that his wife would become aware of the call to be at John Brown University (Board of Trustees Minutes, October 22, 1993); see also interview with Anita Brown in *Threefold Advocate*, February 4, 1994.

11. Gustavson interview; email interview with Shirley Thomas, January 18, 2002; Graham Jones interview with Lee Balzer, November 27, 2000.

12. Interview with Lee Balzer, April 3, 2002; *Threefold Advocate*, September 3, 1994.

13. Jones, "Trust in the Vacuum," 20–23; *Threefold Advocate*, September 3, October 27, 1994; Gustavson interview; Balzer interview, April 3, 2002; Board of Trustees Minutes, October 27, April 12, 1994.

14. Faculty Climate Survey, spring 1995; Crandall interview.

15. Faculty Association Minutes, March 30, 1994; *Threefold Advocate*, September 3, 1994; Board of Trustees Minutes, October 21, 1994.

16. *Threefold Advocate*, September 20, November 1, December 13, 1991; February 21, March 27, 1992.

17. Ibid., December 3, 1998. Board of Trustees Minutes, June 28, October 21, 1994; April 10, 1999.

18. *John Brown University Bulletin*, fall 1993; *Threefold Advocate*, November 5, 1993; November 3, 1994. Board of Trustees Minutes, April 16, 1994; Annual Report, 1999–2000.

19. *Threefold Advocate*, August 31, 1995; Windgate Foundation to Lee Balzer, June 24, 1997 (in the university archives); John Brown University Bulletin, winter, summer 1998.

20. *John Brown University Bulletin*, fall 1998, 1999.

21. Annual Report, 1999–2000

22. *John Brown University Bulletin*, fall 1999.

23. Ibid., April 2000. *Threefold Advocate*, January 20, 2000. On the growing wealth of evangelicalism, see Larry Eskridge and Mark Noll, eds., *More Money, More Ministry: Money and Evangelicals in Recent North American History* (Grand Rapids: Wm. B. Eerdmans Publishing, 2000).

24. Lee Balzer served on the board of directors, and administrators Don Crandall, Al Cureton, Cheryl Kester, and Shirley Thomas have served on various CCCU advisory commissions.

25. *John Brown University Bulletin*, winter 1998; Annual Report, 1999–2000.

26. *Threefold Advocate*, April 27, 2000.

27. Michael Hamilton, "We're in the Money!" *Christianity Today*, June 12, 2000.

28. Ibid.

29. Martin Marty, "Will Success Spoil Evangelicalism?" *Christian Century*, July 19–July 26, 2000; Hamilton, "We're in the Money!"

30. Wesley quoted in Hamilton, "We're in the Money!"; Morgan quoted in Kennedy and Rothrock, *John Brown of Arkansas*, 45.

Epilogue

1. *The Outrageous Idea of Christian Scholarship* (New York: Oxford University Press, 1997), 110.

2. "From Light to Lite to Night," *The University Bookman*. 14, no. 4 (1999): 10–14.

BIBLIOGRAPHICAL ESSAY

John Brown University

Only a few secondary works have been written on John Brown University and its founder. *John Brown of Arkansas* (1966), by Ralph Kennedy and Thomas Rothrock, is an adulatory biography of John Brown Sr. that delves briefly into the university's history. Earl Williams's "John Brown University: Its Founder and Founding, 1919–1957" (Ed.D. diss., University of Arkansas, 1971) provides a year-by-year chronicle of the early decades of the institution's history. In addition, John Brown III and Edward Nichols compiled a volume *By These Stones: Biographies and Writings of Former Faculty at John Brown University* (1984) that includes helpful historical information.

Fortunately, the paucity of secondary sources is outweighed by a wealth of primary documents that are available in the library stacks and archives of John Brown University. Throughout his adult life, John Brown Sr. produced a steady stream of books, articles, and sermons, all of which are available on paper or cassette tape. Tapes and photographs of John Brown Sr. are also available at the Billy Graham Center Archives, located on the campus of Wheaton College in Wheaton, Illinois. The John Brown University archives also contain personal correspondence of the three John Browns, press clippings and photographs of John Brown Sr.'s revivals, minutes of faculty and trustee meetings, and tedious but informative self-studies for accreditation compiled in 1961, 1971, 1981, 1991, and 2001. Complete collections of university publications begin with John Brown Sr.'s evangelistic newsletter the *World Wide Revival* in 1907 and continue with the *American Evangelist*, the *Southwestern*, the *Ozark American*, the *American Wayshower*, the *Christian Fellowship*, the *John Brown University Bulletin*, and the student newspaper, the *Threefold Advocate*. For this book, primary documents were supplemented by interviews with John Brown Jr., John Brown III, Don Crandall, Bill George, Pat Gustavson, Ed Klotz, Jan Lancaster (Goring), Arnie Mayer, John McCullough, Lee Netherton, Jim Pearson, Cal Piston, Larry Seward, Shirley Thomas, and Jim Walters.

American Higher Education and Religion

The historical study of higher education in America took a great step forward with the publication of Frederick Rudolph's *The American College and University: A History* (1962). Rudolph portrays the history of American colleges and universities as a gradual liberation from the shackles of religion, social elitism, and impractical curricula. More recently, George Marsden has documented the shift from Protestant to secular control of American higher education in *The Soul of the American University: From Protestant Establishment to Established Nonbelief* (1994). Marsden and Bradley Longfield have also edited a volume, *The Secularization of the Academy* (1992) that focuses on the pivotal years from the late-nineteenth to early-twentieth centuries. Michael Dennis's *Lessons in Progress: State Universities and Progressivism in the New South, 1880–1920* (2001) traces the transformations to southern public higher education during this era.

In recent years, a number of historians have explored the history of Christian colleges in America. The seminal study remains William Ringenberg's *The Christian College: A History of Protestant Higher Education in America* (1984). A counterpart to Marsden's *Soul of the American University* tracing the secularization of denominational colleges is James Burtchaell's *The Dying of the Light: The Disengagement of American Colleges and Universities from Their Christian Churches* (1998). Also helpful is a collection of historical essays edited by Joel Carpenter and Kenneth Shipps, *Making Higher Education Christian: The History and Mission of Evangelical Colleges in America* (1987). Concerning the origins and nature of fundamentalist Bible colleges, Virginia Bereton's *Training God's Army: The American Bible School, 1880–1940*, provides a lucid analysis. Mark Noll explores the changing philosophical underpinnings of

Christian higher education in *The Scandal of the Evangelical Mind* (1994), especially chapters 3, 4, and 5. A fascinating study of recent trends in evangelical Christian colleges is found in John A. Schmalzbauer and C. Gray Wheeler, "Between Fundamentalism and Secularization: Secularizing and Sacralizing Currents in the Evangelical Debate on Campus Lifestyle Codes," *Sociology of Religion* 57, no. 3 (1996): 241–58.

In order to understand John Brown University, it is important to consider other fundamentalist and evangelical endeavors in higher education in the twentieth century. Fortunately, many good secondary sources exist that shed light on the John Brown University experience. *Models for Christian Higher Education* (1997), edited by Richard Hughes and William Adrian, provides a collection of case studies of dozens of other institutions. Two institutions in particular that have resembled John Brown University at times are Northwestern College in Minneapolis, Minnesota, founded by John Brown Sr.'s colleague William Bell Riley, and Bob Jones University. The stories of these institutions are told in William Trollinger's *God's Empire: William Bell Riley and Midwestern Fundamentalism* (1990) and Mark Dalhouse's *An Island in the Lake of Fire: Bob Jones University, Fundamentalism, and the Separatist Movement* (1996). Wheaton College is typically regarded as the flagship evangelical college throughout the twentieth century. Its history is best told in Michael Hamilton's *The Fundamentalist Harvard: Wheaton College, Evangelicalism, and American Higher Education* (2003). Wheaton's counterpart among Bible colleges is Moody Bible Institute, the story of which is recounted in Gene Getz's *MBI: The Story of Moody Bible Institute* (1989).

As a revivalist, John Brown Sr. had many models, peers, and successors. The most complete study of American revivalism is William McLoughlin's *Modern Revivalism: Charles Grandison Finney to Billy Graham* (1959). A host of individual biographies of evangelists supplement McLoughlin's survey. Among the best are Harry Stout's *The Divine Dramatist: George Whitefield and the Rise of Modern Evangelicalism* (1991); Charles Hambrick Stowe's *Charles Finney and the Spirit of American Evangelicalism* (1996); Lyle Dorsett's

A Passion for Souls: The Life of D. L. Moody (1997); Lyle Dorsett's *Billy Sunday and the Redemption of Urban America* (1991); and William Martin's *A Prophet with Honor: The Billy Graham Story* (1994).

Of course, as this study has shown, the history of John Brown University is unintelligible apart from an understanding of the religious, social, and cultural odyssey of American evangelicals in the twentieth century. For an understanding of the era in American religion that produced modern evangelicalism, two books are especially noteworthy—Ferenc Szasz's *The Divided Mind of Protestant America, 1880–1930* (1982), and Martin Marty's *Modern American Religion: The Irony of It All, 1893–1919* (1986). The most influential movement in mainline religion during this early twentieth century was liberal Protestantism. While liberalism has not received as much attention as fundamentalism, there are nonetheless some excellent studies of this movement. Two of the most significant works are Kenneth Cauthen's *The Impact of American Religious Liberalism* (1983) and William Hutchison's *The Modernist Impulse in American Protestantism* (1976). Hutchison has also edited a book entitled *Between the Times: The Travail of the Protestant Establishment, 1900–1960* (1991), which traces the fate of Protestant liberalism in the decades after the tumultuous 1920s.

Concerning twentieth-century evangelicalism, any study of this movement must begin with George Marsden's groundbreaking work, *Fundamentalism and American Culture, 1875–1925: The Making of Modern Evangelicalism* (1980). Marsden built on the first historical work to take fundamentalist religious ideas seriously, Ernest Sandeen's *The Roots of Fundamentalism: British and American Millenarianism, 1800–1930* (1970). Also helpful in understanding the fundamentalist mentality is C. Allyn Russell's *Voices of American Fundamentalism: Seven Biographical Studies* (1976). While the above studies attempt to remain dispassionate, two other works combine historical analysis with more overt theological assessment. David Beale's *In Pursuit of Purity: American Fundamentalism since 1850* (1987) tells the history of fundamentalism from the perspective of an insider, while Douglas Frank's *Less Than Conquerors: How*

Evangelicals Entered the Twentieth Century (1986) combines historical analysis with theological critique of the religious and cultural developments that contributed to fundamentalism.

After their seeming defeat in American culture in the 1920s, fundamentalists entered an era of retrenchment and growth. This story is best told in Joel Carpenter's *Revive Us Again: The Reawakening of American Fundamentalism* (1997). Marsden traces the evolution from fundamentalism to evangelicalism in *Reforming Fundamentalism: Fuller Seminary and the New Evangelicalism* (1987). A number of particular features in twentieth century evangelicalism have attracted the attention of historians. For example, Margaret Bendroth explores religious conservatives' ambivalence toward gender in *Fundamentalism and Gender, 1875 to the Present* (1996). Ronald Numbers focuses his attention on evangelical opposition to evolution in *The Creationists: The Evolution of Scientific Creationism* (1992). Evangelicals' continuing fascination with biblical prophecy is amply chronicled in Timothy Weber's *Living in the Shadow of the Second Coming: American Premillennialism, 1875–1982* (1987), and Paul Boyer's *When Time Shall Be No More: Prophecy Belief in Modern America* (1994). Finally, no study of an evangelical Christian college would be complete without consideration of the rising social and economic status of modern evangelicals, a phenomenon studied in Larry Eskridge and Mark Noll, eds., *More Money, More Ministry: Money and Evangelicals* (2000).

INDEX